"Were the first religions in the world polytheistic or monotheistic? As someone who has spoken on college campuses for decades, I can attest to the fact that most faculty and students would select the first option rather than the second. Win Corduan provides a service to scholarship on religion by making the case for the second option. Many start with an evolutionary assumption that naturally leads them to the conclusion that the first religion was animism or polytheism. But early on in the book Win Corduan makes the case that no matter what view you have about the origin of human beings, you cannot escape the fact that the first religion was monotheism. As the title says, in the beginning was God, a monotheistic God. This book deserves a hearing and a wide audience. I commend it to you."

Kerby Anderson
President of Probe Ministries
Host of the *Point of View* radio talk show

"*In the Beginning God* deals with an immensely important topic in an in-depth and thoughtful manner. It is well researched and deals with all of the relevant sides in the scholarly discussion concerning the origin and development of humanity's religious quest. Building on the work of Wilhelm Schmidt and others, the book adds a new and powerful voice in support of the belief that the human race's original spiritual focus was on one all-powerful and morally inclined creator God. I highly recommend it for any and all who are interested in the topic of our pursuit of the sacred."

Michael J. Caba
Dean of faculty
Kilns College

"What is the origin of religion? I recommend *In the Beginning God* to students of religion who seek to hear from all sides in this important conversation. In it, Win Corduan guides you through a fascinating exploration of the evidence for original monotheism in language, culture, and world religions. He challenges naturalistic theories in the field of religious studies and provides a fresh angle for apologists seeking to make the case for the Christian worldview."

Mikel del Rosario
Speaker and trainer (www.apologeticsguy.com)
Adjunct professor of World Religion and Christian Apologetics
William Jessup University

"This book is one of the most important contributions to religious apologetics in the last generation by the most qualified religious apologist on the topic within evangelicalism. It is a must read for every Christian apologist."

Norman Geisler, Ph.D.
Professor of Apologetics
Veritas Seminary

"*In the Beginning God* is a paradigm-shifting work. Dr. Corduan has penned a persuasive and masterfully argued case for original monotheism. All future research on the origin of religion will need to take seriously and interact with Dr. Corduan's argumentation."

Dayton Hartman
Adjunct professor of Religious Studies
Judson College

"Dr. Corduan has provided readers with one of the most unique —and most sorely needed—apologetics works that has come along in years. Having addressed this topic on many a university campus myself, I can say that to assert that humanity's original religion was monotheism draws disagreement—if not ridicule. In this impressively researched book, Corduan lays out a riveting history of monotheism, and persuasively defends Christian theism, and refutes the common tendency to interpret religion through an evolutionary lens. Many apologetics books are being released these days, but this one is a 'must have.'"

Alex McFarland
Christian apologist
Host of *Exploring the Word* radio program

"A fascinating journey through the history of language, cultures, and morals. Professor Corduan provides an exhaustively researched argument for the early existence of monotheism in many cultures. Moreover, he offers a sound apologetic that counters evolutionary theories of religion that scholars such as Wellhausen popularized and used to dehistoricize the Bible. I enthusiastically recommend his book."

Ravi Zacharias
Author and speaker

IN THE BEGINNING GOD

A FRESH LOOK AT THE CASE FOR ORIGINAL MONOTHEISM

WINFRIED CORDUAN

B&H
ACADEMIC
NASHVILLE, TENNESSEE

To
Daniel and Mary Muppidi
and
Paul and Nancy Reid

Table of Contents

Preface

Although I do not remember the exact day on which the idea for this book first became a reality, I remember the circumstances well. Just that morning, as I was leaving the house for my daily teaching duties, I remember remarking to my wife, June, that I would really like to start focusing on writing only technical books. Specifically, I said words to the effect that "if it isn't about modal logic or Sanskrit, I don't think I want to write about it anymore." A little later that day I received an e-mail from Steve Bond of B&H Publishing Group, asking me if I would be interested in writing a complete book on original monotheism. I had devoted a short amount of time and space to that topic off and on in some previous books and articles. In a review of my *A Tapestry of Faiths* (InterVarsity Press, 2003), someone had suggested that it would be nice if I were to write an entire monograph treating the subject. Steve thought that was a good idea.

Obviously the entire picture of what I would or would not like to write immediately changed upon receiving a direct note of encouragement from a publisher. Still, I was just a little reluctant to agree to the project, though my reluctance did not last more than a day or so at best. I was fully aware of the fact that writing an entire book on this topic would be a lot different from writing a few paragraphs or even a chapter in a more general book. I would have to immerse myself in the literature of anthropology to a much larger degree than I had before. The only way I could see giving the topic any further treatment was to attempt to engage the experts in the field on their own level. Actually, few of the main participants in this story, other than the Americans in the twentieth century, had formal academic backgrounds in anthropology, and so I joined the many figures coming to the field from the "outside," in my case with an M.A. in philosophy of religion and a Ph.D. in religious studies. I spent the next few years buying books and reading massively in the areas of ethnology and the anthropology of religion, particularly in connection with the phenomenon of monotheism. I realized that in some of my own earlier expositions, I had made some of the same mistakes I will point out in the writings of others over the course of this book. Slowly I started to feel that I was beginning to get a handle on this topic in the context of the debate that began more than 150 years ago and on its place in the current discussion within its anthropological context. My older son, Nicholas S. Corduan, who, among the many hats hanging from his rack, has one labeled "anthropologist and archaeologist," has been of invaluable help to me in pointing out important details and connections. Even more importantly, he kept me from moving into one of the many fantasy worlds into which anthropology loves to entice researchers.

Still, when I finally got to the point of starting to write, it immediately became obvious to me that I was not as ready as I had previously thought. To a great extent this book focuses on those who analyzed the reports and tried to make sense of them: Tylor, Lang, Schmidt, Eliade, and so forth. But I realized that I need to give far more attention to the work of A. W. Howitt, K. Langloh Parker, A. L. Kroeber, E. H. Man, Friedrich Strehlow, and the many other field-workers who documented the facts that gave rise to the theory of original monotheism. Ultimately, their work (though not necessarily their own interpretations of the data) makes the theory stand or fall. I also realized this was an area that was almost entirely untouched by today's experts.

Wilhelm Schmidt is the centerpiece of the story in this book. One simply cannot get around that fact because no one advocated original monotheism as strongly and effectively as he. I will not restate much of Schmidt's argument, which is impossible, since there is no way I could summarize all twelve volumes of *Der Ursprung der Gottesidee*. We need to take a look at what happened before his time and afterwards and to make corrections to his conclusions insofar as they become inevitable. Ultimately, Schmidt's role is precisely what I believe he wanted it to be; he is a guide to truth, which, in theory, took a higher place for him than his own conclusions.

To understand the case for original monotheism under scrutiny, one must understand the culture-historical method of ethnology. Schmidt's conclusions clearly pivoted on it. People often call it the method of culture circles, but these circles are not the method but the result of the method. In chapter 6, I try to take the mystery of this method and show that it ultimately relies on our common faculties of drawing reasonable inferences. Although this method was at the heart of Schmidt's writings, it is often completely left out of summaries of his work, possibly because for various reasons it has remained obscure. I hope that by my using simple examples, readers will come to understand the method better, thereby, coming closer to accepting the conclusions of its application as well.

Wilhelm Schmidt and his work have frequently been dismissed on the grounds that he was a Catholic priest and was, therefore, merely attempting to endow Catholic dogma with a certain amount of academic respectability. I recognize that I may be risking a similar liability as an evangelical scholar who believes in the inerrant truth of the Bible and in the exclusive redemptive work of Jesus Christ. Like Schmidt, I also believe that the doctrine of original monotheism carries a lot of weight in terms of demonstrating the truth of Christianity, yet it may still not gain any hearing whatsoever from certain quarters.

It is nothing new to me to have the truth of something I have written questioned by people who have not read a word of it, simply on the basis of my personal beliefs. Such folks are accountable for themselves. One could point out that they are guilty of the alleged prejudice of which they are accusing Schmidt or me, but what else can one say? I am reminded of Schmidt's memorable phrase in the first volume of *Der Ursprung* in connection with the offhand rejection of reports by missionaries just because they were missionaries: "This nonsense has got to stop!" Also, it occurs to me that it might help to remind these folks that a lot of people will notice that they are putting their biases ahead of scholarly interaction. Scholars are not as likely to receive applause for elitist laugh lines as they were even twenty years ago. The issues discussed here, whether right or wrong, are intended to be factual and scientific; therefore, supposed refutations based on a priori prejudice will ultimately reflect on the person making cavalier statements of unreflective rejection. The same thing applies to the empty dismissal of the topic on the grounds that one's discipline is no longer concerned with it. The dark ages in which both the natural and social sciences have assumed the working presuppositions of atheism may be coming to an end.

My gratitude to Taylor University can only be an indirect one for this volume. I do want to thank my former colleagues at Taylor University for their farewell gift upon retirement, which consisted of several volumes of Schmidt's *Der Ursprung*. I also want to acknowledge that it would not have been possible for me to write this book if, during my many years at Taylor University, I had not had the opportunity to travel and study, both at home and abroad, various aspects of the subject matter addressed in this book.

Over the last few years, after retiring on disability, it has not been easy to maintain the schedule of regular study and writing I had envisioned. I must express my deep gratitude to the editors at B&H, in particular Chris Cowan, the acquisitions editor, for their infinite patience with me. I also want to acknowledge Steve Bond, Terry Wilder, Ray Clendenen, Jim Baird, Dean Richardson, and a number of people whose names are not known to me.

I want to thank various members of the International Society of Christian Apologetics for their words of encouragement along the way. The same thing applies to any number of people, many of whom

I have never met in person but who have been extremely kind in cheering me on in e-mails and on Internet social media.

As always, one thing is sure. This book would never have seen print if it had not been for the constant encouragement from June, my dear wife. In addition to giving up much time and, as always, proofreading my prose, she has now had the additional job of monitoring me so that I would not spend all of my writing energy for one week on a single day.

Concerning Terminology

The discussion on which I am reporting in this book began in the middle of the nineteenth century, and, as we will clearly see, many of the scholars involved in it were convinced that they and their European culture constituted the apex of human development. People of other cultures were deemed to be inferior on two different levels. On the lowest level were the "savages," by which they meant people living on a foraging level with virtually no technological developments. Actually, the word *savage* is derived from a word meaning "man of the woods," a purely descriptive term at one time, but one that certainly has taken on highly negative and derogatory connotations. On a higher level, but not attaining to the glory of Victorian England, were the so-called barbarian cultures, a term invented by the Greeks to refer to those people whose language they did not understand. Again if, a neutral meaning was ever associated with this word, it is long gone. Other terms, such as *primitive*, are also no longer considered appropriate. However, having acknowledged all of that, I feel the debate I am describing would make no sense if I purged my report of all the expressions based on the perception of a hierarchy of cultures. That was the point of the debate in many instances, and for many of the leading figures, the inferiority of the people, not just of their hunter-gathering economy, was a given. So, in order to tell the story accurately, I need to convey their attitude and at times use their words.

I would like to beg for your understanding that such expressions carrying such negative evaluations do not reflect my personal attitude. In fact, the bottom line of Wilhelm Schmidt's argument, which I endorse, is that those people who have been looked down upon to such an extent manifest more honesty, more integrity, and a greater devotion to God than do their self-appointed superiors. Still, for the sake of historical accuracy, I need to report the thoughts of the various parties as they conveyed them. When we eventually come to Wilhelm Schmidt's "culture circles," his designations become technical terms rather than descriptive evaluations, and I will indicate that this is how they are intended to be understood by capitalizing and italicizing them; as in, e.g., *Primitive*. I trust the alert reader will be able to discern that in contrast to the evolutionists by virtue of their position, the scholars who were advocating an original monotheism, including the present author, could not possibly have intended to say anything derogatory about the cultures in question.

With regard to capitalization, I have obviously followed the standard rule that we capitalize "God," the one and only God, as revealed in the Bible, and that we do not capitalize "god" or "gods" when the reference is to false or invented deities, or perhaps just the idea of a supreme being. However, the point of this book is to show that some cultures worship a divine being who is in many ways the equivalent of the God of the Bible. Only when I hoped that such an equivalence was clear in my discussion did I feel free to refer to that being as "God" with capitalization; otherwise I left the designation in the lower case. Since this procedure involved a certain amount of subjectivity, it will be quite easy, no doubt, to find fault with its application at various points. I trust that the reader will see past the size of the letters to the magnitude of the issue.

As you go through the book, you will run into certain sections of various sizes marked by an asterisk. This sign indicates to you that the material covered in this section is particularly technical, and it is possible to skip it without missing the flow of the argument. (I am happy to say that in a few such places I did manage to make some reference to Sanskrit, but modal logic will have to wait for the sequel.)

This year marks the centennial of the first publication of *Der Ursprung* in German. It is time to look once more at the debate (or the lack thereof) on the important topic that Wilhelm Schmidt sought to bring to the attention of the world.

Winfried Corduan

August 5, 2012

CHAPTER 1

Origins and Beginnings: Confusion in the Making

A good story is worth telling well, and to tell it well, one may have to bring in a lot of detailed information, even if we would prefer to get to the action right away. This is one of those stories where many details are inevitable.

Our story's plot concerns a number of scholars attempting to find an answer to the question, How did religion come about? and, sad to say, how their theories on the topic simply did not work. The story continues with a handful of men who came up with a scholarly answer to this question; it made sense and fit all of the data provided by various sciences. But then we learn about how these good ideas were discarded for nonscholarly reasons. Finally, we will conclude by showing that these supposedly discarded answers are still valid today and that they can make a difference to us.

A Straightforward Question

I think you and I would agree that the two questions, When did religion first become a part of the life of human beings? and, What form did the first religion take? are straightforward and objective questions that deserve straightforward and objective answers. Whether we have the answers is a different matter, but the nature of the questions does not change.

However, we need to be clear from the outset that *straightforward* is not synonymous with *easy*. A question such as, What is the cube root of 343? is straightforward but may not be easy to answer, depending on your skill in math. Of course, it would be wrong just to make up an answer or to say it is not a valid question just because you cannot answer it.

The question of the origin of religion strikes me as a straightforward one, inquiring after some information concerning the history of human beings. It is safe to say there was a time when no human on the earth held any beliefs or carried out any practices we would consider to be religious. One of the easiest explanations for such a religionless period could be that at that time there were no human beings; consequently, no one would have been around to practice any religion. Then—continuing that easy explanation—as soon as human beings were created, they were aware of their Creator and thus held to a religious belief. This is the biblical view.

If one wanted to become a little bit more precise within this framework, one could say that Adam and Eve really did not practice "religion" because they had an immediate relationship with God; further, perhaps religion in a more formal sense did not begin until the time of Enosh, the son of Seth, of whom the Bible tells us, "At that time people began to call on the name of the LORD" (Gen 4:26 NIV).

This response seeks to base itself on the Bible, and the reader is entitled to know that this author holds fast to it. However, I want to do more in this book than simply declare my belief, to which other people could then respond by declaring their beliefs. I also want to show why my belief is plausible. Most of the scholars with whom we will occupy ourselves in this discussion subscribed to the theory that human beings are the products of nature, not a Creator, and that religious awareness emerged alongside the process of human cultural evolution. Even scholars who did not buy into Darwinian evolution still said that religion came about as a part of human development. Without believing in a personal Creator, the question of the origin of religion becomes a difficult one.

Sticking to the Right Question

We must make sure we do not allow ourselves to get sidetracked into trying to answer a question we did not mean to ask. What is the origin of human beings? and, What is the origin of religion? are two different questions, even if for many people the answer to the second question is virtually identical with the answer to the first. My contention is that **Regardless of how one explains the origin of human beings, one cannot get around the fact that the first religion of human beings was monotheism, the recognition and worship of one God.** Obviously, world views make a lot of difference, and questions such as whether we accept the truth of the Bible, whether the Genesis account is factual, whether humans were created by God in his image, or whether they are the product of a currently ongoing process of adaptation and development, are extremely important ones. But we need not answer every possible question every time we consider a related topic. For our purpose, we are assuming the presence of human beings on the earth, and we want to know what they believed and practiced as their religion. The point is that even without believing in creation or revelation, the answer still comes out the same.

Ambiguity Arises

What makes this story complex is that after a time of debate in the late nineteenth and early twentieth centuries, neither the question nor the answers were considered to be straightforward in academic circles. Due to the manner in which scholars treated this topic, the theories became increasingly complicated and—dare I say—evasive. One change was that the word *origin* took on an equivocal meaning.

Imagine a fantasy novel that begins with a hero looking for a long-lost magical sword called "Victor." It is clear that what everyone means by *Victor* in the first part of the book is the traditional weapon made of metal with a two-edged blade coming to a sharp point, mounted on a grip. However, unbeknownst to the reader, somewhere toward the middle of the novel, the author changes the meaning of the word; suddenly *Victor* is no longer a weapon but the name of the hero's younger brother, who has disappeared! While the readers are still thinking about the weapon as the novel progresses, it stops making sense to them because they do not realize that for some unknown reason the author changed the object to which the word *Victor* referred from a weapon to a person. This story has become incoherent, and the reader will presumably toss it to the side and find something more consistent to read.

However, if the reader is a budding scholar in the academic world, maybe as a graduate student or as a beginning teacher, and if he discovers that the ambiguity (or really, incoherence) concerning the word *Victor* is an essential principle in his discipline, he may decide it must be profound, assent to it without necessarily understanding it, and defend it in his writings so that a doctorate, a professorship, tenure, and promotion will all be in his reach.

A large part of the upcoming story revolves around the fact that scholars have allowed themselves to redefine the word *origin* in new and novel ways. What precisely does *origin* mean? It may be difficult for you, just as much as for me, to understand the word to mean anything other than some kind of a beginning in time, the first appearance of something, the particular moment when something new came into existence. However, in the discussion on the origin of religion, for many scholars the word *origin* can also refer to something else less clearly defined.

Let me quickly cite one example in the context of our topic. Joseph Kitagawa, a leading scholar of religions in the twentieth century, affirmed with confidence: "The question of the origin of religions is not a historical one, but a metaphysical one."[1]

What does this statement mean? I do not blame you if you cannot make sense of this assertion because surely the one making it seems to be redefining words. How can an "origin" not be an event in time and space, and, therefore, historical? At a minimum the statement may strike you as a gesture of misdirection, as when a stage magician tries to get you to look the wrong way.

So it could be possible to write off Kitagawa's pronouncement, and others like it, as evasive double-talk. Perhaps it is. Still, many people accept what he said, whether they understand it or not. It sounds "deep," and people love "deep" sayings, even if they are unintelligible or maybe especially if they are so.

We can counter such profound-sounding declarations with plain biblical ones. But there is no good reason to ignore the other resources at our disposal. We can go a step further and show that the biblical version is true not only because we say it is divine revelation but because it is also based on scholarly criteria. The information others have tried to use to debunk the biblical account will actually support the Bible. If someone who makes a statement inconsistent with the Bible is wrong on scientific grounds, then we should be able to show on scientific grounds where he is wrong because God did not create a world in which the facts contradict his Word. If the person is wrong because he is allowing his predispositions to dictate his answers, we should be able to expose such sleight of hand. If the person is talking gibberish, we should be able to expose it as such. And if someone should claim it is neither possible nor even permissible to demonstrate the nature of the origin of religion, we should be able to counter by saying, "We just did."

---

[1] Joseph M. Kitagawa, *The History of Religions: Understanding Human Experience* (Atlanta: Scholars Press, 1987), 23.

Mircea Eliade: The Sky Becomes God

We are getting far ahead of ourselves here, and we should start travel-
ing back in time, about 150 years, to the beginning of the debate. But,
as we travel back, let me pull the "stop" switch at a place about half
a century ago for a quick look at an example of the outcome of the
discussion after about 100 years. I am inserting this example for two
reasons: (1) because it illustrates how persuasive, almost hypnotic,
some theories on the origin of religion can be, and (2) because it
illustrates the manner in which the overall academic mind-set had
shifted by then, preparing us to look through the prism with which
contemporary scholars view the discussions that began 150 years ago.

Here is a summary based on the speculations of the well-known
scholar of religion, Mircea Eliade:[2] Once upon a time, when the economic level of human beings could only be described in terms of
mere subsistence, people were highly aware of their natural environment. Among the many things that intrigued them was the splendor
of the sky. They realized the sky with its brilliant light, which illumi-
nated every part of the world, was different from anything else they
encountered. They were aware of the many items that populated the
universe such as trees, mountains, and rivers, as well as people and
their implements. But those were all different from the sky. When
the people saw a rock, they simply saw a rock; when they beheld the
sky, they saw something so vast and so beyond anything that they
could touch or understand that they were simultaneously fascinated
and intimidated by it. In many ways they feared the sky, but they also
saw the sky as friendly to them, at least most of the time. The sky
brought sunshine, it brought rain, and it was their constant companion, whether they were hunting or fishing or collecting edible vegetation. The sky was always present.

Sometimes the sky would be angry, and it might send thunder
and lightning and possibly even downpours so harsh they resulted in

---

[2] Mircea Eliade, *Patterns in Comparative Religion*, trans. Rosemary Sheed
(Denver: Bison Books, 1996), 38–41.

harmful floods. But after the sky had worked off its temper, the rain and the cool its tantrum had produced contributed to making further life possible and bearable.

The sky, people said, is great. We cannot conceive of anything greater than the sky; and, what's more, if we pray to it, it often fulfills our desires. It knows and understands us. Because it is so great, nothing is beyond its capability. Understanding these amazing qualities of the sky, it seemed that it was more than just an object: it was a great being, who was not just a thing up there, but who in some ways resembled a human person, except that its powers exceeded anything we humans are capable of. The people began to think of the sky as the home of a super person and considered him to be "god." They thought they could call him by his name and approach him if they were careful. Having come to think of him as a supreme god now, they recognized that he was still the Great Shining One, who is beyond our understanding, and they continued to be in total awe of him.

Thus, according to Eliade, the sky had become one of the important manifestations of what is sacred in the world. He called such disclosures "hierophanies," which means literally, "manifestations of the Holy." The little narration above is based on his exposition of the sacredness of the sky, which he says "symbolizes transcendence, power and changelessness simply by being there. It exists because it is high, infinite, immovable, powerful."[3]

As we saw above, in the perception of the people, the sky then underwent a transformation from being a disclosure of sacredness itself to becoming the residence of a Supreme Being. Eliade explains, "When this hierophany became personified, when the divinities of the sky showed themselves, or took the place of the holiness of the sky as such is difficult to say precisely."[4]

Let us look carefully at this declaration of a lack of precise knowledge. It seems to imply that we are looking at an event or a period in

---

[3] Ibid., 39.
[4] Ibid., 40.

time during which this transition occurred. What else could one possibly mean by asking "when" something took place? There can hardly be any doubt that this event is the "origin" of belief in gods of the sky or of a single supreme God of the sky. Thus, Eliade seems to have committed himself here to the idea that we can reconstruct a minimal historical sequence, certainly not in the sense of being able to provide a date and place when the shift from sky to sky-god occurred, but, inasmuch as we can state that somewhere along the line of human development, there must have been such an occurrence.

However, prepare to be startled! In other places Eliade has asserted in unequivocal language that it is impossible for us to find a historical origin of religion, or for that matter to identify the origin of any part of religion. As indicated in the statements above, by "historical origin" he obviously did not mean being able to provide a date for the origin of religion, which seems to be impossible, but even to describe the process which it took in the course of history. To wit, "So, after more than a century of untiring labor, scholars were forced to renounce the old dream of grasping the origin of religion with the aid of historical tools, and they devoted themselves to the study of different phases and aspects of religious life."[5]

So, even though Eliade himself had provided a scenario by which belief in God may have originated, he also said that doing so is impossible. So either we are misunderstanding him or Eliade was contradicting himself, apparently dismissing some of the material he was writing simultaneously.

Going Back to the Beginning of the Discussion

Similar to Kitagawa, his colleague at the University of Chicago, Eliade is giving new and different meaning to words. I shall add one more comment: If it appears that the intent of this wordplay is to escape

---

[5] Mircea Eliade, *The Quest: History and Meaning in Religion* (Chicago: Chicago University Press, 1969), 50.

the consequences of a historical investigation in the traditional sense, we may just be on the right trail.

We noticed that Eliade had referred to the hundred years or so prior to his statement when researchers had actually treated the question and its potential answers as historical in nature; therefore, being forewarned of the confusion that will eventually be in store for us, let us resume our trip back in time to the point when *history* still referred to what happened in the world, *events* were still actual occurrences, and *origins* were still beginnings in time.

I am not going to describe and criticize all of the theories prominent in the late nineteenth and early twentieth centuries. To do so would be a needless repetition of the thorough work of Wilhelm Schmidt, who has provided such a summary in his readable, and sometimes even entertaining, book, *The Origin and Growth of Religion*.[6] Schmidt's works are going to be major sources for our pursuit, but I shall try not just to restate his material. I will limit myself to a few of the more prominent figures in the debate, though I intend to salute in passing those writers whose ideas were so quixotic that readers might feel deprived of getting the full enjoyment out of following the discussion if I completely ignored them.

---

[6] Wilhelm Schmidt, *The Origin and Growth of Religion: Facts and Theories*, 2nd ed., trans. H. J. Rose (New York: Humanities Press, 1936). These ideas were fleshed out and documented further in his monumental twelve-volume work, *Der Ursprung der Gottesidee* (Münster: Aschendorff, 1912–55), as well as in numerous other works that will be cited as they become relevant.

CHAPTER 2

Max Müller: Mythology as a Disease of Language

How did religion come about? Let us be clear on one matter: the theories that were proposed in the nineteenth century for the most part were intended to be "scholarly," and, unfortunately, that term implied that they were intended to rule out a supernatural origin of religion. As Evans-Pritchard says:

> We should, I think, realize what was the intention of many of these scholars if we are to understand their theoretical constructions. They sought, and found, in primitive religions a weapon, which could, they thought, be used with deadly effect against Christianity. If primitive religion could be explained away as an intellectual aberration, as a mirage induced by emotional stress, or by its social function, it was implied that the higher religions could be discredited and disposed of in the same way.[1]

We can leave to the side whether the intent was always outright hostility to Christianity or the antagonism was based on the

---

[1] E. E. Evans-Pritchard, *Theories of Primitive Religion* (New York: Oxford University Press, 1965), 15.

misconception that academic studies had to rule out supernatural explanations by definition. In either case, the whole point was to find a "natural" explanation for the origin and characteristics of religion. Simultaneously, the theology departments in the universities of Europe were imposing their negative criticism on the Bible and were raising doubt concerning biblically based doctrines by substituting a religion of good works. Thus, in the universities, resorting to the Bible as a source of reliable information was becoming disreputable.

Not all of these scholars were complete atheists. Specifically, Max Müller (1823–1900), the subject of this chapter, accepted some vague, ill-defined, perhaps pantheistic, notion of God. Underlying his writings was a vague, fundamental sense of "spirituality," which he accepted as given among all human beings. The object of his critique was "mythology," by which he meant stories in which spirits and gods have personhood and relate actively to the world; the perspective would certainly include most religions, including biblical Christianity. In particular, Müller focused on Roman and Greek myths, attempting to find clues on how to understand them by consulting Sanskrit,[2] the language of ancient Indian scriptures. He generalized from what he concluded on the basis of this method to other cultures around the world.

Socrates and Mythology

In one of his essays, Müller began by citing the beginning of the *Phaedrus*, a dialogue written by Plato.[3] As usual, it narrates a con-

---

[2] More specifically, Müller focused on the earliest Hindu compositions, the Vedas, of which the Rig Veda is the oldest (c. 1500 BC). The language of the Vedas is somewhat older than classical Sanskrit and manifests some differences as well as signs of being a language in transition. Insofar as this distinction may come up, we shall distinguish between the older Vedic Sanskrit and classical Sanskrit. Vedic Sanskrit was preceded historically by a language we shall call Indo-Iranian, which, in turn, found its roots ultimately in the most ancient Indo-European language, to which we refer as proto-IE. Both of the latter two have left no records and must be reconstructed by experts in linguistics.

[3] F. Max Müller, "Comparative Mythology" in *Chips from a German Workshop*, vol. 2 (New York: Charles Scribner, 1871), 1–141.

versation between Socrates and another person, in this case a man named Phaedrus. They were strolling along a grassy meadow, situated next to the cliffs of the sea. Phaedrus mentioned that right in that area a mythological event took place, namely that the god of the north wind, Boreas, carried off the girl, Oreithyia, to be his wife. Then he asked Socrates what he thought of dismissing supernatural stories by explaining them as exaggerations of natural events.

To Phaedrus's surprise, Socrates, who was not known for his piety, thought it was a waste of time. It would be possible, of course, to mine all such stories for some nonmiraculous core events in history, but once you got started along that route, he asserted, there just was no stopping. The world was filled with supernatural legends and myths, and Socrates saw no point in occupying himself with finding historical kernels behind all of them. He declared that he did not have the leisure to explain what other people should believe when he had hardly scratched the surface of his own personal mandate: "Know thyself."

So we can see that the process of "demythologizing" religious stories in the light of modern enlightenment began no later than the fifth century BC, and it has continued ever since. Most of it has been done on the basis of the philosophical presumption that miracles or other supernatural events simply cannot happen, and so disbelievers have substituted their presumptions for the supernatural elements in the stories.[4] For some reason, it never seems to occur to these skeptics that in the process they have made the stories pointless and have removed any reason they should have been created, let alone propagated for a long time. E. B. Tylor referred to such a move as "rationalizing Jack the Giant Killer by leaving out the giants."[5] For example,

---

[4] One of the best examples is Rudolf Bultmann, *Kerygma and Myth* (1953; repr., New York: Harper & Row, 1961), 5, where he asserts that "it is impossible to use electric light and the wireless and to avail ourselves of modern medical and surgical discoveries and at the same time to believe in the New Testament world of spirits and miracles."

[5] Tylor here is quoting G. W. Cox, though he gives no reference for the quip. E. B. Tylor, *Primitive Culture*, vol. 1, 2nd ed. (New York: Holt, 1889), 279.

Socrates mentioned that for the myth above, one could say that at some time, perhaps, a girl was playing too close to the cliffs and a powerful gust from the north made her lose her balance so that she fell down the cliffs and died. But, sad to say, people fall down cliffs all the time. What would be so special about this unfortunate event for a mythology to develop around it?

Max Müller and Philology

Müller contended that there was a third alternative between simply accepting the mythology as factually true and trying to explain its origin without any supernatural elements. Taking his cue from Socrates's dictum, "Know thyself," he believed we should use mythology as a guide to getting to know ourselves, by which he referred not just to individuals but to the entire human race. What he had in mind was a reciprocal process by which we learn about ourselves through mythology and, at the same time, use what we have learned about ourselves to clarify the nature of mythology. That second part, the analysis of mythology, actually became the centerpiece of his studies.

Max Müller was a German philologist who lived most of his life in England at Oxford University. The field of philology can be described as linguistics, the study of languages, combined with the study of the historical and cultural settings in which an ancient language functioned. Philology adds to linguistics the insight that for any distinct group of people, its language is bound to reflect specific traits of its material and spiritual culture.

Thus, philology is the discipline that teaches us to learn about the content of different cultures by analyzing the language within each culture, sometimes supplementing information we do not get directly from historical sources or from archaeology. For example, if we do not know the main weapons of a given culture but we see that in their language they have a word for bow, we can safely infer that the bow was a part of their armaments.

Müller would have preferred to live in his native Germany. However, his passion was to work on translating Sanskrit manuscripts of Indian religions, and only in England did he have access to these documents, which were owned by the British East India Company. He held a teaching position at Oxford University, though the fact that he was not a member of the Church of England kept him from occupying an endowed chair in Sanskrit.[6] Müller remained at Oxford, and years later, when his line of thought had become popular, the university created a chair specifically for him in "comparative philology." He devoted most of his life to translating Sanskrit texts as well as to editing the fifty volumes of the *Sacred Books of the East*.[7] From time to time, Müller would take a respite from his translation and editing projects to write some essays in which he expressed his theories concerning religion and mythology. Since these essays were a by-product of his major tasks, he called them "Chips from a German Workshop," and a number of his collections of essays bear that title.

The Discovery of the Indo-European Connection

The big news in philology at the time was the discovery of the family of Indo-European languages. Of course, it had been known for quite a while that, say, Greek and Latin, or French and Spanish, or German and English, to pick just a few pairs, seemed to have a lot of attributes in common, in both vocabulary and grammar. In fact, it became clear that these languages had enough in common that it made sense to stipulate an earlier common language from which they were derived.

---

[6] Sir Monier Monier-Williams (1819–99) was appointed to this chair. He was hardly a lightweight in Sanskrit studies. Undoubtedly anyone from the English-speaking world seriously studying Sanskrit today is making use of his Sanskrit-English dictionary, which has now been turned into a web-based instrument as well: http://www.sanskrit-lexicon.uni-koeln.de/monier.

[7] This large series was published originally by Oxford University Press from 1879 until 1910. Various volumes and extracts of the *SBE* have been excerpted and reprinted. However, the entire set is available at the Sacred Texts website: http://www.sacred-texts.com/sbe/index.htm.

Then, in the eighteenth century, the scholarly world learned about Sanskrit, the ancient language of India. Sanskrit, they discovered, had many similarities to those same Western languages, but it seemed to be older and more complex. The initial jubilation went so far as to believe that Sanskrit was the original version of all of these related languages, but that idea was not tenable.

This complete family of language was then called "Indo-European," a term commonly abbreviated as "IE." If all the languages in this family are related to one another, it was supposed, they must have had earlier languages in common, from which they branched off. Ultimately, there must have been one language from which they all derived, which we can call proto-Indo-European. Thus, all current IE languages had their roots in this original "proto-Indo-European" (proto-IE) language. (See appendix A for a simplified glimpse at the developments and relationships among IE languages.)

Max Müller and many other scholars believed Sanskrit was far older than Latin or Greek and thus closer to proto-IE. Therefore, he reasoned, if there were puzzles in Greek or Latin literature on the meaning of certain myths, they might well be solved by taking recourse to Sanskrit and allowing that language to shed light on Greek or Latin mythology.

The classification of languages into various families is not without controversy. However, the disputes are on the fringe, not in the core. For example, there is no question that there is an IE family of languages. The arguments focus on whether some particular minor language should be classified in that category. Other language families alongside IE include the Semitic (e.g., Hebrew and Arabic), Altaic (Turkish, Korean, and Japanese), or Sino-Tibetan (Chinese and Burmese) families. Some languages whose geographical distribution seems to be rather limited, e.g., Basque or Tamil, appear not to have many broader affiliations. Basque seems to be completely separate from any other language, and Tamil, the language of South India, is classified as a part of the Dravidian language family; the extent of this family, both in the past and the present, is uncertain, and the scholarship on this point is marred by ideological bias.[8]

*Attributes of Indo-European Languages

The following few sections are fairly technical in nature, and knowledge in depth of the subject matter is not required for the flow of the story. It is good, though, to have some basic knowledge in this area because

1. It is integral to Müller's theory. One frequently sees Müller's system described as "naturism," with the linguistic issue mentioned as an incidental by-product. However, if one wants to follow the argument of the "Father of Comparative Religion," then his approach to language must stand front and center. The fact that his conclusions frequently involved nature myths, particularly solar myths, is not nearly as important as the theory of language that led him to those results.
2. It is the foundation for identifying Indo-European monotheism, as we shall describe it in chapter 10.
3. Linguistics and language families were the door through which Wilhelm Schmidt entered the study of other cultures, which led him to the confirmation of original monotheism.
4. A basic knowledge of the nature of language families is required to understand the relationship between different cultures and their religions.

---

[8] See, for example, the works by J. D. Baskara Doss: *Dravidian Philosophy* (Chennai: National Institute of Leadership Training [NILT], 2004), *Trinity in Indian Thought* (Chennai: NILT, 2004), and *Six Darshanas and Christianity* (Chennai: NILT, 2008). Baskara Doss includes among the Dravidian languages the as-yet-untranslated language of the early Indus Valley civilization and even Greek and Hebrew. Such claims have no validity, but they illustrate the extent to which linguistics can become the tool of an ethnocentric ideology.

5. It serves as an example of how in any language family similarities and differences are recognized and principles are discovered.
6. It also supplies a blueprint by which the attentive reader, even without technical training, may be able to recognize the spurious claims for imaginary language families made up by some writers.

The affiliation of various languages with one another can be established by means of comparing vocabulary and grammar. Obviously, there will be major differences between languages, or we would not be differentiating them, but in a family certain stems and patterns reappear in their representative languages. Let us see how this looks by taking the words for "water" from different languages. The result is table 2.1. Please note that I have included only a few IE languages. This is merely an example, which should in no way be construed as a proof for the reality of the IE family of languages.[9]

If we took any two variations and nothing more, such as *watra* and *vand*, we would probably not be likely to think they belong to the same language family. But the large number of similar words gives us a clue that we can stipulate earlier languages from which these languages developed, which, in turn, developed from earlier languages, until we get all the way back to proto-IE. This original language is obviously a reconstruction by scholars; nobody speaks proto-IE today, and we have no documents written in proto-IE. But a reconstruction is possible not only on the basis of ancient written records testifying to earlier languages and dialects but also because we can detect patterns and trajectories on how a word in a specific earlier language would have become transformed into its form in a later language. To try to go back from there to a language from which proto-IE, proto-Semitic, proto-Altaic, etc., developed does not seem

---

[9] The data come from Isidore Dyen, "Comparative Indo-European Database," ed. Isidore Dyen, Joseph Kruskal, and Paul Black, 1997. Available on the Internet at "Wordgumbo.com": http://www.wordgumbo.com/ie/cmp/iedata.txt.

Language	Word
Afrikaans	water
Belorussian	vada
Bulgarian	voda
Danish	vand
English	water
Frisian	wetter
German	wasser
Greek	hudor
Hindi	pani
Icelandic	vatn
Latin	aqua
Lithuanian	vanduo
Sanskrit	vari
Sinhalese (Sri Lanka)	watura
Swedish	vatten
Takitaki (a form of Creole)	watra

Table 2.1. The word *water* in various IE languages.

to be possible—even though some scholars are mounting hypothesis on hypothesis trying to achieve such a result. The distinctions between the proto-languages seem to be irreconcilable, and this phenomenon furnishes a good reason to accept the account of the Tower of Babel (Gen 11:1–9). If it had not happened, linguists would have to invent one to account for the differences in language families.

*More on the Indo-European Connection

Focusing again on the table of words for *water* in IE languages, we must be sure not to make the English *water* the paradigm from which all others are derived. The paradigm would be the proto-IE word, which, according to the linguist Glenn Gordon would have been *wódr*, which became *wádr* as IE developed and *wádar* by the time the various tribes were separating and each of their languages was undergoing further changes.[10]

Obviously, the claim is also not that all of these languages were the direct offspring of proto-IE but that they developed through stages. As an easy example, we can point to the changes in the English language when we compare how we speak and write today with the language of the King James Bible and Shakespeare and, going back further, with the English of Chaucer.

It is not too difficult to reconstruct how most of the words in that table may have gone back to proto-IE by reconstructing intermediate stages just by using our imagination, though many of the later intermediate stages are illustrated in ancient documents. Still it does not seem too easy to connect the Latin *aqua* and its derivatives in Romance languages, such as *agua* in Portuguese, to any of the words I have listed. As a matter of fact, though, there is no problem in the case of the Latin word because there appears to be another proto-IE word referring specifically to running water, which may have been *ek*, from which another word, *akuā*,[11] may have been derived. This word could likely have been the ancestor of the Latin *aqua*. The idea is not that there is a word-for-word resemblance among all of these languages but that there are many resemblances, which we can recognize once we understand the patterns of development. Müller recognized only two families, Indo-European and Semitic; he thought all other languages were too chaotic to be capable of classification. We have come a long way from his time.[12]

---

[10] Glenn Gordon, "Paleoglot: Ancient Languages, Ancient Civilizations," http://paleoglot.blogspot.com/2008/01/syncope-and-qar-in-mid-ie.html.

[11] "Indo-European Lexicon," University of Texas, Linguistics Research Center, http://www.utexas.edu/cola/centers/lrc/ielex/PokornyMaster-X.html.

[12] Language distribution is often tied to ethnic retaledness but not necessarily. When it came right down to it, Müller did not think these language classifications should be used to draw fundamental distinctions, let alone hierarchies, among

Again, merely as illustration, not as proof, let me mention some of the fascinating grammatical similarities. Here are some easy, obviously handpicked, ones.

1. In Latin, in the second declension, the nominative case of singular masculine nouns frequently end in -*us* and the accusative case in -*um*. The same endings occur in some nouns in Sanskrit. Thus, we have in Latin, *deus* (God) in the nominative and *deum* in the accusative, and in Sanskrit, say, *shatrus* (enemy) in the nominative and *shatrum* in the accusative in one declension.

2. Neuter nouns in Latin, Greek, and Sanskrit, as well as in German (where the article before a noun is declined) always have the same form in the plural nominative and accusative cases.

3. In fact, in both Latin and Greek neuter nouns, the nominative and accusative plural endings are always -*ā*. This ending is not found in later classical Sanskrit, but it occurs in the older Vedic Sanskrit.[13]

These particular similarities do not occur in other language families. Those languages have their own resemblances, which allow linguists to classify them together as their own family.

Müller's Interpretation of Mythology as a Confusion in Language

Max Müller took advantage of the new insights of his time into the IE languages and attempted to explain the development of Greek mythology, not by questioning the facts but by analyzing the language used in mythology. His main point was that mythology arose

---

ethnicities. He opposed the growing misconception throughout Europe at the time to turn membership in an IE language group into a sign of ethnic superiority.

[13] William Dwight Whitney, *A Sanskrit Grammar*, 5th ed. (1895; repr. Delhi: Motilal Banarsidas, 1924), sec. 329c, 113; sec. 428d, 159.

because people misunderstood poetic language used in the admiration of nature and interpreted it as narrative language about divine beings.

Let us take a closer look at how Müller proceeded by following his argument in one of his most famous essays in the second volume of *Chips from a German Workshop*.[14]

1. Müller contended that the mythologies of the early IE-speaking people were too bizarre and morally offensive to think they could have arisen as a corruption of an original revelation. There are so many accounts of gods seducing human women, devouring one another, and other unacceptable and irrational actions that Müller said, "it seems blasphemy to consider these fables of the heathen world as corrupted and misinterpreted fragments of a divine revelation once granted to the whole race of mankind—a view so frequently advocated by Christian divines."[15] Müller was convinced that people in cultures suffused with mythology, as bizarre as it might be, were as intelligent as we are, so they would not necessarily believe all of their myths to be true. Many stories that are a part of our culture (legends, novels, films) we all recognize to be fiction, and the same would have been true for the people back then.

2. Instead, mythology must have arisen as a degeneration in language. With this assertion Müller postulated that there must have been a time when humans did not yet believe in myths but expressed something with their language that could easily be turned into mythology, namely a poetic description of the world around them. Müller believed that all of humanity at one time went through this stage, which he called the Mythopoeic age. It was preceded by two earlier eras, the Rhematic[16] age, in which language was so primitive that it could

---

[14] Müller, "Comparative Mythology," 1–141.

[15] Ibid., 12.

[16] From the Greek work *rhem*, which means "word" in the purely linguistic sense, as opposed to *logos*, which has deeper implications.

only express thoughts necessary for survival and in which grammar was merely a matter of sticking words together, and the Dialectic age, in which at least the Semitic and Indo-European languages developed distinctive patterns of grammar. The Mythopoeic age was followed by the Mythic period, the time in which people started to believe in the myths as realities referring to the actions of gods, goddesses, and spirits. These periods are summarized in table 2.2.

Period	Vocabulary	Grammar	Mythology
Rhematic	Only adequate for survival	Clustering of words	None
Dialectic	Survival and some descriptive	Patterns developing in IE and Semitic families	None
Mythopoeic	Descriptive, poetic, metaphoric	Concrete subjects and action verbs	None
↓ Misunderstanding of Poetic Language as Narrative ↓			
Mythic	Descriptive and abstract	Complex	Narratives

Table 2.2. Müller's periods of the development
of language and mythology

3. Now we need to clarify what occurred in the Mythopoeic period. According to Müller, during this time language still was not capable of expressing anything that required conceptual thought. It contained no abstract nouns, such as *beauty*, or any adjectives, such as *beautiful*, because such

words generalized concepts from direct observations. Thus, he claimed that the earliest languages consisted entirely of nouns that referred to substantial objects and verbs describing actions.[17]

4. However, certain intangible realities would of necessity have been spoken of by these early people, even though the language had no words for them. Such realities would include manifestations connected to time, such as *day, night,* or *dawn,* and what Müller called collective words, such as *sky* or *mountains.*[18]

5. So, how does one speak of the dawn without having a direct word for it? One uses poetic metaphors. To make up an example, not directly cited by Müller, we can speak of the morning by saying, "The sun begins its journey." Furthermore, we could speak of dusk as, "The evening star has conquered the sun." Again, "The sword of fire has sliced the clouds," might refer to lightning. Thus during this time, due to the limitations of early language, people thought and spoke as poets.[19]

6. As Müller continued his argument, the fact that he clearly focused on IE languages becomes obvious. His next observation is that the nouns used during this alleged Mythopoeic period had grammatical gender, either masculine or feminine. There was no "neuter" category yet. It was an easy step from speaking of objects with grammatical gender to thinking of them as being either male or female in sex.[20]

7. Thus, Müller envisioned the language of the Mythopoeic period to be thoroughly colorful and animated. People spoke

---

[17] Ibid., 54.

[18] Ibid., 54–55.

[19] Ibid., 55.

[20] Ibid. Since it's such an obvious point, I may as well confirm now that the question of how grammatical gender developed before people thought of things having either male or female sex is a definite weakness in Müller's argument.

of the world in ways that for later generations would sound as though they thought that the entire universe was populated with personal beings.[21]

8. A further complication for the language of people during this period was the absence of auxiliary verbs, which, again, require a level of abstraction that had not yet been attained. So, Müller claimed, abstract relations such as (my own examples again) "John *is* good" or "Betty *has* a hot temper," also had to be expressed in more concrete ways, such as (still my own examples), "John clothes himself with sweet honey," or "Betty wields her club."[22]

9. To add one more area that could lead to confusion in the future, there is the factor of synonyms and homonyms. A language usually has multiple words for certain things, which can be used interchangeably. Later on it may happen that one of those words becomes dominant, and the previous synonyms fall by the wayside. Also, languages usually have some words that sound alike, though they mean different things, and it is possible that over time such a homonym may replace the original word.[23]

10. Then, Müller's reconstruction continues; as the various segments of humanity proceeded from the Mythopoeic period to the Mythic period, they turned the poetry into prose. The descriptions of the various aspects and forces of nature were misunderstood. *Lightning* represented metaphorically perhaps as a sword, using masculine grammar, became the god Lightning, bearing the name of *Sword*, to use another simplified example. The various descriptions of the sun, moon, and stars became personalized into actual deities performing the actions ascribed to them with poetic phrasing. The colorful imagery that had been used to refer to the streams and rivers,

---

[21] Ibid., 56–60.
[22] Ibid., 60–70.
[23] Ibid., 71–73.

the mountains and rocks, the sky and the darkness of night, and so forth, now became the names of personal spiritual beings who supposedly inhabited the world. Therefore, what once was simply poetic language now turned into mythology.

Thus, to use a common summary of Müller's analysis, according to him, religion came about due to a mistake in grammar. People confused grammatical gender with biological sex and misunderstood metaphors as literal descriptions. He asserts:

> After the laws that regulate the growth and decay of words have once been clearly established, instead of being any longer surprised at the breaking out of mythological phraseology, we almost wonder how any language could have escaped what may really be called an infantine disease, through which even the healthiest constitution ought to pass sooner or later. The origin of mythological phraseology, whatever outward aspects it may assume, is always the same; it is language forgetting herself.[24]

Mythology, then, is the measles of a language growing up.

Müller's Method Applied

Müller had created a tool to understand problematic parts of mythology without turning the stories themselves into historical occurrences devoid of their supernatural elements. As mentioned above, he took note of the fact that many ancient myths ascribe such dark and revolting actions to the gods that even the people who supposedly believed in them were offended by them. Others appear contradictory or senseless. According to Müller's analysis, it might be possible to clear up such awkward tales by going back to the myths' origins in language.

Furthermore, Müller had provided the means to show that in general, when a myth claims that supernatural events have occurred, its linguistic roots will reveal to us that initially no such claim was

---

[24] Müller, "Greek Legends," in *Chips*, vol. 2, 160.

intended. In theory, every piece of mythology should be able to be translated back into a metaphoric statement meaning nothing more than such declarations as, "The sun rises," or "Dawn is coming."

Let us say that we are considering a Greek myth that describes the actions of a hero. Probably, but not necessarily, those actions will include miraculous deeds. Müller will take the name of the hero and the words used for the action and trace them back to their original premythological meaning. Doing so appears to be a rather daring endeavor. How can one possibly bring about this retransformation since the people living in the Mythopoeic period did not leave any written records? We can do so in some cases, Müller believed, simply by constructing a plausible etymology for the Greek terms. In many other cases the etymology can make progress only by looking for the Greek language's equivalents in Sanskrit, which is much closer to proto-IE.

Even though Müller did not believe Sanskrit was the proto-IE language, he did think it came closer to it than other languages. He did not think that Greek, Latin, or German were directly derived from Sanskrit. However, if Sanskrit was more closely related to proto-IE, from which the other languages took their own paths, one might be able to get insight into expressions that may not make sense to us in the other languages. We can demystify them by looking at their parallels in Sanskrit and finding their original meaning in nonmythical discourse. As we shall see shortly, some of Müller's critics never came to terms with the fact that Müller never said anything as silly as that Sanskrit influenced Greek, let alone that Hindu mythology influenced Greek mythology. His point was that both languages must have had a common ancestral language and that Sanskrit reflected that earlier language more closely than Greek.

Let us look at an example. There is a Greek myth in which Apollo, unquestionably a sun god, chased Daphne, a nymph. He loved her, but she refused his advances. He insisted, and so she ran away, but he continued to pursue her. There are, as usual, several versions of the myth, in some of which Daphne dies or is swallowed up by the earth. According to a common variant, when Apollo was just about to catch her, she prayed to the other gods to save her, and they did so by turning her into a laurel tree. Our task, if we want to follow Müller's analysis, is to see what the original language would have said before the episode turned into a story of gods and supernatural events.

1. Since Apollo's identity as a sun god is clear, the original in the Mythopoeic period must have said something about the sun. Furthermore, his name can be traced back by way of looking at a possible Sanskrit etymology. *Apavaryan* or *Apavalyan* can mean "he who opens the sky," an interesting way of referring to the sun. Regardless, there is no question that Apollo represents the sun.

2. A more difficult task is to discover what *Daphne* could have meant in the Mythopoeic period before she became personified as a myth later on.[25]

3. There are no further clues in the Greek for an etymology of *Daphne*. However, when we look at Sanskrit and postulate its development out of the precursor language to both Sanskrit and Greek, we can make further progress.

   An important caution is in order here: We need to emphasize that Müller is looking at the language in which eventually India's own mythology would emerge and grow, not at classical Indian mythology itself. The stories of the Hindu gods and their exploits developed long after the groups that were going to speak Greek and those that would speak Sanskrit parted from each other. Thus, taking recourse to Indian mythology is not going to help much, if at all, but by looking at Sanskrit, or—more precisely—the earliest form of Sanskrit in which the Rig Veda was composed, along with the archaic names of the gods in the Rig Veda, we may make some progress.

---

[25] Müller, "Comparative Mythology," 89–93.

4. A Sanskrit word for "day" is *ahan*. Müller states that *ahan* should actually be *dahan* with the letter *d* having dropped out. I assume he is basing this judgment on his acquaintance with the seemingly hundreds of principles for euphonic combinations—rules that smooth out the pronunciation of combinations of words in Sanskrit. He states that it is possible, then, that the root of the word would be *dah*, which means to burn, which can be connected to the red and violet colors of the dawn. But then, surprisingly, he does not particularly pursue that path. Instead, Müller demonstrates that in many IE languages, the word for *day* is used as a verb to refer to the dawn. For example, in German, the word for *day* is *Tag*, and when dawn is coming, one says, *Es tagt*, "It is 'daying.'" Thus, *dahan*, presumably the original form of *day* in the precursor to Sanskrit, can also function as *dahana*, "the dawn," and, of course, *Dahana* can then be personalized into a goddess of dawn.

5. Now, if we follow the rules of transformation, by which we can estimate what a word in one IE language would be like in another IE language, turning the Sanskrit *Dahana* into a Greek word yields the result: *Daphne*.

6. So now we have a pretty good idea of what the ancient pre-mythological poets were saying when they stated that Apollo chased Daphne. They were describing the phenomenon that the sun chases the dawn away, no matter how intensely the dawn, with its exhilaratingly fresh air and sparkling dew, tries to resist.

7. So far the version according to which Daphne dies fits in well with the analysis, but what about the part where she is turned into a laurel tree? For this point Müller's appeal to homonyms and synonyms comes into play. In Greek the word for "laurel" is also *daphne*. Laurel wood burns easily; Daphne was in danger of being burned (and I can't help but remember the possible Sanskrit root *dah*, to burn); so,

in a highly likely confusion, the laurel tree and the goddess became interchanged. Thus, in the story, Daphne turns into a laurel tree.

Let us summarize Müller's case. He addressed himself to what we might call "conventional religion," by which I mean beliefs about personal gods and spirits as described in a collection of mythological stories, ranging all the way from animism to monotheistic religions. How did these mythology-based religions arise? Müller claimed it all began with a misunderstanding that is a natural part in the development of any language. There was a time when a culture's language was capable of expressing abstract concepts only by using metaphors composed of nouns referring to substantial objects and verbs. The nouns had grammatical gender. At a later time these metaphors were no longer recognized as such, but people interpreted the nouns as personal beings with superior powers and the verbs as real actions. Thus, mythological narratives were born, and they expanded from there.

Andrew Lang's Critique

All this was too much for Andrew Lang (1844–1912), a folklorist and disciple of E. B. Tylor, the best-known advocate of the evolution of religion. (We shall focus more on both Lang and Tylor later.) There are two aspects to Lang's reaction to Müller: the weakness of the philological method and the claim that an evolutionary theory can give a better explanation of the content of mythology than philology.

Lang thought philology, as exemplified by Müller, was highly arbitrary. He found Müller's conclusions to be unconvincing, particularly in light of the fact that other scholars using the same method came to radically different conclusions. Lang asked rhetorically:

> Why, then, do distinguished scholars and mythologists reach
> such different goals? Clearly because their method is so
> precarious. They all analyze the names in myths; but where one

decides that the name is originally Sanskrit, another holds that it is purely Greek, and a third, perhaps, is all for an Accadian [*sic*] etymology, or a Semitic derivation. Again, even when scholars agree as to the original root from which a name springs, they differ as much as ever as to the meaning of the name in its present place.[26]

It appears to me that Lang is making a valid argument, at least up to a point. We must insist that logically Müller's interpretations could be true even if no other philologist ever agreed with him. Nevertheless, his etymological derivations often (not always) appear forced and not entirely convincing. The problem Lang exposed was that we do not have a clear set of standards with which to judge which interpretation is correct. Perhaps we are confused because we have not immersed ourselves in the subject matter to the extent Müller had; then again, those that seem to have done so do not seem to help us find clear lines either.

The second part of Lang's case, that developmental anthropology provides a better explanation for mythology and religion, we will discuss extensively in the next chapter.

Lang also brought up some factual issues with Müller's theory. There is no evidence of a "Mythopoeic period" in which people spoke in metaphors because their language was too underdeveloped to express abstract notions. One might say that given the nature of this hypothetical period, no historical record could be possible, but such an argument from silence does not carry much weight. In fact, going beyond Lang, we must question whether there even can be such a thing as a "pure" metaphor.[27] For a metaphor to communicate something, it must have a core of meaning behind its images with which its users are familiar. Otherwise, people would just be making speech-like noises that only they understood. But if there is a

---

[26] Andrew Lang, *Custom and Myth* (1885; repr., New York: AMS Press, 1963), 2.

[27] See Paul Edwards, "Professor Tillich's Confusions," *Mind* 94 (April 1965):197–206, for a good exposition on the idea of "irreducible metaphors."

commonly understood concept underneath a metaphor, surely it can be expressed, if not with its own word or sign (an idea that seems obvious to me, but that Müller did not accept). If you can think an abstract idea, you can say it, at least by circumlocution. Metaphors only convey a meaningful point if others are familiar with the same abstract notion the metaphor illustrates.

Still there was something positive in Müller's analysis that Lang and others abrogated. Müller attributed the development of myths to a stage in language, not to the supposed simplemindedness of people in the Mythic period. He gave them credit for not inventing the bizarre events of Greek mythology or accepting them as factual history. In fact, Müller was upset with the way in which the growing field of anthropology relegated so-called primitive people to an unacceptable level of stupidity.[28] Lang, however, following the dictates of an evolutionary theory, could not avoid the distinction between the way earlier human beings thought and the way in which we now think.

So we can come back to the story of Daphne turning into a laurel tree. Lang saw this myth as a case of metamorphosis, which, he said, is a common theme in myths around the world and is embraced as truth by those who tell it. Lang's argument on this point can be divided into three parts:

1. The thesis that Greek mythology arose out of a misunderstanding of an unsubstantiated early phase of IE language is highly implausible and without credible proof.
2. Since similar myths arise all over the globe, the notion that in all those cases the mythology came about due to the same kind of linguistic breakdown strains anyone's credulity.
3. It is far easier to believe that unenlightened people in the early stages of human culture actually believed such myths,

---

[28] See, for example, Max Müller, "Physical Religion" extracted from "Gifford Lectures on Physical Religion, 1890," in John R. Stone, *The Essential Max Müller* (New York: Palgrave Macmillan, 2002), 271–72.

regardless of how monstrous they may appear to us, because such primitive people make little distinction between themselves and the objects of nature around them.[29]

Lang accounted for these apparently absurd stories by saying that to the savage mind, which draws no hard and fast line between man and nature, all such things are possible—possible enough, at least, to be used as incidents in a story. Again, as has elsewhere been shown, he said the laxity of philological reasoning is often extraordinary while, lastly, philologists of the highest repute flatly contradict one another about the meaning of the names and roots on which they agree in founding their theory.[30]

Lang would eventually change his mind in some respects, as we shall see.

Müller's philological approach, though popular for a while in academic circles, was embattled on two fronts. Scholars of a traditional Christian persuasion took exception to the idea that Müller's theory of the origin of myth also relegated biblical accounts to the same level of linguistic mix-ups. On the more liberal side, the new anthropology with its Darwinian presuppositions was waging fierce warfare on Müller's philology. The idea that mythology was simply a malfunction of language could not stand up to newer trends in scholarship.

Nevertheless, we should not lose sight of Müller's genius in blazing trails in Sanskrit studies. And it is to Müller's everlasting credit that he resisted the idea that people in other stages of religion were dull witted and primitive. But anthropology, coming along with Darwinian presuppositions, was taking the day; with the evolutionary model also came a derogation of many other human beings as inferior. We need to turn in that direction in the next chapter.

---

[29] Please see my comments on this terminology in the preface.
[30] Lang, *Custom and Myth*, 2012.

CHAPTER 3

E. B. Tylor: Religion from a Darwinian Perspective

As I stated at the end of chapter 1, it would be redundant and not particularly helpful if I recounted all of the many theories of the origin of religion and their advocates during the late nineteenth and early twentieth centuries. As mentioned, Wilhelm Schmidt's work *The Origin and Growth of Religion*[1] does so well, and there is no need to recite the entire catalog again. E. B. Tylor, who advocated an evolutionary model of religion wherein a universal and simplistic belief in spirits (animism) would develop and culminate in the worship of powerful deities, will serve as our main representative in this chapter. We will, of course, make reference to other scholars as we move along.

During the same time period when philology was dominating the discussion on the origins of mythology, evolutionism was growing in stature and eventually taking over as the reigning paradigm. "Darwinism" became an uncontestable presupposition for many scholars in the analysis of religions.

---

[1] Wilhelm Schmidt, *The Origin and Growth of Religion: Facts and Theories*, 2nd ed., trans. H. J. Rose (New York: Humanities Press, 1936).

The Early Anthropological Method

Max Müller, as we saw, focused on the historical legacy of the cultures in the IE-speaking cultures. Studying the past is certainly a reasonable approach to solving a puzzle located in the past, such as the origin of religion; however, much of the past is inaccessible to us. Archaeological artifacts, for example, are not self-interpreting.[2] However, under the label of "uniformity," nineteenth-century anthropology proceeded on the premise that the ancient past has preserved itself. We can still see it in full bloom in the cultures of tribal people. Human beings who are now living on a stone-age level must have preserved stone-age culture, they argued.[3] And as a corollary, the beliefs and practices of people whose material culture has not grown as far as others[4] have sustained the beliefs and ritual practices of those human beings who were on the same level of material culture in the past. Thus, if we want to learn about the religion of the earliest humans, we do not need to travel back in time; we may simply have to travel across the ocean and visit various cultures in the bush, desert, or jungle. This area of study is also frequently called "ethnology," the study of various ethnically diverse populations, and *ethnology* is many times used synonymously with *cultural anthropology*, even though the two are not actually the same.

---

[2] To put it simply, there seems to be a pattern among archaeologists to designate an artifact as a ritual instrument if they cannot identify any other practical function for it. They are probably correct in many cases, particularly if there are analogous objects in use in contemporary cultures. Moving further back in time to the Paleolithic era, the cave paintings that presumably depict magical hunting rituals do not come with captions. Such interpretations that have practically become conventional wisdom today were read into the pictures by nineteenth-century anthropologists and are actually quite arbitrary.

[3] See E. B. Tylor, *Researches into the Early History of Mankind* (New York: Henry Holt, 1870).

[4] By "material culture" I mean the basic mode of living. Included in that category are the manner of supplying food (hunter-gatherer, agriculture, etc.), and forms of dwelling (huts, caves, tents, etc.). Anytime we attempt to group different cultures together, we must consider the materials of which they produced implements (stone, pottery, metals) as well as the skill evident in making them functional and ornamental.

This method clearly incorporates some assumptions that can be questioned. For one, it makes distinctions between various levels of material development among human cultures. This assumption needs to be neither controversial, as long as we maintain some common sense and do not impose unnecessary values on different stages nor evolutionary if we do not ascribe development to natural laws. There can hardly be a question that a culture living with pottery and bronze implements is materially more advanced than one that only uses stone tools and is less advanced than one that utilizes plastic bottles and DVDs. Moral or intellectual superiority does not need to (nor should it) have anything to do with such an observation—though for some nineteenth-century anthropologists, it did.

Another, more questionable, assumption is whether the present-day, less-developed cultures really represent the early cultures of humanity. To maintain this assumption we need to stipulate that such cultures spent millennia virtually unchanged. Now, it is not unknown for a tribe or other population group to be forced to reverse their material situation, perhaps due to warfare, an epidemic, or environmental catastrophes. But we know about such instances because there is evidence for such reverses with or without recoveries, which one can take into account. (We will discuss the nature of what constitutes evidence in a later chapter.) However, on the whole it is reasonable to believe that most cultures that are now on a materially less advanced level did not go through a roller coaster of substantial major changes. Still it is an assumption, at least for now.

The third assumption is that the material level of a people group runs parallel to its religious culture. Darwinian anthropology made that assumption its starting point, coming to the subject matter with preconceived notions of what primordial religions must have been like: simplistic, childlike, credulous, magical, and irrational. As we shall see shortly, this picture became an unassailable dogma for many people. In response, because of the arbitrary way in which they filled in what the earliest religion must have looked like, we may be tempted to dismiss this assumption and say that anthropology can tell us nothing plausible about the religious culture of early humans. However, an outright rejection would be going too far; indeed, it would actually deprive us of some strong evidence against the Darwinian view. It is not really either the assumptions of the method that we need to put into question, just the preconceptions with which these scholars assumed their conclusions prior to full investigation. Eventually this process would be turned back on them by one of their own highly vocal defenders.

The Dogma of "Primitivity"

Not everyone followed this scheme of the evolution of religions. We have already seen that Max Müller did not believe people who lived in ages dominated by mythology were less intelligent than modern humans. Sadly, we saw that his unwillingness to take the supposed intellectual inferiority of the so-called savage mind into account was considered to be an obvious point against him by his critics. It became a matter of alleged conventional wisdom that "primitive" people were only capable of "primitive" thoughts, and, thus, their religions could only be "primitive," viz. childish and magical without having a rational distinction between the natural and the supernatural.

Other writers attempted to counter the Darwinian approach by insisting that religion began with the awareness of a single God, the Creator, and that later developments were instances of degeneration from this original monotheism. After all, this was the teaching of the Bible and, despite the general antibiblical attitude that was developing in the academy, some scholars still thought this was the most plausible way of understanding diversity and change in the world's religions. E. B. Tylor referred to it as the "Degeneration Theory."[5]

One advocate of such a theory of a primitive monotheism was the Swiss linguist Adolphe Pictet (1799–1875). Pictet wrote a lengthy treatise on the early Aryans, the Indo-European people who settled in India and Iran, in which he employed philology as a kind of

---

[5] E. B. Tylor, *Primitive Culture*, 2nd ed., vol. 1 (New York: Gordon Press, 1889); and *Primitive Culture*, vol. 2 (London: John Murray, 1889), *passim*.

archaeological tool.[6] He called his method "linguistic paleontology" (*paléontologie linguistique*), and his goal was to attempt to reconstruct the proto-Indo-European language (proto-IE), which he believed to have been spoken on the Indian subcontinent (an idea whose day is long past), to which he referred—as many scholars did at the time—simply as "Aryan."[7] Then, following the method of philology, he attempted to use the language of the people who spoke "Aryan" in order to reconstruct their culture, trying to go back to the time before they split into the two groups who eventually settled in India and Iran respectively.

In the pursuit of his goal, Pictet had to deal extensively with the religious elements in Vedic Sanskrit and its hypothetical precursor, the elusive proto-IE or simply "Aryan." His study directed itself against those writers who advanced a theory of gradual development of religion, according to which the people of the early Aryan tribes turned the recognition of a spiritual element in nature into the worship of the gods of nature. Pictet discerned a serious linguistic problem with this idea. Let me illustrate with a simple example.

Numerous words in Sanskrit refer to the sun; one of them is *suriya*. In later mythology "Suriya" becomes the name of a personal sun god who rides his chariot across the sky every day. Pictet, in a manner not all that different from Müller's, believed he could discern that in its earliest usage *suriya* referred merely to the sun as the physical bright and hot object in the sky without any attributes of deity. So, Pictet asked rhetorically, how could it be that, if the religion supposedly started out as a polytheistic nature religion, the idea of *Suriya* as a sun deity is a later development tagged on to the earlier meaning of *suriya* as the physical sun?

---

[6] Adolphe Pictet, *Les origines indo-européennes; ou, les Aryas primitifs: Essai de paléontologie linguistique*, 2nd ed., 3 vols. (Paris: J. Cherbuliez and Sandoz & Fischbacher, 1877).

[7] See the essay by E. F. K. Koerner, "Linguistics and Ideology in the Study of Language," accessible at http://www.tulane.edu/~howard/LangIdeo/Koerner/Koerner.html.

Pictet answered his own question by raising doubts about the notion that the gods and goddesses were derived from the object with which they were associated. He maintained that the practice of endowing a god with the names of its object was a later development. This undermined the notion that the god emerged out of divinization of physical entities.

But in that case the identities and original attributes of the supernatural beings must have come from somewhere other than the natural entities. It seemed to Pictet to be a natural conclusion that if the supernatural beings were not derived from the natural realm, they must have emerged out of a previously accepted supernatural realm. The early Aryans must have believed in a supernatural reality that was not tied to natural objects. Thus, at one time they must have recognized the reality of a single spiritual being.

Pictet concluded that the religion of the earliest Aryans began with an ill-defined but undeniable monotheism. The conception of this primeval single god was vague, however; thus, it was easy for the early Aryans to isolate aspects of him and turn them into the numerous and more concretely describable gods and goddesses of polytheism. Only secondarily, then, did they attach these "parceled out" divine beings to phenomena of nature based on some resemblances in attributes. Pictet believed that in the overall process leading to polytheism among the Aryans, "supernature" preceded nature; a single god preceded multiple gods.

Another scholar, John Muir (1818–82) was an expert in Sanskrit and Hinduism and had spent a large part of his life in India, much of it promoting education.[8] He responded to Pictet rather conservatively, namely by stating that Pictet had simply not made his case. Muir argued that

1. Even if there were a simpler religion earlier than the polytheism of the Vedas, such a possibility would not necessitate

---

[8] John Muir, *Original Sanskrit Text on the Origin and History of the People of India*, vol. 5 (London: Trübner, 1872), 412–20.

a monotheism; it could simply have been a much simpler nature worship.

2. Even if the original references to the heavenly bodies seem to focus mostly on their physical characteristics (which would not be surprising), this possibility would not rule out that from the beginning the people may also have endowed them with spiritual powers and attributes. They may not have stated that they were doing so explicitly.

Note that Muir himself did not claim directly that Pictet was wrong, only that his arguments were unconvincing. He did not bring up any actual evidence against Pictet. However, he did quote a number of other writers who shared neither Muir's nor Pictet's credentials in Sanskrit. They simply repudiated Pictet's ideas on the basis of speculative and philosophical presuppositions. Their objections were based almost entirely on the dogma that polytheism must have preceded monotheism because early humans were not capable of a monotheistic religion.

One of these critics, the German theologian Otto Pfleiderer (1839–1908), took the route of postulating that any hints at a monotheism in an early culture were an anticipation of future developments, a line of argumentation that would become increasingly popular. Pfleiderer gave the following explication of the spiritual state of the early Aryans:

> We thus see that in this original form of piety, there already exist general powers, to which the devout spirit is directed, powers which, in consequence of their relative infinitude, were well calculated to present and render comprehensible, to the childlike spirit, the idea of absolute infinity. For to the childlike contemplation of the earliest races, the heaven and earth were not, what they are for us, for the educated understanding, a system of finite causes standing in a relation of orderly reciprocal action to each other; but living beings, endowed with soul, acting, after the manner of men, with knowledge and will, to

whom consequently men could quite properly pray with the
firm belief that they would be heard, and their wishes granted.[9]

Before proceeding, I cannot help but register my curiosity as
to what the distinction between "relative infinitude" and "absolute
infinity" could possibly mean. Furthermore, I do not believe children
in any culture, let alone adults, are ignorant of the difference between
the sky and God who lives in the sky. Nobody expects the physical
sky to answer prayers.

Still, the same thought underlay the critique by the French
apostate and ex-theologian Edmond Scherer (1815–89), who had
by this time turned stridently against all religion. Muir quoted him
from a review of Pictet's work, in which Scherer first of all asserted
that Pictet based his argument on a strict distinction between
monotheism and polytheism. "[Pictet] thinks the human mind must
have proceeded from the simple to the complex, from unity to
diversity; that polytheism has arisen from the need of seeking other
beings intermediate between the Supreme Being and man, and that
it has thus been able to establish itself without destroying altogether
the first or monotheistic idea."[10]

Then Scherer attempted to take the wind out of Pictet's sails by
claiming that "there never has been, and doubtless there never will
be, either a pure polytheism or a pure monotheism."[11]

The word "pure" is essential in this assertion because it is flexible and subject to ad hoc modifications as needed. No doubt, in
cultures in which the dominant religion is monotheistic (Judaism,
Islam, Christianity), it will be possible to find people who have not
entirely subscribed to the idea of a single supreme god; similarly, in
polytheistic cultures there may live a monotheist or two. But the possibility of such minor anomalies is surely compatible with declaring

---

[9] Otto Pfleiderer, *Die Religion, ihr Wesen und ihre Geschichte*, ii. 45 ff. (Leipzig: 1869), cited in Muir, *Original Texts*.
[10] Edmond Scherer, *Melanges d'Histoire Religieuse*, 35 ff., cited in Muir, *Original Texts*.
[11] Ibid.

that a given religion is fundamentally monotheistic or polytheistic or neither.

Then Muir turned to a theologian named Albert Seville:

> If we had before us positive facts attesting that the march of the human mind has been such (as M. Pictet describes), we should only have to surrender, and admit, contrary to all probability a priori, that man, while still sunk in the most profound ignorance, was better able to grasp religious truths than he was at the epoch when he began to reflect and to know.[12]

Seville conceded that if there truly were evidence in favor of Pictet's theory, there would be no choice but to concede Pictet's case to him. However, he contended that up to such a time one should refrain from the a priori absurdity that human beings, "while still sunk in the most profound ignorance," could have held a monotheistic religion. One could point out that if the earliest humans held to a basic monotheism, they might just turn out not to have been sunk in that pit of ignorance, at least as far as their religious views go. Again, the contest appears to be between Pictet's admittedly meager evidence on the one hand and a dogmatic assumption on the other.

Muir continued to cite Seville:

> In short, it is clear that the human mind, in proportion as it observes and reflects, rises more and more towards monotheism, in obedience to that imperious law, hidden in the depths of its being, which leads it to the logical pursuit of unity. But this movement is very slow, greatly retarded by the force of tradition and habit, and we ought not to place at the beginning that which can only be found at the very end of the process.[13]

Seville appealed to a "fundamental law." He called it "imperious" and "hidden in the depths of the being [of the human mind]." But how hidden is it really? Seville obviously thought he knew about

---

[12] Albert Seville, *Revue des Deux Mondes* (February 1864), 721 ff., cited in Muir, *Original Texts*, 412–15.

[13] Ibid., 415–20.

it. In fact, he seemed to assume it was obvious to well-educated people. Now this alleged law leads the mind to the "logical pursuit of unity," though we must be careful to recognize that such unity, expressed perhaps by monotheism, can only be attained after a lengthy process. Where did Seville get such an idea? Who discovered this law? Where is the independent evidence for it that does not merely beg the question? The fact is that there is no law to the effect that the human mind will slowly and with great difficulty strive for conceptual unity, which may then manifest itself in embracing monotheism. This "law" is merely a restatement of the ever-growing evolutionary mentality of Muir's day. Uttered in properly unctuous tones, such a statement will sound convincing, but it is nothing but a fiction created to support a point of view. These early enthusiasts for an anthropological Darwinism were, as we have seen now, dogmatic and not scientific. It was E. B. Tylor's distinction that supported this position by amassing a huge amount of facts, thereby enabling him to speak not just by delivering messages from an academic Mount Olympus but by appealing to evidence.

E. B. Tylor: Master of the Details

Today's scholars who disagree with the outcome of E. B. Tylor's (1832–1917) work should not overlook the contribution he made in establishing anthropology as a legitimate field of scholarship in academics. His penchant for supporting his conclusions with details based on reports from all over the world gave anthropology a degree of credibility that went beyond the appeal of its philosophical presuppositions.

In fact, Tylor's interest in studying other cultures began with a trip to warmer climates, on which he encountered some of the indigenous people of Central America.[14] When he showed the symptoms of

---

[14] A. C. Haddon, "Introduction" in E. B. Tylor, *Anthropology*, vol. 1, 14th ed. (1881; repr., New Delhi: Cosmo Publications, 2004), v.

early tuberculosis, his parents had sent him on this journey rather than having him take over the family business. When he returned to England, he began studying at Oxford University but never finished a complete course of study. Instead, based on his publications and obvious ability, he was soon invited to give regular lectures, and eventually he became Oxford's first professor of anthropology. He earned all the usual honors available to British scholars at the time, such as becoming a member of the Royal Society and delivering the Gifford lectures. He seems to have been competent in Greek, Latin, and French, but his Sanskrit appears to be secondhand,[15] as would be the many other languages to which he made reference in his writings.

Tylor worked within the paradigm of Darwinian evolution, but he makes little reference to the scientists and thinkers who built this theory. His reason is simply that his cultural work and the geological and biological work of Darwin, Lyell et al., do not actually cross one another's territory. Tylor was willing to assume the biological evolution of human beings but thought their cultural development could not be subsumed under the same pattern without serious adjustments. Unfortunately, the natural scientists did not necessarily see it this way and saw themselves as social engineers as well.

*Darwin and Human Beings

We have already made the point that in the middle of the nineteenth century evolution was a theory many people longed to accept though it had not received the desired scientific grounding. For many scientists the "fact" that biological species could transform into other species was a given, but they were in need of a method that would

---

[15] See Tylor, *Primitive Culture*, 315. Here Tylor tries to make an etymological connection between the English word *waddle* and the Latin *vado* ("to go") and the Sanskrit root √*vad*. Unfortunately, *vad* in Sanskrit means "to speak" or "say," and it was frequently the first verb used as a paradigm in Sanskrit textbooks of the nineteenth century. My point is not to make Tylor look unintelligent—that would be impossible—but to emphasize how much of his evidence is derivative.

explain how such a change could transpire. Virtually everyone who followed the evolutionary line accepted the idea of the inheritance of acquired characteristics that is usually associated with the French biologist Jean-Baptiste Lamarck (1744–1829).[16] This theory held that animals that would exert themselves in exercising one of their abilities would likely see that same ability in strengthened form inherited by their offspring. On the other hand, disuse of a capacity would weaken it in subsequent generations, and it would eventually disappear. Lamarck's contribution was to provide a metaphysical basis for such changes. He did not think that such changes occurred purely by either the organism's own will or random chance but were driven by two natural forces, one that pushed life forms constantly to diversify and another one that enabled them to adapt to their environment in their new forms. Few people went along with the idea of these forces, but the concept of self-directed changes in organisms was widely received.

Herbert Spencer (1820–1903), who eventually coined the phrase "survival of the fittest," stated in an earlier essay concerning the basic mechanism of the inheritance of acquired traits that "it is the *only* law of organic modifications of which we have any evidence."[17] Not that there really was any evidence for this "law," but it had become regarded as true simply by repetition and lack of competition. Since Darwin had no knowledge of genetics he made use of it himself from time to time. The idea of an opposition between Lamarck and Darwin is a myth based on events that transpired in the twentieth century.[18]

Obviously such changes in the population of a particular species would require a lot of time, and the contribution of the geologist

---

[16] Jean-Baptiste Lamarck, *Philosophie zoologique: ou Exposition des considérations relative à l'histoire naturelle des animaux.* English version: *Zoological Philosophy: An Exposition with Regard to the Natural History of Animals,* trans. Hugh Elliott (London: Macmillan, 1809).

[17] Herbert Spencer, "Progress: Its Law and Cause," 1857, in *Essays: Scientific, Political and Speculative* (London: Williams and Norgate, 1891), 55.

[18] Michael T. Ghiselin, "The Imaginary Lamarck: A Look at Bogus 'History' in Schoolbooks," http://www.textbookleague.org/54marck.htm.

Charles Lyell (1797–1875) made such a framework possible.[19] Studying the different layers in Earth's crust and the embedded fossils, he concluded that Earth was millions of years old. Given that amount of time, the slow and gradual changes needed for evolution seemed to be available. He exercised a profound influence on Charles Darwin (1809–82) and Alfred Russell Wallace (1823–1913), who had arrived at the concept of natural selection independently and who presented it for the first time together at a conference in 1859.

For Darwin the conclusions of his observations also led to practical consequences. Having established a hierarchy among animals, he also believed in gradations of inferiority and superiority among human beings. These rankings could be found both among different races and among people belonging to the same race. We read at the conclusion of *The Descent of Man*:

> Both sexes ought to refrain from marriage if they are in any marked degree inferior in body or mind; but such hopes are Utopian and will never be even partially realised until the laws of inheritance are thoroughly known. Everyone does good service, who aids towards this end. When the principles of breeding and inheritance are better understood, we shall not hear ignorant members of our legislature rejecting with scorn a plan for ascertaining whether or not consanguineous marriages are injurious to man.[20]

So Darwin was convinced that any two human beings, either of whom might bear the marks of inferiority, ought not to marry, lest the human race become downgraded. Darwin lamented that this idea was only Utopian, but still he called on people to advance this end.

To whom was Darwin addressing this hope for a ban on marriage between those whom he considered to be incompatible? Surely not

---

[19] Charles Lyell, *Principles of Geology, Being an Attempt to Explain the Former Changes of the Earth's Surface by Reference to Causes Now in Operation*, 3 vols., 2nd ed. (London: John Murray, 1832).
[20] Charles Darwin, *The Descent of Man and Selection in Relation to Sex*, vol. 2 (London: John Murray, 1871), 403.

just to the hypothetical mismatched couple, who would not even read his book anyway; as we can see in the next sentence, he was overtly wishing for a social program. The first step in this program would be a government-sponsored test of the effects of consanguinity in marriage on offspring. In other words, the government ought to sponsor some practical experiments on the empirically verifiable effects of incest. Presumably, if it can be shown that a brother and sister with highly superior intellect can have offspring without genetic repercussions, such marriages should be encouraged. Thank God for the "ignorant members of the legislature" who rejected this experimentation "with scorn"!

Did Darwin, then, support eugenics? It would appear that even when he tempered his ideas by invoking moral principles, it is pretty clear what his preferences were when he referred to a ban on mismatched couples as "Utopian." Darwin carried on with his musings: "The advancement of the welfare of mankind is a most intricate problem: all ought to refrain from marriage who cannot avoid abject poverty for their children; for poverty is not only a great evil, but tends to its own increase by leading to recklessness in marriage."[21]

This line of thought led him to the more radical ideas of a cousin of his. If inferior people should be kept from procreating, superior people should be freed from any bonds or restrictions. Francis Galton (1822–1911) believed that not only should there be nothing standing in the way of the superior person's efforts to advance the human race, but the world should welcome him as a messiah-like figure. To quote Galton (who, unsurprisingly classified himself with these one-in-a-million individuals):

> If a man is gifted with vast intellectual ability to work, eagerness
> to work, and power of working, **I cannot comprehend how such
> a man should be repressed.** The world is always tormented
> with difficulties waiting to be solved—struggling with ideas
> and feelings, to which it can give no adequate expression. If,

---

[21] Ibid.

then, there exists a man capable of solving those difficulties, or of giving a voice to those pent-up feelings, he is sure to be welcomed with universal acclamation.[22]

Darwin contemplated Galton's ideas as he continued with his own concluding thoughts:

On the other hand, as Mr. Galton has remarked, if the prudent avoid marriage, whilst the reckless marry, the inferior members tend to supplant the better members of society. Man, like every other animal, has no doubt advanced to his present high condition through a struggle for existence consequent on his rapid multiplication; and if he is to advance still higher, it is to be feared that he must remain subject to a severe struggle. Otherwise he would sink into indolence, and the more gifted men would not be more successful in the battle of life than the less gifted. Hence our natural rate of increase, though leading to many and obvious evils, must not be greatly diminished by any means. There should be open competition for all men; and **the most able should not be prevented by laws or customs from succeeding best and rearing the largest number of offspring.**[23]

This is a pretty scary conclusion. If truly implemented, it would mean that the superior people could kill those whom they considered inferior. Rape and other acts of violence promoting the supposedly superior people would be justified. Remember now that this situation would bring about what Darwin considered to be a Utopia. Nonetheless, he recognized the moral restraints that made the implementation of such radical ideas unacceptable.

Important as the struggle for existence has been and even still is, yet as far as the highest part of man's nature is concerned there are other agencies more important. For the moral qualities are advanced, either directly or indirectly, much more through the effects of habit, the reasoning powers, instruction, religion, than

---

[22] Francis Galton, *Hereditary Genius: An Inquiry into Its Laws and Consequences* (New York: D. Appleton, 1871), 39 (emphasis added).

[23] Darwin, *Descent*, vol. 2, 403 (emphasis added).

through natural selection; though to this latter agency may be safely attributed the social instincts, which afforded the basis for the development of the moral sense.[24]

Darwin definitely turned down Galton's heat, but he did not shut him down completely either. He was simply saying that other considerations were more important than mere existence, namely superior morality. After all, if the superior people became brutish in their struggle for survival, then the moral superiority would be lost, and not a whole lot would be gained. However, we should not make the mistake of thinking that Darwin was opposing the advancement of the superior people in the battle for survival through manipulation. He was just not as radical as Galton. Here his recourse to Lamarckian inheritance becomes important. He invoked a combination of methods by which superior humans can advance themselves: First, natural selection provides the social instinct that brings about the moral sense. Then, by cultivating the moral qualities through habit, reason, education, and religion, the superior people will propagate themselves because such acquired moral skills are supposedly heritable. He may not have approved of any radical implementation of his ideals, but he certainly labeled such a state as his Utopia.[25]

E. B. Tylor's Methodology

Tylor's Levels Among Human Beings

In contrast to some of the natural scientists who immediately connected their theories to practical implications on a social scale, the anthropologists by and large considered themselves to be students and observers of other cultures in relationship to their own. They certainly recognized a hierarchy of people groups, but they did not

---

[24] Ibid.

[25] Please see n27 below for a distinctively different view in the context of evolutionary biology in the twentieth century.

usually counsel intervention in the process of growth, if for no other reason than that they thought natural selection was hardly an appropriate method of dealing with human culture. There was no question that willful, human selection, beyond the choice of one's mate, played an important role in the development of human culture.

On the intellectual capacity of preliterate human beings, Tylor was ambiguous. In large strokes he appeared to divide humanity into three great divisions: the "primitive" people or "savages," who were the tribal groups living basically on a subsistence level; "barbarians," who had made serious advances in material and intellectual culture but were still stuck in a world of misconceptions and superstitions; and "civilized" people, who had permanent residences, successful economies, and intellectual cultures based on advanced stages of reasoning. Among the "barbarians" might be the Aryan tribes as they immigrated into Iran and India, while the crown of civilization was, of course, the British people with their refined culture and manners.

As to the "savages," Tylor made an attempt not to dehumanize them as radically as some of his contemporaries. He asserted:

> Few who will give their minds to master the general principles of savage religion will ever again think it ridiculous, or the knowledge of it superfluous to the rest of mankind. Far from its beliefs and practices being a rubbish heap of miscellaneous folly, they are consistent and logical in so high a degree as to begin, as soon as even roughly classified, to display the principles of their formation and development; and these principles prove to be essentially rational, though working in a mental condition of intense and inveterate ignorance.[26]

Unfortunately, as he goes on with his exposition, this appreciation of the mental capacity of preliterate people gets lost in his consistent reference to them as childlike and incapable of understanding higher concepts than their present ones. In fact, in his two-volume work *Anthropology*, Tylor presents a description of so-called human

---

[26] Tylor, *Primitive Culture*, vol. 1, 22–23.

races,[27] in which he makes a correlation between their different skull capacities and the alleged complexities of their brains on the one hand and their alleged intelligence on the other.[28] So, whatever Tylor says about the intellectual equality of all human beings in *Primitive Culture* makes little actual difference. His conclusion to the subject is that "it may perhaps be reasonable to imagine as latest-formed the white race of the temperate region, least able to bear extreme heat or live without the appliances of culture, but gifted with the powers of knowing and ruling which give them sway over the world."[29]

Despite Tylor's occasional attempt to distance himself from the Darwinian hierarchy, Tylor was not able to bring it off consistently.

---

[27] I need to observe that according to scientific terminology, it is no longer legitimate to recognize different "races" among human beings. In order for there to be two races of a species, you must have two populations capable of interbreeding but that manifest a clear discontinuity in their outward appearances (phenotypes) so that there are two groups that look different from each other without a significant number of intermediate individuals between the groups. It may be possible to defend the identification of two races within, say, one species of salamanders, but it is not difficult to recognize when, under this criterion, there is insufficient discontinuity to claim that there are two races. *Homo sapiens* is a good case in point. Human physical characteristics, including coloration, if graphed on a map of the world, show smooth transitions on both the north-south and east-west axes. The two exceptions to the continuity of human appearance are found: (1) On the two sides of an imaginary line east of Indonesia and west of Papua, New Guinea. This line marks the end points of migration by Asiatic people moving west to east and of Melanesian people moving east to west. In the former case, however, there is continuity going back in a westerly direction, and in the latter case the continuity can be traced by going eastward with a connection to African people. In fact, going backwards along the lines of phenotypical continuity without stopping along the way will eventually lead you to the other side of this dividing line. Continuity can be established along either longitude or latitude. (2) In the forced rearrangement of natural population patterns due to colonialism, slavery, imperialism, and other disruptions. However, since they are due to direct human intervention, they cannot count against the fact of natural phenotypical continuity. Human beings changed in appearance in the process of migrating all over the world, but they still constitute only one species and one race. I need to thank my former professor Dr. Richard Highton, a prominent evolutionary biologist, for this insight that saves evolutionary biology from Darwinian racism. I am, of course, forced to continue to use the word *race* in the context of reporting on the debate in question.

[28] Tylor, *Anthropology*, vol. 1, 46–49.

[29] Ibid., 91.

Anthropological Evidence

Tylor did believe his theses needed to be based on empirical evidence. Even though he never went on another foreign trip, he meticulously accumulated and studied the reports from travelers and explorers all over the world. Consequently, every point he made in the course of his discussions was illustrated by examples from cultures ranging from the least developed to the highest developed, from ancient reports to newest discoveries, and spanning the entire globe. He acknowledged in the preface to the second edition of *Primitive Culture* that some people found his unrelenting compilation of instances in question annoying; however, he was convinced progress could only be made if as much evidence as possible could be presented. (We shall return to this point below.)

Survivals

An important tool for Tylor's research was the discovery of "survivals." These are parts of a culture's heritage that have lost their original function but are still maintained, even if no one remembers their meanings. Poems, nursery rhymes, rituals, ceremonial practices, festivals, and many other intangible aspects of a culture are maintained just because they have "always" been done. An anthropologist can examine these survivals and reconstruct their original meaning, thereby shedding light on the past practices and beliefs.

Animism

Undoubtedly one of the reasons Tylor's theory became as popular as it did was that it was compatible with a number of other theories. Even though various writers began with different starting points, they wound up erecting similar pyramids of religious stages, and his animism was broad enough to accommodate their original points of beginning without toppling over anything else. His starting point for religion was the idea of a world filled with personal spirits. For Herbert Spencer, it was the fear of ancestor ghosts (Latin: *manes*); for Muir, as we saw, it was the veneration of natural phenomena; for Sir J. G. Frazer (1854–1941),[30] it was the practice of magic, requiring a spiritual reality that could be manipulated; for John H. King, it was *mana*, an impersonal spiritual force.[31] Granting the integrity of their differences, they still were not so different that they could not be integrated—with some adjustments—into the general scheme advocated by Tylor: beginning with the most simplistic and moving up the ladder to the most advanced (monotheism).

Tylor argued that it was highly doubtful whether there ever was or could be a culture without a religion. People who claimed they knew of such cultures usually made one of two mistakes: either they just didn't know the culture well enough, or they equated the concept of "religion" with some specific doctrines, such as belief in a Creator. However, by allowing a fairly broad definition of religion, there seemed to be no known religionless culture. And the one item all human cultures have in common in their religions is the belief in spirits. Tylor moved easily back and forth between the terms *spirit* and *soul* and their synonyms. He revived the term *animism*, which is derived from the Latin word *anima*, "soul" and means the belief that the world is inhabited by many personal spirits. Since the veneration of spiritual beings seemed to him to be a universal element in all religions insofar as they had been observed, he inferred that, consequently, there was a good probability that it may have been the original form of religion and that one could trace from there an "unbroken continuity into high modern culture."[32] Thus, the rude beginnings of

---

[30] Sir James George Frazer, *The Golden Bough*, 1-vol. ed. (1922; repr., Central, Hong Kong: Forgotten Books, 2008).

[31] First described by C. H. Codrington, *The Melanesians* (Clarendon: Oxford, 1891), 118–20. John H. King, *The Supernatural: Its Origin, Nature, and Evolution*, 2 vols. (New York: Putnam's, 1892).

[32] Tylor, *Primitive Culture*, vol.1, 426.

a simplistic belief in spirits would develop and culminate in the worship of powerful deities.

The following summary is based primarily on Tylor's discussion of animism in *Primitive Culture*, volumes 1 and 2.[33] Tylor attempted to reconstruct the reasoning processes of a person in the earliest stages of human culture. He proposed that the earliest preliterate people were puzzled by two profound questions:

1. What makes the difference between a living body and a dead one?
2. What are the human shapes that appear in dreams and visions?[34]

In the process of contemplating these issues, it occurred to our hypothetical early man that he seemed to consist of two parts—his body and his "phantom," viz. his immaterial part, of which he may think as either "soul," "ghost," or "spirit." The words in his own language would, of course, have been different. Furthermore, it appears plain to him that there is a direct connection between the life of his body and the presence of this noncorporeal component. Regardless of the proper word for it, the concept seemed to be similar in many cultures.

The Nature of the Soul

Tylor summarized the nature of a soul in this way:

> It is a thin unsubstantial human image, in its nature a sort of vapour, film, or shadow; the cause of life and thought in the individual it animates; independently possessing the personal consciousness and volition of its corporeal owner, past or present; capable of leaving the body far behind, to flash swiftly from place to place; mostly impalpable and invisible, yet also manifesting physical power, and especially appearing to men

---

[33] Ibid., vol. 1, 417–502; vol. 2, 1–361.
[34] Ibid., vol. 1, 428.

waking or asleep as a phantasm separate from the body of which
it bears the likeness; continuing to exist and appear to men after
the death of that body; able to enter into, possess, and act in the
bodies of other men, of animals, and even of things.[35]

Tylor does not claim that this definition is universal. It is simply a
general summary of how spirits or souls are most often conceived of
in strictly animistic cultures. He provides further descriptions of the
common understanding of a soul on this level of culture:[36]

1. A person's soul bears the image of the human being, but it is
   materially unsubstantial.
2. It possesses the personal consciousness and volition of its
   owner, even when it is removed from the body.
3. A soul is capable of leaving the body not just after death but
   during sleep or trances.
4. Despite the fact that it is not physical, souls can at times
   manifest physical power.
5. A soul may appear to people in dreams, in induced visions, or
   even in unexpected surprise encounters.
6. It can possess other human beings and even act within them.
7. It is often interpreted as "shade," and correlated to a person's
   shadow, viz. a person's shadow signifies that his soul is present. The unusual absence of a shadow alongside a person
   indicates that his soul has left him.
8. The soul is often interpreted as or equated with a person's
   "breath."
9. There are distinctions between different kinds of spirits,
   depending on the person's status in life.
10. Spirits can depart, and they can also be retrieved by experts.
11. After death, if a soul appears to people, it looks like the
    departed person's physical body.

---

[35] Ibid., vol. 1, 429.
[36] Ibid., vol. 1, 431–92.

12. Frequently the soul manifests personal marks when it becomes visible, such as a scar from an injury suffered earlier in life. In certain cases a fatal injury inflicted by an enemy, such as a decapitation, may keep a soul from proceeding into the more pleasant aspects of the afterlife.
13. Souls or spirits often have voices.
14. Spirits are usually considered to have certain physical limits. For example, they may need an open window in order to enter or leave a house. Furthermore, even though they are incorporeal, they frequently appear in the clothes worn by their earlier physical persons.

Expansion and Growth

Once humans had come to understand that they were embodied spirit-beings, it became an easy step from there to believe that a similar scheme was true for animals. They, too, must be indwelled by souls. To quote, "The lower psychology cannot but recognize in beasts the very characteristics which it attributes to the humans so, namely, the phenomena of life and death, will and judgment, and the phantom scene in vision or in dream."[37]

In fact, why not widen the possibility of the realm of spirits to further venues? Why not include plants as well? Well, plants do not look or act like people. It's possible to think of a plant having a soul like a person, but it makes more sense to imagine a personal spirit that lives within the plant as his or her home, like a dryad might. By taking this step, Tylor has ascribed to the people under consideration the independent existence of certain spirits. They are not tied to bodies or human beings. They may appear in human form with human attributes, but they do not have a human origin.

Thus, we have come to an important new stage: the belief in nature spirits. Furthermore, if these spirits can live in plants and trees,

---

[37] Ibid., vol. 1, 469.

there may also be spirits living in rocks, rivers, and other natural phenomena. Now we are in the realm of true, full-blown animism, the belief that the whole world is populated by a multitude of different spirits.

In most of the second volume of *Primitive Culture*, Tylor tells the story of the advancement of animism into higher forms of religion. Personal spirits may be particularly attracted to specific objects that concentrate their power. Such objects would be considered fetishes and given special veneration. If the spirits within an object are considered to have superior powers to others, and particularly if the object is fashioned into the form of a living being, we now have idols in which they live. Idols are big fetishes.

Fetishism and idolatry are the gateway to polytheism. Certain spirits are elevated in esteem and power so that they are now considered gods. Rituals develop; superstitions give way to prayers and sacrifices; relationships among the deities are recognized and get complicated. Nevertheless, polytheism is still just animism on a bigger scale.

Eventually, one of the gods may be considered to be superior to the others. Not that most of such occurrences are clear or particularly meaningful according to Tylor: "In surveying the peoples of the world, the ethnographer finds many who are not shown to have any definite conception of a supreme deity; and even where such a conception is placed on record, it is sometimes so vaguely asserted, or on such questionable authority, that he can but take note of it and pass on."[38]

However, Tylor recognized that some cultures worked out the belief in a supreme god a little further: "There are many savage and barbaric religions which solve their highest problem by the simple process of raising to divine primacy one of the gods of polytheism itself."[39]

Actually, Tylor recognized a multitude of ways in which the idea of a supreme god can arise out of polytheism in the mythology

---

[38] Ibid., vol. 2, 334.
[39] Ibid.

of the people. One god could be considered to be the head of a hierarchy among the gods of the polytheistic pantheon. He may be the glorification of a primeval ancestor. He could have come about by means of elevating, say, the sun or heaven to divine status. He may be the soul (*anima*) of the world as a whole. On the other hand, his derivation may be more abstract as the result of a fusion of the best attributes of the gods of polytheism, together with the removal of any limits placed on them.[40] Ultimately, in some cultures the idea of monotheism became more well-defined and permanent.

Thus, for Tylor, animism is not only the original form of religion, but all forms of religion are really more or less complicated versions of animism. The monotheist may look down on the tribal animist without realizing that his own doctrines are merely an extension of the other person's beliefs.

The Need for Closer Study

I have attempted to stress that E. B. Tylor's advocacy of an evolutionary development of religion was more than the robotic assertion of a dogma but that he stressed supporting all of his assertions with evidence gleaned from explorers all over the world. His motto appeared to be, "The more supporting material, the better." As a matter of fact, he considered it to be a flaw in the work of the philologists that they focused too closely on specific language families and did not take a universal global approach. Tylor did not care about direct connections. He began with the assumption of the uniformity of human nature and its evolution, and he considered any similarities among human cultures as more significant if there was no connection between them than if there was. He thought disconnected similarities revealed abiding traits of humanity as mandated by the laws of evolution.

However, simply piling up data without regard to time and place can ultimately mislead both the scholar and his audience. Tylor

---

[40] Ibid., vol. 2, 335.

combined all the reports into one large heap of data with the intention of discovering the patterns that would emerge. It would have been hard for him not to see the patterns he was looking for, given the indiscriminate admixture of data he created. Therefore, his case loses credibility. With the amount of undifferentiated "evidence" and the undeniable reality that he was deliberately selecting examples that illustrated his case (who wouldn't?), the plausibility he created was more apparent than real.

Tylor would have been better off looking more closely at some of the specific cultures he lumped together with hundreds of others in order to find general truths. This blemish in his method apparently caused him to set aside an important factor in the search for the origin of religion, namely, the morality of preliterate tribes. Tylor's animistic theory prevented him from taking seriously the moral standards of the people in question.

> Savage animism is almost devoid of that ethic element which to the educated modern mind is the very mainspring of practical religion. Not, as I have said, that morality is absent from the life of the lower races. Without a code of morals, the very existence of the rudest tribe would be impossible; and indeed the moral standards of even savage races are to no small extent well-defined and praiseworthy. But these ethical laws stand on their own ground of tradition and public opinion, comparatively independent of the animistic belief and rites which exist beside them. The lower animism is not immoral, it is unmoral. For this plain reason, it has seemed to be desirable to keep the discussion of animism, as far as might be, separate from that of ethics.[41]

There are two ways of looking at this quotation. One is to take it at face value as an observation by Tylor that animistic people can only have an arbitrary or conventional moral code, even though it may be a rather good one. The other is to see in it an unintended confession by Tylor that his animistic theory cannot account for the

---

[41] Ibid., vol. 2, 360.

high levels of morality that one may often find among the materially least developed people. It is certainly difficult to derive a coherent ethic from animism as he described it; animism per se may very well be amoral, though that's a difficult point to defend. But the fact is that among the so-called lowest cultures, we find some of the highest moral standards among humans.[42] If animism cannot account for that fact, maybe it's time to take another look at Tylor's theory of animism. Tylor says, "So far as savage religion can stand as representing natural religion, the popular idea that the moral government of the universe is an essential tenet of natural religion simply falls to the ground."[43]

But this is an evasive statement. As he himself admits, the people who are supposedly practicing a natural religion are indeed subscribing to some notion of "the moral government of the universe." Tylor is faced with the fact that there are preliterate people who have high moral standards. If it is not possible for people to have a high moral code unless their religion is at a higher level than animism, and if there is a group of people with such a high moral code, logically it would lead us to think their religion must have been on a higher level than animism. To ascribe those moral norms merely to peer approval or tradition is arbitrary and contrary to the evidence. But Tylor did not know about the evidence because his occupation with the forest of general principles obscured his vision of the particular trees.

Clearly there could be no further progress unless someone would examine some of the "trees" individually. What was needed was for another scholar to take a much closer look at the particulars of what some of those tribes actually believed, at the risk that his discoveries might put Tylor's general theory in question. Such a person came along, and it could not have been a less likely individual who wound up challenging Tylor.

---

[42] See Wilhelm Schmidt, *Primitive Revelation*, trans. Joseph J. Baierl (St. Louis: Herder, 1939), 109–15.

[43] Tylor, *Primitive Culture*, vol. 2, 360.

CHAPTER 4

Andrew Lang:
Turnabout Is Fair Play

The last time that we met Andrew Lang (1844–1912)[1], he was a defender of Tylor's developmental school of religion vis-à-vis Max Müller (1823–1900) and the philological approach to religion. In contrast to Lang, Tylor (1832–1917) had always been deferential in his references to Müller throughout *Primitive Culture*. He observed the distinction between himself, the anthropologist, and Müller, the philologist,[2] and where Tylor's readings of his colleague in Oxford coincided with his own view, he cited him with approval and respect.[3] However, as we saw at the end of chapter 2, Lang did not restrain himself in disparaging the entire philological approach in general and the work of Max Müller in particular.

This observation gives us an insight into the personality of Andrew Lang, and it is impossible to separate the man from his writings. He

---

[1] I am providing these dates to make apparent that most of the Europeans involved in this early debate were roughly contemporary with one another. They also knew one another personally.

[2] E. B. Tylor, *Primitive Culture*, vol. 1, 2nd ed. (New York: Holt, 1889), 299.

[3] Ibid., vol. 2, 258.

was always passionate, personal, and never wrote without a certain amount of sting in his writings toward those he saw as his opponents. His own views went through numerous changes, and it is only possible to summarize the beliefs he expressed in any one particular book.

Lang was a Scotsman, and some of his writings concern Scottish history. He started his higher education at Saint Andrews University and then moved to Oxford where, upon completion of his studies, he remained for seven years lecturing on classical literature. Then he left the formal academic world to begin a career as a writer, which spanned many decades and many topics. His popular reputation was based on twelve collections of fairy tales, known by their colors, beginning with the *Blue Fairy Book* and ending with *Lilac*. In his huge mountain of books and articles, he addressed the Greek and Roman classics, folklore from around the world, poetry ancient and modern, and, of course, the history of religions. As he progressed in age, he became increasingly interested in psychic phenomena and the occult; he was even the president of the Society of Psychical Research a few years before his death.[4]

As a student at Oxford, Lang became an ardent disciple of E. B. Tylor, and he never completely gave up that loyalty even when his views were patently incompatible with those of his teacher. In many places in his writings, when he accused the defenders of animism of shoddy work, he added a phrase exempting Tylor, even where such an exemption was not necessarily warranted.

I closed the previous chapter with the observation that Tylor was faced with a serious dilemma. On the one hand, he posited the beginning of religion to be animism, which is by nature incapable of providing a consistent moral system. The spirits are fickle, demanding, and

---

[4] Andrew Lang's major works pertaining to the history of religions include: *Custom and Myth* (London, 1884; repr., New York: AMS, 1969); *Myth, Ritual and Religion*, 2 vols. (1887; repr., London: Longmans, Green, 1913); *Modern Mythology* (New York: Longmans Green, 1897); *The Making of Religion* (New York: Longmans Green, 1898; repr., Charleston, SC: Bibliobazaar, 1968); *Magic and Religion* (New York: Longmans Green, 1901); *The Secret of the Totem* (New York: Longmans Green, 1905).

selfish; further, in practice if not in theory, they cannot be associated with a moral code. A genuine standard of right and wrong required a much higher level of development in culture, intellect, and religion than he was willing to grant to his "primitive" cultures. Certainly they could not have the notion of a god, the provider of a divine law to whom people were accountable. Still, on the other hand, he could not help but notice that in many tribes a fairly rigorous moral climate prevailed. Thus, Tylor, in company with other writers, held the opinion that whatever standards of morality the animistic cultures might have had were simply due to social convention.[5]

I suggested that it would take someone who would take a much closer look at the individual cultures in question to see whether the facts would leave us with Tylor's unsatisfactory solution of the dilemma or would allow us a credible escape. Shockingly, it turned out to be Andrew Lang, perhaps Tylor's most vociferous defender, to call the world's attention to the facts that (1) certain people on the simplest level of material culture had some of the highest moral standards found anywhere in the world, and that (2) those standards were based on their belief in a single God who created them, watched over them, gave them his laws, and enforced them.

Lang did not make the anthropological discoveries on which his theory was based, but he relied on the reports of various travelers and scholars. His interest became particularly piqued when he read reports from observers[6] who had studied the indigenous people of

---

[5] Tylor, *Primitive Culture*, vol. 2, 360.

[6] The largest contribution came from the work of A. W. Howitt, an Australian government official and "amateur" anthropologist. His reports, which at first appeared in journals, raised the bar for anthropologists on how to investigate and describe a culture, both for the detail he provided and for his attempt to do justice to the perspective of the indigenous people. The journal articles, which were the basis for Lang's conclusions, were eventually collected into one massive volume of more than 800 pages: A. W. Howitt, *The Native Tribes of South-East Australia* (London: Macmillan, 1904). Other important sources were Baldwin Spencer and F. J. Gillen, *The Native Tribes of Central Australia* (London: 1899); idem, *The Northern Tribes of Central Australia* (London: 1904); Carl Strehlow and Moritz Freiherr von Leonhardi, *Die Aranda- und Loritja-Stämme in Zentral-Australien*, 5 vols. (Frankfurt: Städtisches

Australia.[7] These were people living on a bare level of subsistence. They were nomadic in the sense that they had no fixed places of residence and were constantly roaming about in small clans within their territories but not because they were herding animals, such as sheep or cattle. They lived by hunting and gathering and dwelt in temporary camps, which consisted of little more than a central fire. Sleeping accommodations were provided by the ground.

In the early nineteenth century, many people of Western origin, including those who had taken up residence in Australia, assumed these people had no religion whatsoever. This judgment was undoubtedly influenced by the fact that the British colonists saw what they expected to see, but it was also due to the fact that many indigenous people kept the core of their religion concealed, except from those men in their groups who had officially become initiated into adulthood. This secrecy hid the fact that they did, indeed, recognize a Supreme Being. His name was hardly ever uttered except by the male members of the clan in the context of their mysteries. The women were not allowed to know much about him, except in vague terms, specifically with reference to the fact that their god had provided the

---

Völkerkunde-Museum, 1907–20); K. Langloh Parker, *The Euahlayi Tribe: A Study of Aboriginal Life in Australia* (London: Archibald Constable, 1905). Again, please keep in mind that the books were usually published several years after the information had appeared and had been discussed in journals. Thus, they may be out of chronological sequence with the actual discussion. We shall take note of other sources as the discussion proceeds.

[7] As I understand the proper use of terminology, the currently preferred designation for the people as a whole who are subject to these studies is "indigenous people of Australia," though "Aboriginal Australians" need not be considered disrespectful if used in a proper context. Unfortunately, in the course of reporting the views expressed in the past, I cannot avoid repeating the terms used by their authors, which once were honorable appellations but were rendered inappropriate by the way they were used. E.g., from its etymology, a "savage" initially simply referred to a forest dweller, but etymology does not give one the present meaning of a term. Thus, since it is now incorrectly associated with inhumane behavior, it is no longer a respectful word.

basis for their moral code and interpersonal relationships among the clan's people.

As Lang collated the various reports, he came to the conclusion that such a high God could not have been the product of an evolution beginning at some "lower" form of religion, such as animism. If it had an origin other than revelation (and Lang was not supportive of the idea of revelation), it must have been in the human capacity to experience the supernatural.[8] Here we see a major dividing line between Lang and most of his former teachers and colleagues. For them the object of their quest was to account for the phenomenon of religion without having to take recourse to the reality of the supernatural. Lang contended that they had foreclosed the possibility of a supernatural realm unscientifically and that, at a minimum, a hypothesis concerning the origin of religions could not be considered scholarly if it immediately ruled out the abundance of evidence for the supernatural in the world of the past and the present.

The Making of Religion

Starting Point: The Inexplicable

Andrew Lang's major work on this topic was *The Making of Religion*, issued in 1898 and followed up with a new edition just a few years later. There Lang fortified his case and responded, at least obliquely, to some of the early criticisms. The thesis was clear: in some of the least developed cultures, one finds an extremely clear and refined understanding of God, equal to that of Jehovah, the God of the Bible. However, Lang did not actually get to that topic until a little more than halfway through the book. Before he approached his main point, he recounted numerous so-called psychic experiences, such as instances of precognition, not all of which he accepted as

---

[8] Lang clearly ties the belief in spirits to such a capacity. *Making of Religion*, 150; *Myth, Ritual and Religion*, vol. 1, 332.

factual but many of which he believed to be well documented. Lang charged that not only did science have no explanation for them but that scientists erred by ignoring or dismissing such events as superstitions rather than attempting to account for them fairly and with an open mind. Tylor, in connection with his animism theory, had specifically stated, "First, as to the religious doctrines and practices examined, these are treated as belonging to theological systems devised **by human reason, without supernatural aid or revelation**; in other words, as being developments of Natural Religion."[9]

In other words, Tylor simply took any questions concerning the reality of the supernatural off the table. To Lang this attempt at closing off the importance of the supernatural, whether in Christian beliefs or in some other form, stymied the scientific search for truth. Lang, who also ultimately rejected the reality of divine revelation, still advocated that accepting at least the *possibility* of supernatural reality would expand science into a broader enterprise that would do greater justice when it examined religion. After all, it was precisely the belief in the supernatural that all religious people had in common. At the end of the first part of the book, he provided this summary:

> We have now finished a study of the less normal and usual phenomena, which give rise to belief in separable, self-existing, conscious, and powerful souls. . . . Again, these faculties have presented . . . just the kind of facts on which the savage doctrine of souls might be based, or by which it might be buttressed. Thus, while the actuality of the supernormal facts and faculties remains at least an open question, the prevalent theory of Materialism [sic] cannot be admitted as dogmatically certain in its present shape.[10]

Whether including this line of argumentation really helped Lang's case, either by strengthening it internally or by making it more persuasive, is hard to say.

---

[9] Tylor, *Primitive Culture*, vol. 1, 427–28 (emphasis added).
[10] Lang, *Making of Religion*, 158.

The High Gods of Australia

At the time Lang wrote this book, Australia was a British colony, and much of the interior of this continent had yet to be explored. Consequently, little was known about the cultures and practices of the Aboriginal people, which made it easy for the experts in the history of religion to use them as examples of their theories since not enough information was available to contradict their doctrines. As mentioned, the tribal people of Australia were living on an extremely simple level of material culture, and so the Darwinian preconception dictated that if they had any religion at all, it could only be of the most rudimentary kind. Further, they could not possibly have a genuine set of moral standards. Thus, T. H. Huxley pontificated:

> In its simplest condition, such as may be met with among the Australian savages, theology is a mere belief in the existence, powers, and disposition (usually malignant) of ghostlike entities who may be propitiated or scared away. And, in this stage, theology is wholly independent of ethics. The moral code, such as is implied by public opinion, derives no sanction from the theological dogmas, and the influence of the spirits is supposed to be exerted out of mere caprice and malice.[11]

As mentioned previously, the indigenous people were not interested in disclosing the true facts of their religion to anyone; many of them even excluded their women and children from knowing about their full beliefs. Thus, it is not surprising that a team of anthropologists exploring Central and North Central Australia came away saying that one of the major tribes of that area, the *Aranda* (called *Arunta* by them), showed no signs of having any religion at all, while another large tribe, the *Katija* (*Kaitish*), might have had some religious

---

[11] Thomas Henry Huxley, *Science and Hebrew Tradition* (New York: D. Appleton, 1896), 346–47. Lang wrote in response, "Remarks more crudely in defiance of known facts could not be made" (*Making of Religion*, 174).

beliefs,but it was not clear that this was the case.[12] We shall return to them below.

Other scholars made more intense efforts to get to know the local people. A. W. Howitt, initially with the collaboration of the missionary Lorimer Fison, was an Australian government official who carried out thorough anthropological investigations as his pastime. In his own words, "Circumstances later enabled me to **acquire considerable influence over** the tribes in South-East Australia, and to become acquainted with their sacred ceremonies and to be present at them."[13] His relationship to the tribes was always close and cordial, but, even after going through tribal initiations, he still remained an outsider, namely as a government supervisor and researcher. The local people always were first and foremost subjects of investigation to him. Still, over the years, he became intimate enough with a considerable number of tribal individuals who were willing to serve as his "informants."

The initiation ceremonies involved boys around the age of puberty being told the true name of their supreme god, some of his history and attributes, and their ethical obligations as expected by this god. They would be commanded not to share this information with anyone else lest they be killed and the whole tribe be destroyed as a consequence. In some tribes this initiation would include a physical ordeal, such as breaking two front teeth. Howitt's observations were corroborated by other investigators.

What struck Lang was that these gods could not have evolved out of any prior phases of the religious cultures for the simple reason that there weren't any discernible prior phases. Breaking allegiance with his former school of thought, Lang asserted that these conceptions of a god could not conceivably have arisen out of animism since, where the

---

[12] Spencer and Gillen, *The Native Tribes of Central Australia and The Northern Tribes of Central Australia*. It would not be long before their observations would be definitively overthrown by Strehlow and von Leonardi in *Die Aranda- und Loritja-Stämme in Zentral-Australien*. Nevertheless, they continued to be cited as authoritative for a long time to come by those who were in sympathy with their presuppositions, while Strehlow's direct observations were ignored.

[13] Howitt, *The Native Tribes of South-East Australia*, vii (emphasis added).

belief in this god was purest, there was no animism. In his own words, "The more animism, the less theism, is the general rule."[14] This rule also works backwards as long as we are careful how we formulate it.[15]

Ignoring the all-important differences between tribes, we can construct a general picture of the "typical" supreme god of Australian indigenous religion. We will use Lang's summaries and arguments, which are mutually intertwined with one another.[16] Please keep in mind that no one is saying that such a belief in a supreme god has been documented in all Australian tribes[17] or that the god of each tribe meets all of the descriptions. However, this list of traits does apply directly to numerous tribes, once one looks beyond the

---

[14] Lang, *Myth, Ritual and Religion*, vol. 1, 333–34.

[15] What logicians call the "contrapositive" of the statement holds true. We can say, "The more theism, the less animism." But "less theism" does not imply "more animism" since, instead of theism or animism, some other form of religion could be dominant, for example, polytheism. For the same reason, we cannot reason from "less animism" to "more theism" since there are other logically possible alternatives including, once again, polytheism.

[16] Lang, *Making of Religion*, 160–204.

[17] The enduring textbook formerly known as Frank B. Noss, *Man's Religions*, published now as David S. Noss and Blake R. Grangaard, *A History of the World's Religions*, 13th ed. (Upper Saddle River, NJ: Prentice Hall, 2008) uses a tribe known as the *Dieri* as a case study of indigenous Australian religion. The Dieri are known for their fierce customs, magic, and animism, and they do not appear to have the concept of a supreme being as so many other tribes do. Nevertheless, Noss ventures, "It begins to appear, when all of the evidence is considered, that practically all of the Australian tribes held a belief in some kind of high god, and the Dieri probably did too" (ibid., 23). As odd as it may sound, since my goal is to document original monotheism, and as much as it pleases me to have the author of such a popular text book draw that conclusion, I need to be careful in evaluating it. I am happy to go along with Noss's assertion but based on inferences on a far more global level (for which we are not yet ready in this book). Hesitancy is called for if it is a generalization based on Australian cultures alone. We must keep in mind that at the time of observation, the Dieri culture, though undeniably on a minimal level, also showed signs of having moved away from the even more austere level in which a supreme being has a more pronounced presence. Thus the problem that will become the outcome of this entire chapter rears its head: In a given geographic area, how can we assess whether a culture has arrived there earlier or later than others in the vicinity? When we have a faint representation of a cultural element among a group of people, how can we discern whether it is just starting to become significant or is in the process of vanishing? So, at least from the viewpoint of an objective scholar, at this point in our discussion, I still need to be open to the logical possibility that the Dieri never had a concept of a supreme being.

superficial mythology.[18] This description is admittedly based on selective data referring to the nature of the supreme being where he is clearly found in a group's belief system. The overwhelming amount of such data from which we can select fitting examples makes compiling this list more than just an exercise in subjective interpretation.

1. The supreme god is described in highly anthropomorphic terms. Sometimes the secondary stories about him, which are disseminated among the women and children, are grotesque. However, as we shall see, the human-like characteristics ascribed to him do not actually limit any of his powers or abilities, but they aid the people in a graphic way to understand the nature of a supreme being. Furthermore, they serve as an outlet for the creative fantasies in which human beings love to engage. At serious religious occasions, such as initiations or prayers in times of emergency, which are not times of entertainment, the mythology usually plays little role. It is interesting to note that in this discussion Lang makes use of a distinction he would not allow for Max Müller (see chap. 2), namely between what people truly believe and practice (their religion) and the oftentimes absurd or even repulsive stories that accumulate on top of the religion: the mythology,

---

[18] Anyone familiar with "Australian religion," as it is usually described today, will immediately notice the absence of a reference to the "Dreamtime," *Alcheringa*, in this summary. This term refers to the mythological time when the gods and totemic beings arose and created Earth and people. "Dream," in this context, has little, if anything to do with what we visualize when we are asleep; it is more synonymous with "being spiritual." I am not including this idea in this list because, even though the early investigators knew of it, it did not play a significant role in most of their reports, and it is only a sidelight to our discussion, which concerns more the "who" of the gods than the "when." Nowadays the concept often leads the descriptions of *the* Australian Aboriginal religion, as though there were such a thing. The specific word and concept, like everything else, varies from tribe to tribe. There is no "Australian religion," and there is no "Aboriginal Dreamtime," just as there is no "Australian Supreme Being," only different groups with varying cultures and religions that display certain similarities—something that is the case anywhere else in the world as well. We must be careful not to turn a generalization based on handpicked data, as is admittedly the case for the list we are about to construct, into universals of the entire religion.

which even the practitioners themselves frequently don't
take seriously.[19]

2. These cultures do not show evidence of having moved up
   or down from some previous level. No previous levels are in
   evidence. So if their concept of God had any prehistory, we
   do not have access to it. Lang states, "From all this evidence
   it does not appear how non-polytheistic, non-monarchical,
   non-Manes [ancestor ghost]-worshiping savages evolved the
   idea of a relatively supreme, moral, and benevolent Creator,
   unborn, undying, watching men's lives."[20]

3. The supreme god in question is not a spirit.[21] By denying that
   the god was a spirit, Lang meant to indicate that the very
   nature of the deity is different in kind from any of the finite
   spirits of which the animism school claims are the building
   blocks of all religions. Remember that Tylor believed that the
   so-called god of monotheism was merely an inflated version
   of one of the spirits of animism. But the supreme god of the
   Australian people, claimed Lang, was different in all respects
   from the entities that Tylor called spirits. Lang declared that it
   would be best to refer to him generically as a "being" without
   imposing on him the character of a spirit as used by the animistic school. The worship practices (called "cult" or "cultus"
   when referring to the entire religious structure) directed to
   the supreme god contrast sharply with the veneration of spirits, which ultimately crowded out monotheism. The spirits of
   animism need attention. They want to be informed, honored,
   and—in most cases—fed. Spirit veneration, where it occurs,
   almost always includes various food offerings as well as possibly far more demanding sacrifices. Then, if one is fairly certain
   the spirits are satisfied, one can present them with petitions
   and prayers. However, if they are not happy, the spirits may

---

[19] Lang, *Myth, Ritual and Religion*, vol. 1, viii.

[20] Lang, *Making of Religion*, 180.

[21] Ibid., 182–88.

cause harm instead. So it requires constant vigilance to make sure one is on the good side of the spirits.

None of these practices apply to the supreme being. He is said to have created the world and people. Then, for reasons that vary in the mythologies from tribe to tribe, he withdrew from the world. If he interacts with it at all, it is most likely through an intermediate being, such as a son, except for in extremely critical emergencies. He is considered to be intrinsically good, so he does not need to be appeased; and since he rarely gets involved with people, he does not need to be enticed with offerings and sweet talk to answer prayers. The one thing one does have to watch out for is that the supreme being has given a set of moral standards, and he may punish humans who transgress them. Moreover, in many cases, he may reward them if they obey faithfully. These commandments are absolute, and the god will not soften them or allow human beings to deviate from them. He cannot be bribed or flattered. No rituals, prayers, or offerings can ameliorate the results of deliberately violating a rule, but a person can usually expect forgiveness based primarily on the god's intrinsic benevolence. In short, for the most part there is no worship or other regular devotion associated with the supreme god, except possibly, when a serious emergency has occurred on a virtually cosmic level and, of course, during the initiation ritual. Later on we shall see that the absence of any worship of a supreme being is not a universal rule.

4. Lang argued that the idea of a supreme being in the sky could not have been thought up as a counterpart to the headman or chief of a tribe of a clan because it appeared that these groups made their decisions based on the collaborations of the elders; they had no chiefs. (He later had to modify this point to a certain extent.)[22]

---

[22] See ibid., 318.

5. The supreme god could not have been an elaborated version
   of a great ancestor or culture hero.[23] The English word *ancestor*, traditionally used in this context, is somewhat misleading
   because where ancestor worship is practiced, an "ancestor"
   does not usually need to have left progeny. The one essential
   requirement to be an ancestor is to have been born, lived,
   and died. However, the stories concerning the supreme being
   place him outside the possibility of death. There are no stories concerning his birth, and he will never die; therefore, he
   cannot be an ancestor, not even in the role of a departed person of note.

   As a matter of fact, the response above is actually irrelevant to the tribes in question because they had no ancestor
   veneration and did not maintain records of supposed culture
   heroes. They did not even keep track of the names of departed
   relatives of, say, two generations ago. So, we can rule out the
   theory of the god-concept arising out of the fear of potentially
   harmful ghosts of people in general, as Huxley intimated, following the theory of Herbert Spencer, or of the gods being
   derived from the idealization of great persons of the past.
   Some tribes had elaborate funeral customs, even outfitting
   the deceased for an afterlife, but they did not subsequently
   observe regular duties toward the departed. Unfortunately,
   the idea of the gods as having originally been culture heroes
   has been a temptation too hard to resist by many anthropologists today, though it does not fit in with the ideas brought
   out in the nineteenth-century reports.

6. The supreme god knows everything. Lang was chastised by
   E. S. Hartland not to use terms such as *omniscience* in reference to the being because that vocabulary allegedly carried
   too many Christian connotations, which supposedly could
   lead to the notion that the Australian cultures worshipped

---

[23] Ibid., 164.

the Christian God of biblical revelation.[24] In later discussions he avoided the traditional terms so as to quiet this shallow critique, which may have been more of a concession than he intended in the eyes of his opponents. He also stopped using other terms like *creator, omnipotent,* or *eternal* in subsequent works, though they certainly apply in a descriptive sense. Furthermore, Lang clarified needlessly that obviously the indigenous people did not mean that the god's omniscience entailed primarily that he knew a lot of bare facts about the world; for example, that the god knew the latest developments in European science. It basically came down for them to the idea that he knows all we do, think, and intend to do.

7. The supreme god made the world and living beings, including people.

8. The supreme god has always existed and will always exist.

9. There are no limits as to what the supreme god can do. This attribute was not intended to mean that the supreme god did everything or even much of anything at present, but he had the power to do whatever he wanted to do.

10. The supreme god is the author of a moral law and sometimes its enforcer, though at other times his emissaries (who are not subject to worship) may enforce it. For example, the high god of the tribe called the Kamilaroi is called Baiame. He directed that there are three unpardonable sins: killing another human being, lying to a tribal elder, and illicitly approaching someone else's wife. Furthermore, he enjoined all men to act in a good and caring way toward anyone in need, those who are too old to care for themselves, and those who are too weak, perhaps due to a disease.[25]

I might mention in this context that it is a pervasive ethical obligation among the Australian people to share their

---

[24] E. S. Hartland, "The High Gods of Australia," *Folk-Lore* 9 (1898): 290–329. See Lang's summary of the debate in *Myth, Ritual and Religion,* xix–xxiv.

[25] Lang, *Making of Religion,* 173–79.

goods with everyone. This does not mean that all property is communal but that if someone is successful in a hunt, for example, he is morally obligated to share the meat with those who were unsuccessful or unable to hunt for themselves. At the time of first contact with Europeans, they were practicing this duty faithfully, but the critics who wanted to show that the Aboriginals picked up their monotheism and ethics from Europeans pointed out that such sharing represented a good instance of how they had learned Christian ethics from white people. One wonders: even if such direct contact had been physically possible, where could they possibly have seen Europeans act in such a way? To be sure, at certain times and locations they observed some missionaries practice altruism, but those instances certainly would not have set a pattern observed just a few years later by all of the inhabitants of an entire continent! To the contrary, when Howitt observed the Gunai initiation ceremony,[26] the elders added one ritual due to the fact that the young candidates had been in contact with white people. The headsman went from boy to boy and with a symbolic gesture pulled something out of their chests. This thing that he removed, as it were, was the greed that they might have picked up from European-originated people.

11. To become more general, the whole idea of a supreme being as encountered in these cultures evolving out of the worship of something inferior goes contrary to logical sense. It would be plausible if people invented a supreme being out of a polytheistic or animistic context because they thought he could do more for them than the spirits, in which case one would expect regular worship of him. Being realistic about it, if there were any profitable ceremonies attached to the worship of the supreme being, it would make sense that shamans or priests would promote the notion because they would see

---

[26] Ibid., 177.

gain in it. However, as we said above, there are no regular and few irregular observances for the supreme god; furthermore, there are no disgruntled animistic priests, shamans, or sorcerers hanging around, complaining that they were put out of business or trying to recruit people to return to spirit veneration. By contrast, in materially more complex cultures, the supreme god fades from memory, spirits and ghosts become the center of attention, and the religious professionals flourish in their trade.

12. On the other hand, there is a lot to be said for the idea of a culture moving from this relatively bland monotheism to the colorful world of animism. The supreme god seems not to be accessible, and though he may look down upon us benignly, particularly when we obey his commandments, he doesn't usually answer prayers, heal sick people, bring rain, make children behave, or help you find game to hunt. The only thing you can plan on is that he is going to punish you if you violate his commandments. How much easier it is to turn to spirits that are supposedly all around you for help! People who are particularly adept at relating to the spirits, then, are soon going to maintain a thriving business!

Lang allowed that this scheme could be counted among the degeneration theories, against which Tylor had argued profusely.[27] What else can you call it if you move from the conception of a supreme creator in connection with a high set of moral standards to the veneration of multitudinous spirits coupled with a serious relaxation of ethical expectations? In fact, Lang argued that "degeneration" in this sense was virtually inevitable, even without abandoning God in favor of ghosts and spirits.

a. For example, suppose two bands of people from different tribes merge for some reason, such as proximity and/or

---

[27] Ibid., 241–52.

routine interaction. Each of their supreme gods may be similar to the one of the other tribe, but they also have different names and different secondary mythologies. It is possible that the two ideas of the god could merge into a single deity, but it is more likely on this level that the two gods retain their identities, though one may be considered superior to the other one. At that point, of course, monotheism has started to fade because there are at least two gods, and in this way "degeneration" into polytheism has taken place. We shall see a powerful example of such a scenario below.

b. In light of the preceding descriptions of the supreme being, there is little attraction in maintaining the monotheism and a lot of incentive to turn to the world of spirits. As Lang says:

> A moral creator in need of no gifts, and opposed to lust and mischief, will not help a man with love-spells, or with malevolent "sendings" of disease by witchcraft; will not favour one man above his neighbour, or one tribe above its rivals, as reward for a sacrifice that he does not accept, or as constrained by charms which do not touch his omnipotence. Ghosts and ghost-gods, on the other hand, in need of food and blood, afraid of spells and binding charms, are a corrupt, but, to man, a useful constituency.[28]

Human beings are naturally motivated to avoid misfortune, to be successful in their relationships, and to be safe from their enemies. (A Christian might add another set of motivations to this list based on the doctrine of our fallenness; but the ones Lang has brought up, based on what he himself calls tongue in cheek "the Old Adam," are sufficient

---

[28] Ibid., 243–44.

to make a persuasive case.) People desire to be in control of their lives, something that is supposedly much more easily facilitated by manipulation of the spirits than living under the watchful eye of a remote god.

Now we need to be careful not to read a stronger conclusion into Lang's work than he himself was prepared to acknowledge. He looked over the reports on the tribes of Australia and found two groups: those on the apparently lower material level with a bare monotheism and those who appeared to be on a slightly higher material level, where the monotheism was at least supplemented, if not displaced, by animism and polytheism. It would appear that, given this description, the more pronounced monotheistic cultures may have resembled an older form of human religion because they seemed to be tied to the older cultures. But how can one decide on the basis of sound scholarship which of the two groups is really the older one? Lang did not think that such a chronological sequencing was possible, and though he left no doubt about his hunch that monotheism preceded animism, he was of the opinion that scholarly criteria did not permit him to decide positively in favor of one or the other. At this point he committed the fallacy of agnosticism; rather than stating merely what he *did not know*, he asserted that such a thing *could not be known*. This kind of statement requires that the person making it knows more than a human can. Still, he averred:

> This point of priority we can never historically settle. If we met savages with ghosts and no gods, we could not be sure but that they once possessed a God, and forgot him. If we met savages with a God and no ghosts, we could not be historically certain that a higher had not obliterated a lower creed. For these reasons dogmatic decisions about the *origin* of religion seem unworthy of science.[29]

---

[29] Lang, *Making of Religion*, 280 (emphasis in the original).

Other than an unusual hesitancy, which seems out of character for the rest of the book, we also see Lang opening the door just a crack for those who would later make a big case for the ambiguity of the word *origin*. Most importantly for our purposes, he is correct in saying that a tight case for an *original* monotheism cannot be made apart from some way of establishing which society represents a level closer to the earliest human culture than others.

*Specific Examples

Let us look at some of the actual information Lang had at his disposal in constructing his theory. Lang's arguments focused most directly on the indigenous people of Australia, but he also drew on reports from other regions. His most important sources were the intense studies made by A. W. Howitt among the tribal people of Southeast

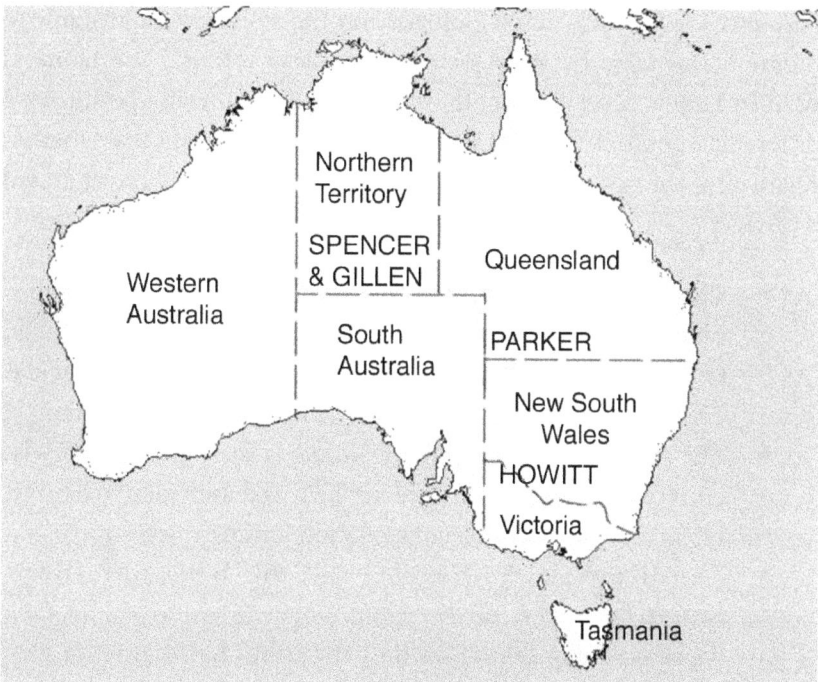

Figure 4.1

Australia. His research covered a large area including the provinces of Victoria and New South Wales but also crossed over into South Australia to its west and Queensland to its north. (See fig. 4.1 for a general orientation.)

It is the case for all of the researchers mentioned below that their initial reports consisted of articles that were published in journals and that the tomes they produced subsequently were largely collections of those earlier pieces. Oftentimes the later collections already included responses to some critics of the article version. By the time the books appeared, their ideas would already have been topics of discussion for several years. Being aware of this fact helps make sense of how it could be that the content of various books could be the topics of discussion in books that were published earlier. The earlier books responded to the articles.

Here is a quick and select survey of some of the tribes and their supreme beings as they were discussed by Lang on the basis of the data provided by the anthropologists on the scene. I will attempt to mention the tribe by its current designation and add the name(s) used in Lang's time in parentheses. Unless I specifically point out a difference, none of the characters mentioned in the myths, whether relatives of the god or ancestors, were either worshipped or venerated as divine.

- The *Narinari* (*Narrinyeri*) believed in a supreme being called *Nurrundere* or *Martummere*. He created everything and taught humans all necessary rituals and means of survival. Then, together with his children, he relocated to heaven.
- The *Maraura* (*Wiimbaio*) say *Nurelli* is the supreme god who created the entire land, gave his laws, and ascended to heaven. He is represented by a constellation among the stars.
- The *Woiworung* (*Wurunjerri*) and the *Wotjobaluk* (*Wotjobaluck*), members of the *Kulin* language group, called their supreme being *Bunjil*. Each of the tribes has their own variations on the mythology, but they all refer to him as "Our

Father," in their respective languages, e.g., *Mami ngorak* (*Woiworung*) or *Mami ngata* (*Wotjobaluk*). The mythology of Bunjil narrates that he divided the people into two clans ("totem groups," "phratries") and that marriage was restricted to someone outside of one's own group (i.e., exogamous marriage). This legend may reflect that historically free marriage without respect to group adherence preceded the restriction of clan exogamy.

- The *Gunai* (*Kurnai*) know their supreme god only by the name of *Mungan ngaua*, "Our Father." He lived on earth and taught people everything good and useful, including the secret initiation rites. He had a son named *Tundun*, who married and became the ancestor of the Gunai. In the course of time, a fickle man disclosed the divine secrets to some women, thereby committing a serious violation of the rules. So Mungan ngaua, who at the time still lived on earth, set the entire sky on fire (*aurora australis*). The people saw this spectacle and went crazy, stabbing one another to death with their spears. Then the ocean overflowed and many more people drowned. A large number of people turned into various land and sea animals; Tundun and his wife transmuted into porpoises. Of the few human beings who were left, a segment became the new ancestors of the revived Gunai. Mungan ngaua left the earth and went up to the sky where he still lives.

- As we look at the tribes still called *Yuin* and *Ngarigo* and the *Awabakal* (*Kuri*), combinedly called the *Coast Murring*, the supreme god is called *Dhuramullan* (*Daramulun*). Specifically these tribes are the ones who recognize him as supreme because in others, where the supreme being goes by a different name, Dhuramullan appears as a subsidiary figure who is not worshipped. Among the tribes in the present category, he may be called *Papang* ("father") and *Biamban* ("Lord"), and under those vague terms, women have some knowledge of him. While still on earth, Dhuramullan planted trees and gave the Yuin their laws and mysteries. Subsequently he receded to heaven, but the people hear his voice in the thunder with which he calls rain. There is no ancestor cult or animism but a belief in souls that join Dhuramullan in heaven after death. The initiation ceremony is called the *Kuringal*. It is distinctive because in its course an image of Dhuramullan is briefly displayed, though immediately destroyed again on pain of death. The participants raise their hands, which sometimes hold their weapons, toward heaven.

- The *Watiwati* (*Wathi-Wathi*) believe their god, *Tathita*, came from the far north and now lives in heaven. He created men, women, and dogs and gave them their languages but subsequently removed the capacity of speech from dogs.

- Moving just a little farther northwest, though still in Queensland, the *Jeithi* (*Wiradjuri*), *Kamilaroi*, and *Ualarai* (*Euahlayi*) worship *Baiame*, who is said to be a large old man with a long beard. The Ualarai call him the "Allfather, whose laws all tribes must obey." Baiame came from the northeast and created people in two ways, first by turning animals into people and then by making human beings from clay. Women, who, again, are allowed some vague knowledge of him, only refer to him as *Boyjerh* (Father); they also pray to *Birrahgnooloo*, one of his two wives, thought of as the resplendent "Allmother." The other wife is *Cunnumbeillie*, whose position is somewhat inferior as a "heavenly housekeeper." The family is completed by two beings who are either supernatural sons or brothers of Baiame (the reports are ambiguous). No worship is associated with either the second wife or these other two male beings. One of these two additional sons or brothers is called *Beilahburrah* or *Dillalee*; the other one bears the name of *Dhuramullan*, the same as the supreme god of the Yurin. The being who here has that name is definitely subordinate to Baiame and has a different personality. This is the case to which I referred earlier, where it is possible that in the contact between two groups of people with two different deities, one emerged as decidedly superior, though we cannot be sure that this is what actually happened. Dhuramullan's official duty in this group of tribes is to stand in for Baiame at the initiation ceremony. At times a stone sculpture, supposedly carved by Baiame himself, represents Dhuramullan's presence. There are different versions of Dhuramullan's mythology among these tribes. The Ualarai say that a long time ago he was charged with the job of knocking out the front teeth of the candidates at the initiation ceremony, called *Bora*. Instead of doing so, however, he started to dig his fangs into the faces of the boys and to consume them. Baiame immediately intervened and turned him into an ugly, poisonous animal. The Kamilaroi's version is not as harsh. For them, Dhuramullan is definitely a son of Baiame, and he does preside over the mysteries, called *Burlung*. However, when he descended from heaven, he landed awkwardly and splintered a leg; thus, the Kamilaroi people picture him as having one good leg and one pointed splinter as his other one.

- The initiates are given a lengthy list of sins to avoid. Among those, three are unpardonable: murder, lying to a tribal elder, and stealing a wife. Lesser obligations include not to lie to anyone, not to play with children, and to behave as adults. They must be good and kind toward the weak and elderly.
- Roughly around the same time as Howitt was learning from the tribes in the southeast, the team of anthropologists, Baldwin Spencer and F. J. Gillen,[30] investigated the tribal cultures of people groups farther west and north. There were two large tribal associations in particular whom they scrutinized. They are known as the *Aranda*, who were occupying the

---

[30] Spencer and Gillen, *The Native Tribes of Central Australia*.

southern part of the northern territories, and their neighbors just to the north, the *Katijas*. (Spencer and Gillen referred to them as *Arunta* and *Kaitish* respectively.) Though doing their best at breaking through cultural barriers and providing a lot of worthwhile information, they returned with minimal results concerning the religion of these people. However, they did not see the lack of information as a shortcoming in their methods; instead, they took it to mean that there was not much information to be had. They concluded that the *Aranda* were most definitely atheists and that it could be that the *Katijas* had some form of primitive religion, though they lacked further clarity on the matter.

- But, even though they were treated as pioneers in their own circles, Spencer and Gillen were not the only ones to have studied the Aranda culture. A German missionary named Carl Friedrich Strehlow (1871–1922) had been living right alongside the Aranda, had spoken their language, and had come to know their religion and customs in intimate detail. In cooperation with the anthropologist Moritz von Leonhardi (1856–1910), he published a lengthy description of Aranda and Katijas culture and religion.[31] Strehlow's intimate knowledge of these tribes seriously corrected the superficial conclusions attained by Spencer and Gillen.

- Spencer and Gillen had learned from the Aranda about a spooky and cartoonish bogeyman-like being named *Twanyirika*, but he was not really a god or a divine spirit, just a being who liked to play tricks on people and punish wayward children. Many of the adult men to whom Spencer and Gillen talked did not take him seriously at all. Nor did the two investigators find a meaningful code of ethics among the members of the tribe. The Aranda seemed to them to be about as religionless as any

---

[31] Strehlow and von Leonardi, *Die Aranda- und Loritja-Stämme in Zentral-Australien.*

people could get. Their conclusion became widely accepted; it fit in pretty nicely with the presumption that these people, who were on a rather low stage in terms of material culture, also had to be on a totally predeveloped level of religion. Spencer and Gillen did not realize how secretive these people were about their beliefs.

- Carl Strehlow was one of a number of people who had little success as a missionary but became close to the tribal people, partially thanks to his medical services to them. He definitely learned more of their religion than they were willing to listen to of his. Strehlow acknowledged that the silly figure of Twanyirika was, indeed, an invention, a convenient fiction to satisfy curious women, children, and uninitiated anthropologists. But, in fact, the initiates of the tribe did recognize a supreme being named *Altjira*. We must picture him with red skin and the legs of a dog, while his wife has the legs of an emu. He rules heaven eternally, and there is no tradition of his being the creator of the earth. He instituted the ritual obligations but did not decree any moral laws. Furthermore, this god had issued a code of ethics, including truth-telling and strict marriage restrictions and fidelity. After people die, they will be judged by him. Good people will be in Altjira's presence until they get ready to be reincarnated once more. Bad people will go to the island of the dead, where eventually their souls will be annihilated by a bolt of lightning. However, there is a serious taboo against talking about these matters to anyone not qualified. Even though the prevailing evolutionary school set Strehlow's observations to the side, he did become known as an expert in Australian languages. His records are still available.

- The Katijas, it turned out, also had a supreme being residing in heaven. His name was *Atnatu*. He created himself and human beings, and at first the people lived with him in the sky. After a time, he expelled the people from heaven. Earth was also already inhabited by further immortal beings. They were not gods but became the totem animals for the divisions in the tribe.

- Let us mention one example outside Australia for this chapter: The Andaman Islands are a chain of islands running roughly parallel to the Southeast Asian peninsula. The Andaman Islanders, a pygmoid group, though richer in their material culture than some of the Australian tribes, were cut off from communication with the rest of the world for a long time. As Andrew Lang states wryly, "Their religion is probably not due to missionaries as they always shot all foreigners."[32] Like some Australian tribes, they drew a web of secrecy around their religion; thus, among Westerners they were known as a religionless people for a while. However, E. H. Man[33] spent eleven years with them, speaking their language and gaining their trust. He was rewarded with learning about their beliefs. Their supreme god is an invisible being named *Puluga*, who is without beginning or end in time, knows our thoughts, and enforces a strict moral code. Among the sins he punishes are "falsehood, theft, grave assault, murder, adultery, bad carving of meat [probably because it is wasteful], and (as a crime of witchcraft) burning wax."[34] However, he also has pity on those who are hurting and may possibly provide relief.

Observations

This is quite an array of deities, which have unmentioned mythologies attached to them. It is obvious as we are looking at this snapshot in time, viz. the second half of the nineteenth century, that we find these groups of people at different stages in the development of their

---

[32] Lang, *Making of Religion*, 190.

[33] E. H. Man, *On the Aboriginal Inhabitants of the Andaman Islands* (*The Journal of the Anthropological Institute of Great Britain and Ireland*, 1882).

[34] Lang, *Making of Religion*, 190.

cultures and religions. Generalizations are to some extent bound to be idealizations, such as in this basic summary of the features of the supreme being. We need to remember that this information comes specifically from the southeastern quadrant of the continent. Many of the other tribes, such as the Dieri, who live close to the Ualarai, do not show monotheism.

To quote Mircea Eliade, "It is useless to multiply examples."[35] Our listing of instances must be continued, but it can wait for later parts of this book when cultures on other continents become more relevant. Specifically, what Eliade referred to was not just the existence of supreme beings among traditional cultures but also the fact that, as Lang had already noticed, their stories usually included their exit from this world, most likely to heaven. This element entailed that normally no permanent, regular set of worship practices was associated with them. To complete Eliade's statement:

> Everywhere in these primitive religions the celestial supreme being appears to have lost *religious currency*; he has no place in the cult, and in the myths he draws farther and farther away from man until he becomes a *deus otiosus* [the remote god]. Yet he is always remembered and entreated as the last resort, when all ways of appealing to other gods and goddesses, the ancestors, and the demons, have failed. As the Oraons [a South-Asian tribal people] express it, "Now we have tried everything, but we still have you to help us." And they sacrifice a white cock to him, crying, "God, thou art our creator, have mercy on us."[36]

Eliade is correct except for the words "everywhere" and "always." There are some places where he does receive worship, and in other places people do not necessarily call on him in times of distress. Still, on the whole this phenomenon that the god has withdrawn seems to reinforce the idea that there was a time when the supreme being

---

[35] Mircea Eliade, *The Sacred and the Profane: The Nature of Religion*, trans. Willard R. Trask (New York: Harcourt, Brace & World, 1959), 125.
[36] Ibid.

received more attention but that his status among the various cultures was taken over by animism, ancestor veneration, and polytheism.

Initial Impact or Lack Thereof

How did Lang fare in the world of scholarship? For the most part the academy simply ignored him, given that his theory was so far out of line with the dominant paradigm. Spencer and Gillen, who had corroborated the prevailing ideas with their incomplete results became celebrities. Howitt was deservedly praised for his excellent work. However, he was proprietary about not only his observations but also of the interpretation he gave to them, and, consequently on uneasy footing, not only with Andrew Lang but also with people who by and large supported him, the so-called "ethnologists of the study" (see the next chapter).

Strehlow received minimal consideration because he was a missionary. The dogma that no Christians, particularly no missionaries, could be trusted for anything they reported, except, of course, when it happened to suit what the academicians in power were advocating, was deeply ingrained in the universities of Europe at the time (and has not vanished). So, except for in a small number of debates in England, few of which had any merit, Lang was written off as an oddball curiosity. We will look at the ones that had some merit in the next chapter.

In other countries, such as France and Germany, Lang was simply ignored or put off with one easy sentence or so. A good example is provided by Émile Durkheim, with whom we will need to deal more extensively later, who declared gratuitously in 1912: "The primitive has no ideas of an Almighty who draws souls out of nothingness."[37] Later in the same book, he provided a fairly accurate description of Lang's theory but then stated that "the facts do not support either Tylor's scepticism [sic] or Lang's theological interpretation."[38]

---

[37] Émile Durkheim, *The Elementary Forms of Religious Life*, trans. Carol Cosman (1912; repr., New York: Oxford, 2001), 198.
[38] Ibid., 213.

One wonders to which facts he was referring. He clarified: "While the great gods are surely superior to the [great ancestors], they are merely different in degree, and we move from the first to the second without any breach of continuity. A great god is, in fact, an ancestor of particular importance."[39]

Durkheim ignored the necessary requirement for being an ancestor, namely to have died, which is a condition not attributed to the supreme gods we have considered. Additionally, as we said above, such an inference is not even operative since ancestor veneration is not even practiced among the groups that have the clearest beliefs about a supreme god. One still wonders to which facts Durkheim was referring.

There were a few serious criticisms of Lang. However, even though there were not many of them, we need to postpone discussing them until the next chapter because it is essential for the purpose of this book that we interact with them directly, especially since the same objections continue to be tossed about casually as conventional wisdom now, a century later.

Let us close with a quotation from K. Langloh Parker, who had lived with the Ualarai and eventually had to wrestle with an overall theory of how to understand what she was witnessing. She occupied an unusual niche as a white woman who had grown up playing with indigenous children and then lived right next to them for many years as an adult. Even though she was a woman, some of the male members of the tribe did not apply the normal taboos to her because she was white and, thus, a nonthreatening outsider. They disclosed matters to her that they would never have told any woman of the tribe. She recounted that "I was first told of Byamee, in whispers, by a very old native."[40] On the other hand, male investigators did not learn much from the women of the tribes, even if they had been

---

[39] Ibid.
[40] K. Langloh Parker, chap. 2, "The All Father, Byamee," *The Euahlayi Tribe*, accessible at the Sacred Texts website: http://www.sacred-texts.com/aus/tet/tet03.htm.

more interested in that perspective than they were.[41] Parker was able to learn their view of their religion as well. She speaks of her younger days when she first learned about the religious culture of her close neighbors: "My anthropological reading was scanty, but I was well acquainted with and believed in Mr. Herbert Spencer's 'Ghost theory' of the origin of religion in the worship of ancestral spirits. What I learned from the natives surprised me, and shook my faith in Mr. Spencer's theory, with which it seemed incompatible."[42]

And incompatible it has remained with other theories based on preconceptions rather than evidence. I might mention that despite her confession of little knowledge of anthropology in her youth, Catherine Eliza "Katie" Parker Stow (Langloh Parker was the name of her first husband) wrote some excellent anthropological accounts and collected an irreplaceable treasure of stories, songs, and lore.

So, despite the evidence that Andrew Lang had accumulated and his plausible interpretation of it, his writing would continue to have limited impact unless someone could find a way of appraising the relative age of the cultures he examined.[43] Did the monotheistic cultures arise before the animistic ones, or vice versa? Or could they have come about simultaneously? Before we can take that step, we need to look at the arguments of those who opposed him.

---

[41] Tomoko Masuzawa, *In Search of Dreamtime: The Quest for the Origin of Religion* (Chicago: University of Chicago Press, 1993) brings out, among other matters, the difference that the point of view of gender makes by contrasting the approach of Mircea Eliade in his *Australian Religions: An Introduction* (Ithaca, NY: Cornell University Press, 1973) with that of Nancy D. Munn in *Walbiri Iconography: Graphic Representation and Iconographic Symbolism in a Central Australian Society* (Ithaca, NY: Cornell University Press, 1973). The title of Masuzawa's book may be somewhat misleading. It is not so much about the origin of religion but about what three white male scholars in the past (Müller, Durkheim, Freud) have written about the origin of religion and what it reveals about these three white male scholars of the past. Then she culminates her self-designated postmodern point with this contrast between Eliade and Munn.

[42] K. Langloh Parker, chap. 1, "Introductory," *The Euahlayi Tribe*, accessible at the Sacred Texts website: http://www.sacred-texts.com/aus/tet/tet03.htm.

[43] Lang, *Making of Religion*, 279–80.

CHAPTER 5

Andrew Lang: Interactions and Totemism

Allow me to come back to my opening remarks in this book. Some stories will not make sense without a lot of detail, and this chapter is one that contains a lot of details, presenting for the most part the debate between Lang and his critics. Fortunately, Lang was an amusing writer, as was Hartland; and, if I may use just a touch of hyperbole, Howitt's apparent attempt to be seen as the foremost authority on Australian ethnology hopefully makes this discussion something a little more than just a recital of "he said; he said."

In the previous chapter we looked at the thesis put forward by Andrew Lang that numerous cultures lived on a minimal subsistence level in their material culture but held a belief in a single god, pictured anthropomorphically, who created the world and watched over the morality of the people. These cultures not only showed no evidence of any previous stages of religion, but their descriptions of the supreme being were such that they could not have evolved out of any previous stage if there had been one.

Lang's thesis definitely went against the grain of the dominant schools of anthropology, particularly the animistic school headed by E. B. Tylor, according to whom a culture could only manifest a supreme being after it had developed for a long period of time, passing through various stages of animism and polytheism first. We closed the last chapter by pointing out that on the whole Lang was ignored, and the same fate befell a number of the reports on which he based his conclusions.

Responses to Lang[1]

However, there were a few interactions of which we shall now take note. I have organized them in such a way that the last issue, which is the most complex one, will lead us into the challenging topic of how to establish a chronological sequence among cultures, a topic that, in this case, will have to get around the interference presented by certain theories on totemism.

The Intelligence of the Indigenous People

Andrew Lang, though not breaking entirely with Tylor in all respects, clearly saw himself as putting forward a new theory on religion, and those who took the trouble to respond to him agreed. The idea of a genuine monotheism being present among the culturally least sophisticated people in the world simply violated the rules of any of the theories popular at this point. Many times, as we already saw in the reaction to Pictet in chapter 3, the rejection took the form of simply writing off such a possibility. E. S. Hartland wrote: "On the antecedent improbability that naked savages, without any organised [sic] system of government, and incapable of counting up to seven, could have attained a conception so lofty, there is no need to argue."[2]

---

[1] Much of the debate here is conveniently summarized by Wilhelm Schmidt in *Der Ursprung der Gottesidee*, vol. 1 (Münster: Aschendorff, 1912), 178–411.

[2] E. S. Hartland, "The High Gods of Australia," *Folk-Lore* 9 (1898): 290–329.

Hartland did not specify how one measures this "antecedent improbability" unless the items he mentioned subsequently count as evidence, in which case the "improbability" is not entirely "antecedent." Thus, there might have been some need to argue, after all. We must leave as a mystery what the ability to count to any integer has to do with having a concept of a single supreme being, though I suppose a person would have to be able to count to one. Would anyone tolerate the inference that Darwin could not maintain belief in God because, according to some rumors, he may have had a learning disability for foreign languages? I seriously doubt it. But then, why must one wear clothes to believe in God?

Hartland, who matches Lang in his entertaining writing style line by line, also overreaches in his description when he refers to the indigenous Australians as not having an organized system of government. The clans usually make do with a council of elders and a headman, who in most cases is just the leader of the council of elders, and the groups that have the most pronounced belief in a supreme god also have the simplest system of social organization. Nonetheless, some tribes that still maintain belief in a high god, though more remote and in heavy competition with animism, maintain social relationships based on totem groups that would take matrix algebra to express in mathematical terms (see below).

Still, all of these rejoinders are obviously beside the point because Hartland's immediate intention is not really about arithmetic but about whether the indigenous people of Australia had enough intelligence to be capable of so lofty an idea as a single supreme being. He did not deny the possibility, but he invoked an "antecedent improbability" against such a case due to their supposed primitive mental state. In raising this point, he followed the idea that it takes a high level of intelligence to believe in God (surely an unverifiable assumption) and the dictum that human beings existing on a simple level of culture have less intelligence than so-called civilized ones. Charles Darwin believed that in order to find evidence of the lower mental capacity of so-called savages, one merely had to look at a person with mental disabilities today. In Darwin's view, contemporary mentally disabled people were manifestations of an arrest in the development of their humanity, thereby giving us insight into the low mental abilities of humans prior to their full development.[3] Let me point out that claims linking "races" of human beings with certain levels of intelligence do not hold water. The common assertion that people from certain geographic origins are more intelligent than others is usually made by people seeking to exalt their own ethnicity and is typically based on experimental data slanted in their direction.[4] Just as human beings of different geographical origins may have hair of different colors or textures, they may have differently shaped skulls, as Tylor described in his *Anthropology*.[5] However, Tylor was wrong in claiming that any of these shapes indicate lesser brain development or lower intelligence.

Let us consider the two competing scenarios by which a group of people could attain to a monotheistic religion, beginning with the process mandated by the animistic theory and its close relations. According to this approach the person who is supposedly of low intelligence is said to have contemplated his nature, analyzed the hypothesis that in his dreams he may be separated from his body, inferred that there is a distinction between his spirit or soul and his body, ascribed the same fact to other people, and concluded that when people are dead, (1) their souls may still hang around and (2) require veneration. Next he would ascribe the same properties to entities other than human beings. From there the succession of tribal philosophers, so to speak, would start to think of some spirits as more dominant than others and, eventually accompanied by an increase in intelligence, attain the insight that some spirits had achieved sufficient greatness to be

---

[3] Steven A. Gelb, "Darwin's Use of Intellectual Disability in *The Descent of Man*," *Disability Studies Quarterly* 28, no. 2 (Spring 2008), http://dsq-sds.org/article /view/96/96.

[4] Leonard Lieberman, "How 'Caucasoids' Got Such Big Crania and Why They Shrunk," *Current Anthropology* 42, no. 1 (February 2001): 69–95.

[5] E. B. Tylor, *Anthropology*, vol. 1 (1881; repr., New Delhi: Cosmo Publications, 2001), 46–49.

considered gods. In the course of time, in the eyes of these sages, one of the gods might eventually emerge as superior to the rest of them. And finally, given the right conditions, a prophet markedly brighter than his ancestors, might arise and proclaim that the superior god is, in fact, the only God. At least a part of this process must have repeated itself the world over whenever a local culture rose above simple animism. I cannot help think of this process as akin to driving from Philadelphia to Baltimore by way of Los Angeles.

We may recall that in his polemic against Max Müller, Lang had no compunction about ascribing an unsophisticated level of intelligence to indigenous people, and he did not need to reverse himself at this point. He contrasted the evolutionist's hypothetical development with one of the most natural questions any person, particularly a young child, might ask in looking around the world: "Who made this?" The answer is easy: "A world maker whose abilities must exceed those of any human being." Even if it were true that the indigenous people of Australia were of lesser intelligence than other people (which it is not), that supposition would hardly stand in the way of their believing in a supreme being.[6]

Missionary Influence

Let us now get to what everyone wants to know: How did E. B. Tylor react to the defection of Andrew Lang from the animistic school of religion? The answer is that he did not respond personally to Lang at all. At least judging by the records available, it appears that Tylor reacted to Lang and Lang's theory, once published, with silence. However, Tylor had previously expressed his opinion on the nature of high gods around the world in clear terms.

Let us go back a few decades to around 1875. At that time there were a few authors who, particularly with regard to the supreme

---

[6] Andrew Lang, *Myth, Ritual and Religion,* vol. 1 (1887; repr., London: Longmans, Green, 1913), 330.

beings in America, ascribed their existence in those cultures to the influence of Christian missionaries by extension. They advocated that the same thing was true for supreme beings everywhere.

If one were to read the defenses of the "borrowing" theory without knowing anything else, it would appear that they had made a good case. One of their main points was that in a number of the cultures in question, a word that simply meant "spirit," such as *manitou* among some Algonquin tribes, was used by missionaries to name the God they were proclaiming. The missionaries ascribed higher attributes to this being, whom they called "Great Spirit" (*Gitche Manitou*). Allegedly this concept then stuck with the local people and spread rapidly.[7] Supposedly, similar things happened hundreds of times all over the world since about AD 1500.

Another leading scholar at that time soundly rejected the borrowing hypothesis (I shall reveal his name and the work in which he made his case shortly): "This view will not bear examination. . . . It can hardly be judged that a divine being whose characteristics are often so unlike what European intercourse would have suggested, and who is heard of by such early explorers among such distant tribes, could be a deity of foreign origin."

In addition to pointing out the incompatibility of the descriptions of the supreme being with the God of Christianity, this opponent also brought up various other instances of high gods in America, where nominal contact with Christians, let alone with missionaries, prior to the expression of belief in the supreme being, could be ruled out. Some cases in point:

- 1558, a report on the Creator *Ondouagni* among Canadian First Nations by an explorer named Thevet.
- 1586, a report by the mathematician Thomas Heriot on the supreme deity of Native Americans in Virginia. His facts were

---

[7] This possibility has been eliminated not only because of the geographic extent in which Gitche Manitou is found but also because of the existence of his analogue in related tribes, which is definitely not restricted to the Algonquin nations.

confirmed in 1612–16, in a report by W. Strachey who found out that his name was Ahone. There had been no missionary activity in the meantime.

- 1623–24, a report by E. Winslow on the creator Kiehtan among the Native Americans of Massachusetts.

The name of this staunch opponent of the borrowing hypothesis was E. B. Tylor, and the work in which he made his arguments was none other than the first edition of *Primitive Culture*.[8]

When the first edition of *Primitive Culture* came out (1873/74), Tylor was firmly in the saddle with his evolutionary scheme. The idea of native high gods was no problem for him because he could fit them neatly into his system as the crown of religious development. In view of the diversity among Native American religions, not to mention the fact that their beliefs were still largely unknown, it wasn't hard to postulate a previous polytheism out of which the supreme beings evolved.

Then, from the early 1880s on, A. W. Howitt started to send his articles to the Anthropological Institute. Since Howitt was in Australia, it fell to one of the officers of this society to read these papers aloud at their regular meetings, and frequently the person to do so was E. B. Tylor.[9] So Tylor would have become familiar with Howitt's account. He would have recognized that even though Howitt's evidence by itself did not necessarily overthrow his theory entirely, the monotheism that Howitt described definitely did not fit in with his scheme, according to which monotheism could only come about after a period of polytheism.

So, what was Tylor to do? In contrast to Andrew Lang, changing his basic doctrine apparently was unthinkable for him. Better to rework the evidence than the theory. When he published the second

---

[8] E. B. Tylor, *Primitive Culture*, 1st ed., vol. 2 (1874), 340.

[9] E.g., A. W. Howitt, "Some Austalian Beliefs," *The Journal of the Anthropological Institute of Great Britain and Ireland* 13 (1884): 185–98. The journal indicates in such cases by whom it was read.

edition of *Primitive Culture*, he expunged the references to the "missionary-influence hypothesis." He neither repudiated it as he had done in the first edition, nor did he embrace it.

Then, in 1892, he published "The Limits of Primitive Religion,"[10] in which he defended the case against which he had argued in the first edition of *Primitive Culture*. He declared that *all* occurrences of an apparent monotheism among people who had not achieved what he considered to be the required level of culture were due to missionary influence. He picked up the arguments of those whom he had previously criticized and dropped his own arguments against them. Needless to say, he did not acknowledge that he was doing any such thing.

Lang and Wilhelm Schmidt subsequently used the arguments Tylor had brought up against the proponents of borrowing.[11]

Furthermore, the scenario now envisioned by Tylor is highly improbable. According to his reconstruction of events, the missionaries came in and did not manage to convert anyone to Christianity; however, the direct audience of the missionary as well as unrelated clans, often hundreds of miles away from any missionary activity, immediately altered their mythology to include a benevolent creator god, though they did not get any benefit from him.

In the case of Australia, the idea is downright self-defeating.[12] For one thing, as we saw above, the tribal myths are highly varied and

---

[10] E. B. Tylor, "The Limits of Savage Religion," *Journal of the Anthropological Institute* 21 (1892): 283–99.

[11] See Schmidt, *Der Ursprung der Gottesidee*, vol. 1, 201–21. Of particular interest is the list of sources left out by Tylor in the American context on p. 203. A solid testament against Christian influence on local beliefs is presented by K. Langloh Parker, who grew up in the company of indigenous children and then lived with her first husband alongside the Ualarai people for many years. K. Langloh Parker, *The Euahlayi Tribe: A Study of Aboriginal Life in Australia* (London: Archibald Constable, 1905), http://www.sacred-texts.com/aus /tet/index.htm.

[12] Also, the most reliable testimony is still the report by A. W. Howitt, who makes a strong case for the native origin of the supreme gods. Again, one must be careful in reading him. His factual reports are beyond question; they are our bedrock data. However, when he gives his opinion as to how the idea of the Supreme Being may have evolved out of animism and magic, he is applying categories to which he

contain a lot of material they could not have learned from Christian missionaries, and here we can now also include the vague idea of a Dreamtime which I made minimal mention in the previous chapter. Even if some missionaries had some success (which was sparse indeed), the notion of this monotheism spreading in just a few years over half a continent and assuming all of the different forms in fitting in with the rest of a group's traditional culture strains one's credulity. Furthermore, missionaries reached out to women and children as well as *all* men; they did not limit their efforts to the initiated men. But—as we have recounted—almost invariably women, children, and the uninitiated were uninformed about the supreme being. And that observation takes us to the final *reductio ad absurdum*: Why would the initiated, having learned about God from the missionaries, subsequently keep that knowledge secret from the people who taught it to them just a few years earlier? The "borrowing" hypothesis is easily defeated by the historical evidence, and it makes no sense. Few people at the time went along with this view because it was obviously untenable; Tylor pretty well stood alone in this opinion among the scholars of his time. Sadly, the theory has continued to maintain a life of its own among those whose knowledge of ethnology is secondary to other disciplines.[13]

The Sanctity of the Supreme Being

We already quoted E. S. Hartland's assertion that there was an "antecedent improbability" in Lang's theory of a possible monotheism among people of preliterate cultures, as exemplified by their

---

has no more privileged access than, say, Lang or Frazer at their desks at home. A. W. Howitt, *The Native Tribes of South-East Australia* (London: Macmillan, 1904), 504–8.

[13] See, for example, Robert F. Spencer, Jesse D. Jennings, et al., *The Native Americans: Ethnology and Backgrounds of the North American Indians*, 2nd ed. (New York: Harper & Row, 1977), 670. This passage, which we will discuss in more detail later on, was written by Jennings, whose specialty was archaeology and who seemed to show little awareness of ethnological matters. He stated that belief in monotheism, once catalyzed by Christian missionaries in the American East, spread by itself and had already been adopted by various tribes once missionaries made contact with them.

deficiency in the ability to count. Taking into account the fact that the supreme deities, as described by Lang, do not usually have a cult associated with them, Hartland quipped that "the description applies particularly to the Australian aborigines, who seem to have been unconscious English Deists in paint and scars and feathers."[14] His main criticism was that Lang created a false impression of these supposedly supreme gods. By using Western terms, which are intimately associated with Christianity, Lang was allegedly giving these deities a seriousness and sacredness they did not deserve. According to Hartland's interpretation, basing himself on the same reports as Lang had, these beings were not "God" (as equivalent to the meaning of the term in Christianity, Judaism, or Islam). They did not manifest divine attributes such as omniscience, omnipotence, eternity, or creatorship.

The debate between Hartland and Lang, both masterful writers,[15] was colorful and lengthy, covering multiple articles and segments of books. Let me try to distill it to two main issues: (1) the importance of the accompanying mythology in the description of a supreme being and (2) the importance of morality in connection to the supreme being. For Lang, these issues came down to a third matter: the importance of discriminating between the distinctive beliefs of each tribe.

To what extent could the mythology of a tribe be considered secondary to their actual religious beliefs and practices? Hartland advocated that it could not and that consequently the so-called high gods

---

[14] Hartland, "High Gods of Australia," 293. Lang responded to Hartland in the next volume of the same journal, and Hartland followed up with a response in the same issue. Lang, "Australian Gods: A Reply," *Folk-Lore* 10, 1 (March 1899): 1–32; E. S. Hartland, "Australian Gods: Rejoinder," *Folk-Lore* 10, no. 1 (March 1899): 46–56. Lang responded to Hartland once more in the introduction to the new and revised edition of his *Myth, Ritual and Religion*, vol. 1 (London: Longmans, Green, 1913), xvii–xxiv. The first edition had been published in 1887.

[15] Wilhelm Schmidt, in his summary of the discussion, concedes that he could not match the writing style exhibited by these authors: Lang was entertaining and genial, even in controversy; Hartland tended to be more compressed and clear, as well as suffused with a dry Anglo-Saxon humor. In fact, Schmidt may have done himself an injustice with this remark. The formal nature of German lends itself to the subtle art of "condemning with faint praise."

of Lang's interpretation were rather comical beings who, while looked upon as esteemed ancestors, bumbled their way through the supernatural world and showed none of the supposedly exalted qualities with which Lang and others had endowed them. But, speaking of "antecedent improbabilities," this conclusion seemed to be in trouble from the start in light of Howitt's description of one of the supreme gods: "As Daramulun, he is said to be able to 'go anywhere and do anything.' He can be invisible; but when he makes himself visible, it is in the form of an old man of the Australian race. He is evidently everlasting, for he existed from the beginning of all things, and he still lives."[16]

After all, Howitt was the source for the data Hartland analyzed. Let us continue to stick with *Dhuramullan* as our example, whom we have encountered as the creator god among the Coast Murring tribes (*Yuin, Ngarigo*, and the *Awabakal* [*Kuri*]). Hartland made much ado about some of the mythology associated with Dhuramullan, playing up the cannibalism associated with him in supposedly consuming the faces of the initiates and the fact that even in more moderated tales he is pictured as having splintered one leg in descending from heaven. Hartland refers to him as "this Creator with a game leg."[17]

But Hartland made a fundamental mistake here, forgetting that Dhuramullan appears in two different groups of tribes playing two different roles. One of them is the above-mentioned group called the "Coast Murring," where he is recognized as supreme, and none of those limitations are ascribed to him. The bizarre mythology concerning Dhuramullan is found among the more northerly "Inland Murring." The *Jeithi* (*Wiradjuri*), *Kamilaroi*, and *Ualarai* (*Euahlayi*) recognized *Baiame* as supreme, and for them Dhuramullan was at best Baiame's son standing in for him at the initiation rite and at worst an evil son who had been punished by Baiame, either by being killed or by being turned into an animal. The temptation to overgeneralize is always present for a serious scholar of religion, and I

---

[16] Howitt, *Native Tribes of South-East Australia*, 500.
[17] Hartland, "High Gods of Australia," 295–96.

suspect few have avoided it completely, but it can lead to propagating some serious errors. In this particular case the difference between the two groups was unequivocally clear. One held Dhuramullan as the supreme god; the other recognized Baiame.

Furthermore, Lang also emphasized the difference between mythology, which is frequently the outcome of creative imagination and the desire for entertainment, and religion, which is the actual cultus (worship practices and rituals) along with the most fundamental doctrines on which those practices are based. For the sake of clarification, Lang asserted that Christianity carries a large bulk of mythology, and he was not referring to the biblical narratives in this context but to the many stories concerning Jesus, Mary, and the disciples that were spun during the Middle Ages. Lang did not use the following example, but I hope it clarifies his point: we can quickly think of a number of additions to the Christmas story that Christians don't really believe but with which they keep themselves entertained: the angry, hostile innkeeper, who grudgingly consigned Mary to give birth to Jesus in the barn; the magi as three kings named Caspar, Melchior, and Balthazar; the animals that adored the Christ child in the manger; and Santa Claus as the representative of the Christian virtue of giving. I shall avoid overgeneralizing and merely say that many Christians know there is no truth behind those legendary accretions but find them to be harmless fictions indulged in as long as they do not detract from what they know to be the essence of Christmas: the incarnation of God in the world, as described by the historical facts of the Bible. Similarly, Lang said that much of the mythology surrounding the supreme beings is highly dispensable, serving for the most part as creative outlets and entertainment, as well as stories to satisfy the curiosity of the uninitiated. In the previous chapter we already encountered one such instance in connection with the spooky-comical figure of Twanyirika among the Aranda.

Hartland was correct in pointing out that Lang was fairly quick to separate secondary myth from practiced religion (particularly if we remember that he did not grant Müller such an easy out).

However, he was not without guidance in doing so. To a large extent he could rely on Howitt, who was able to do so pretty well in his reports—though only after his initiation! The fact that Howitt himself was misguided by the mythology until he had been a part of the central rite of a tribe is extremely important for this topic because it explains why other, uninitiated, anthropologists came up with no results or dubious ones. So Howitt is a good guide to follow in order to separate the religious wheat from the mythological chaff. In an article, which on the whole was quite prickly toward Lang, Howitt asserted, "As to the belief in the Tribal All-Father, which is held by the tribes mentioned by me in my *Native Tribes of South-East Australia*, p. 500, and is not held by any others, I see no reason to alter anything I have said."[18] It almost appears as though, having stated his criticisms of Lang (see below), he now turned toward Hartland and asserted that he was not happy with him either.

But Hartland was not yet done attempting to undermine Lang's contention that the supposedly supreme god was truly a sacred figure. Even granting that Lang could be correct in divorcing the frivolous mythology from the beliefs of the true religion, Hartland did not think Lang's case would stand up if the initiation ceremonies were the yardstick for separating them. According to his assessment, "'Their best religious ideas,' we learn, 'are imparted in their ancient and secret mysteries,' which, let me add, are celebrated with horrible cruelty and worse than beastly filthiness."[19] In short, the supposed relationship between a rigorous tribal morality and belief in the supreme being was just so much whitewash; the initiation ceremonies were filled with blatant immoralities as well.

We do not read about any initiation ceremonies involving "horrible cruelty and worse than beastly filthiness" in Howitt's descriptions of the initiation rituals. In his account of the initiation by the

---

[18] A. W. Howitt, "The Native Tribes of South-East Australia," *Folk-Lore* 17, no. 1 (March 1906): 188. Be sure to observe the distinction between this article and the book bearing the same title, cited above.
[19] Hartland, "High Gods of Australia," 296.

Gunai under the god *Mungan ngaua*, there is not even the compara-
tively simple ritual (by anthropological standards) of knocking out
any teeth. Hartland's source for the supposedly sordid practices was
R. H. Mathews,[20] who studied the Inland Murring. However, there
were some issues of credibility with Mathews's multitudinous reports,
most of which followed similar lines.[21] Apparently, Mathews did not
distinguish sufficiently between what he had actually experienced,
what he had learned from knowledgeable "informants," and what he
picked up secondhand. It seems that he enjoyed the recognition of
supposedly having been the first European to have witnessed this or
that sexually charged aspect of newly discovered cultures, playing
up to the alleged post-Victorian moral liberation of Europe, which
was finding its peak in the mythologies created by Sigmund Freud.
The alleged obscenities were not reported by other investigators, and
Hartland was relying on some fairly dubious material. Furthermore,
it appears that Mathews was misunderstanding much of what he
saw. A number of the initiation ceremonies included pantomimes
of forbidden actions (probably acted out in sketchy form so as not
even to speak of them out loud), and the candidates were expected
to abjure them. It is possible that Mathews did not understand their
prohibitive purpose but thought they were done to entertain the
candidates.[22]

---

[20] R. H. Mathews, *Notes on the Aborigines of New South Wales* (Sidney: Apple-
gate, 1907).

[21] For one thing his descriptions contained more details than one could reason-
ably expect a person to be able to see, remember, or record at first exposure. His
vantage point seemed to be akin to that of the so-called omniscient narrator of a
novel who knows what is happening with all of his characters simultaneously, even
when they are far apart. How could he know precisely what a representative group
from another clan was doing as they were approaching the initiation grounds and
what the host group was doing at the same time in preparing the initiation grounds?
Obviously he was relying on what was being told to him, which is proper procedure,
but he needed to clarify that fact and refrain from slanting what was reported to him
as though he saw it himself, let alone make a good story just a little better.

[22] Schmidt, *Ursprung*, vol. 1, 222.

Thus, Hartland, having constructed a somewhat confusing critique, which clearly was based on some erroneous and unreliable assumptions, played the same card that had become the escape hatch for many others before him. Whatever confusion may not be resolvable, "the reason lies in the vagueness of the savage mind and the shifting nature of tradition."[23]

The discussion between Hartland and Lang went on, but we can leave it there. Once one gets to the point of blaming the local people for not fitting into one's scheme, the debate becomes fruitless.

The Ideal Chief and the Father in Heaven

If in some way I have created the impression that Howitt was pleased with Lang's use of the data he provided, I need to correct that notion immediately. He wrote a rather snitty response article as though Lang had personally attacked him in making use of his reports. A. W. Howitt had a rather proprietary attitude toward his accounts, but everyone who made use of them gave him the credit he deserved. Still, he clearly felt that his *interpretations* of what he experienced should be as authoritative as his descriptions, which is not necessarily how things work in scholarship. To use an example far distant from Australian anthropology, the data used by Watson and Crick in creating the model of DNA as a double helix, which won them a Nobel Prize, came to a large extent from the publications of other scientists.[24] That's how things have to work if science is going to make progress. The overall connecting theories often come from those who did not do the research in the labs. Also, curiously, even though Howitt made use of the reports made by Spencer and Gillen in his explanations,[25] he showed himself displeased when Lang combined

---

[23] Hartland, "High Gods of Australia," 294.

[24] J. D. Watson and F. H. C. Crick, "The Structure of DNA," *Cold Spring Harbor Symposia on Quantitative Biology* 18 (1953): 123–36.

[25] Other important sources were: Baldwin Spencer and F. J. Gillen, *The Native Tribes of Central Australia* (London: 1899) and *The Northern Tribes of Central Australia* (London: 1904).

their results with his (i.e., Spencer and Gillen's with Howitt's), again conveying the impression that by doing so Lang was personally assailing him.[26]

However, Howitt clearly was right in two factual corrections of Lang, which at first seem unrelated, but which actually hang together in the end.

Previously, I quoted Howitt's description of the supreme god and his attributes. I now need to reveal what followed right afterwards. Let us pick up with Dhuramullan's eternity. The god would not have died, but human beings would also not die apart from some witchcraft or curse placed on them. "He is evidently everlasting, for he existed from the beginning of all things, and he still lives. But in being so, he is merely in that state in which, these aborigines believe, everyone would be if not prematurely killed by evil magic."[27]

Note that Howitt in the second sentence is no longer reporting but opining, and, as soon as he does so, he is no longer immune from criticism. This trivialization of Dhuramullan's everlasting existence is an overgeneralization based on a common phenomenon. In many cultures, including Australian ones, accidental deaths or deaths from sickness are ascribed to someone having cast a spell on the departed one. However, they cannot apply this diagnosis universally; two clear exceptions are death in battle and death due to the evident weakness brought on by sheer old age. Regardless of how far this belief encompasses human beings, simply having enough power to ward off death-bringing magic still makes the god unique. But to get to the criticism of Lang, Howitt goes on, "Combining the statements of the legends and the teachings of the ceremonies, I see, as the embodied idea, a venerable kindly Headman of a tribe, full of knowledge and tribal wisdom, and all-powerful in magic, **of which he is the source**, with virtues, failings, and passions, such as the aborigines regard them."[28]

---

[26] See, for example, Howitt, "Native Tribes of South-East Australia," 186.

[27] Howitt, *Native Tribes of South-East Australia*, 500.

[28] Ibid., 500–501, emphasis mine.

Howitt was not going along with Lang's hypothesis that the monotheism of the Australian tribes could have come about without a preceding stage of belief in magic and spirits. He held that it must have been derived from some earlier notion and proposed the theory that the Supreme Being was the idealization of a departed chief or headman. Lang had put that theory aside because the Aboriginal groups had no "headman" who enjoyed special standing in the band and, consequently, could not be the source of belief in a deity.[29] At this point Lang was overstating the information available to him, and Howitt corrected him. He stated that many groups had a headman, usually the oldest man, and that in some tribes he received great honors, particularly at his funeral. Thus, the idea of the god could be based on imagining someone in such a role without the usual limitations to which humans are subject. Lang at least partially acknowledged this oversight on his part and added a short appendix to that purpose to the second printing of *The Making of Religion*.[30]

Still, even if the description of the god incorporated the qualities of a respected chief, there were too many problems to say sensibly that such a chief was *the source* of the idea of the deity. Simply put, to serve as source, the human model must show a close approximation to the divine replication, or vice versa, so that the deity is essentially a larger, less limited, instantiation of the model. Otherwise, the idea that a human person served as source for the idea of God makes no sense. In fact, there are a number of significant differences between Howitt's descriptions of the earthly authorities and of the divine beings.

On the human side, the function of the chiefs was usually to preside over the council of elders, but there was no council of gods with whom the supreme god collaborated. Following the correction Howitt applied to Lang, we must acknowledge that in some cases the office of chief had attained an elevated status in some societies.

---

[29] Lang, *Making of Religion*, 175. Nor, as we mentioned above, did they have genuine ancestor veneration.

[30] Ibid., 318.

However, those groups are the ones in which the belief in the supreme being was less pronounced, and that it received its clearest form in those tribes where the headman simply assumed that role by outliving other men and becoming the oldest male member of the clan.

Furthermore, the functions of chief and magician of the tribe were separate in those groups where the chief had assumed greater prominence. So, if the idea of the god as idealized chief had its source in the cultures where the chief had become an important figure, the human model should prevent him from combining those two offices and cannot be, contra Howitt, the source of the idea of the god.

Moreover, the people and the headman knew other clans had their chiefs so that insofar as he had power, it was geographically limited. If we remain with the idea that the chief was the blueprint for the god, the expected outcome should not be monotheism but "henotheism," a term coined by Max Müller. Henotheism is exemplified by the pagan nations surrounding Israel in Old Testament times, for whom each god was limited to the territory of the people who worshipped him. But the Australians did not follow the example set by the human chiefs and limit their god in such a way; each of their supreme gods was seen as the one and only god over the entire world.

In all cases where there is a belief in a supreme being, once the chief had died, regardless of how high his standing was and how elaborate the funeral might have been, there would be no further cultus devoted to him, and he would be soon forgotten. Thus, the idea of an ancestral chief or culture hero growing into godhood, which is a common belief in other cultures, cannot work here. It could only be sustained by imagining that at one time customs were different from what they were at the time of investigation. In that case we would be adding new, unverifiable facts.

On the divine side, although the god may have embodied some of the ideal traits of both the chief and the powerful tribal magician, he also lacked many of their attributes. He did not engage in acts of magic for anyone's profit, least of all his own, as a tribal magician would. As we have already said, except for his moral supervision, he was not usually involved in the affairs of human beings.

In most cases there is no logical connection between the headman of a clan and the most important function ascribed to the Supreme Being, namely as Creator of the world.

Finally, at the risk of overemphasis, we must not lose track of the fact that where the belief in a Supreme Being was most thoroughly developed, the headman's standing was special only thanks to his age. There was little if any magic, and there was neither ancestor veneration nor animism.

So the thesis that the idea of God developed out of this picture of an ideal chief shows itself to be contrary to the facts, as established by Howitt himself. However, because he was not willing to share Lang's hypothesis of an original monotheism, he had to come up with some way of explaining the origin of this belief, and this "idealization theory" was the result. Whatever else one wants to make of it, it was certainly nothing he observed but a theory and not a very strong one.

The Supreme Being was frequently called "Father," either as his actual name or as a secondary name. It was an easy jump from there to interpret this term in a Christian sense of there being a familial relationship between God and the human person.

But "father" in the various Australian cultures functioned not only as a label for one's biological progenitor but as an honorific term, and overall, particularly in the light of the discussion that will follow, this latter usage may have been the dominant one. In many cases it was bestowed on the headman or other venerable individuals because of their advanced age, high social standing in the clan, or their great wisdom. Initially Lang fell into the trap of interpreting this title in a sense close to the Christian conception of God looking after his children paternally. However, Howitt pointed out to him that such an interpretation went too far. In fact, it would compromise the general remoteness of the Supreme Being. God being called "Father" was also

a title of honor, similar to that given to a chief. It did not particularly refer to his creating or nurturing his people. Lang accepted this
correction.

Societal Arrangements and the Age of Cultures

Howitt understandably took pride in what he had experienced and
recorded. Nevertheless, some of his most fundamental interpretations were not anything that he could have observed directly. They
were theories created by people who "just knew" how things must
have gone but were wrong, as we shall show. Howitt believed the
monotheism of the tribes was a late development, preceded by cultures like those of the Dieri and Urabunna, who showed no evidence
of belief in a Supreme Being.

He and his early coworker, Lorimer Fison, based their chronological sequence on the idea that the earliest social arrangement among
the indigenous people of Australia was "group marriage." Let us stipulate that the entire tribe is divided into two groups (phratries or
clans), and each group contains one-half of both the male and female
population of the tribe. These groups are usually designated by animal
names, such as Eagle Hawks and Crows. "Group marriage" meant that
any man among, say, the Eagle Hawks, could have sexual relationships with any woman among the Crows, and vice versa. The only
restriction would be that "marriage" partners had to belong to opposite groups (exogamy). Which of the two groups a child would belong
to was determined by the mother's affiliation (matrilineal descent).

From there, Howitt's theory continued, the cultures in Australia
advanced into two different directions (see fig. 5.1). One was exemplified by the North Central tribes, such as the Aranda. Each of these
tribes had their individual arrangements, but over the course of time,
some of them followed similar patterns. In this instance cultures multiplied the different marriage groups, first into four and then into eight,
creating subclasses along the way and arranging them into complex
patterns. Some of these same cultures switched to reckoning one's

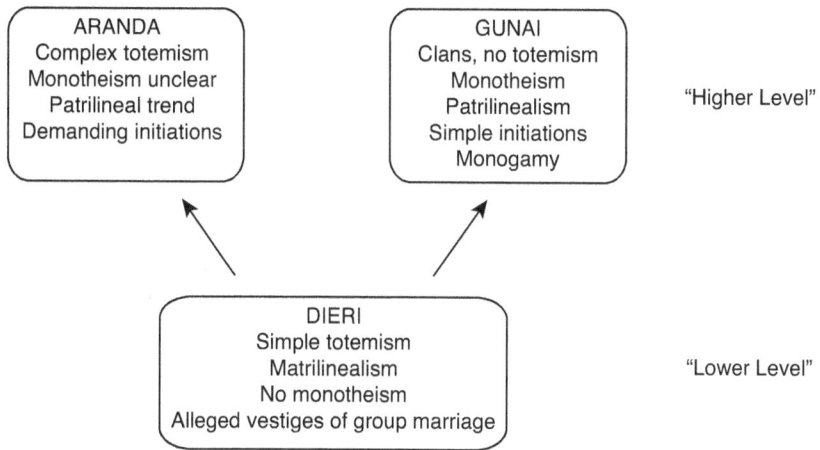

Figure 5.1

group identification through the father (patrilineal descent), and they tended toward a preference for monogamy. In terms of their religions, they elaborated the animistic and magical aspects. The other direction of advancement was exemplified by the Coast Murring and other Southeastern tribes, who became strictly monogamous, simplified the divisions of society or did away with them altogether, and attained the notion of a Supreme Being.[31] Let us call the aforementioned group divisions in a society "totem groups" and the phenomenon of a society living with such a scheme "totemism." We will elaborate on these systems toward the end of this chapter.

Having added the vocabulary in parentheses, we can restate the above description a little more efficiently. Howitt believed that in the past the Australian Aboriginal people practiced group marriage within the context of a rather simple, matrilineal totemic system. Insofar as they had religious beliefs, they were animistic and magical. Two different steps in advancement from there were (1) a much

---

[31] Lorimer Fison and Alfred William Howitt, *Kamilaroi and Kurnai: Group-Marriage and Relationship and Marriage by Elopement* (Melbourne: George Robinson, 1880).

more complex, mostly patrilineal, totemic system, tending toward monogamy, with animism remaining dominant in religion; and (2) the virtual abandonment of strict totemism and animism, a strictly enforced practice of monogamy, and the strong belief in a single creator god.

Howitt's scheme was obviously not based on direct observation since he could hardly have observed the cultural developments of the different tribes over time. One would like to think it was an inference based on his observations, and that's how Howitt wanted it to be perceived; but even that assessment is not really accurate. It truly was the imposition of a theory on the observations, namely the conjectures of L. H. Morgan.

When Western thinkers in the early nineteenth century started to contemplate the nature of humanity's first religion, they usually tended to favor one of these two criteria: (1) fidelity to the Bible, which favored an original monotheism; and (2) a subjective philosophical judgment of "what must have happened," which theoretically could still be an original monotheism, polytheism, or anything else. The options of an original animism, which eventually had to compete with the idea of preanimistic magical practice, were later additions on the whole. The point I am repeating here is the not-so-novel one that people came to the question of early religion once their own theories were already firmly in place.

What I want to add to the above observation is that this backwards methodology was not confined to how people pictured early religions. It also included imaginary views of the earliest social arrangements among humans. How should we picture "uncivilized savages" living together? The criterion appeared to be that the cruder and the more dehumanizing the picture was, the closer to the early reality it must be.[32] In Sigmund Freud's fantasies, the first humans lived in hordes similar to baboons, in which the oldest and most powerful male was

---

[32] As a reminder, despite all of the problems with his theory, E. B. Tylor's biggest contribution was to lift anthropology out of the realm of pure imagination to the reality of the need to adduce evidence for one's claims.

the only person to be allowed to have sexual intercourse with any female members of the group. The younger and less powerful males would either have to wait their turn or fight for the right to become the dominant man in the clan. (Freud's scenario goes on with the young men conspiring to kill and consume the dominant old man, but we need not pursue the story any further at this point.)[33]

Another way of imagining early human beings that makes them appear bestial is to ascribe to them the idea of unrestricted group marriage. The horde lives together. Any man may have access to any woman (or vice versa), circumstances permitting. Women get pregnant and give birth to children; nobody can know precisely who the biological father is, therefore it becomes common practice for all men to address all women as either mother or spouse, depending on the age, and for all women to refer to all men as either father or spouse, again depending on the age differential. Very early on, perhaps because of the problems associated with inbreeding, the group was divided into two phratries, thereby putting some restraint on the sexual free-for-all. Such was the theory of L. H. Morgan.[34] And this was the theory to which Fison and Howitt subscribed. In fact, their correspondence reveals that they saw themselves virtually as Morgan's eyes and ears on the field.[35]

Now, even though personal promiscuity and the societal collapse of sexual standards have been a recurring phenomenon in the history of the human race, there is no evidence that group marriage was ever a social institution. It was Morgan's assumption of what would be appropriate for human beings in the earliest stages of their existence as so-called savages. It would not be inappropriate at this point to remind ourselves of Howitt's derogatory remarks concerning

---

[33] Sigmund Freud, *Totem and Taboo* (1918; repr., New York: Random House, Vintage Books, 1948).

[34] Lewis H. Morgan, *Ancient Society* (1877; repr., New Brunswick, NJ: Transaction Publishers, 2000).

[35] Bernhard J. Stern, ed., "Selections from the Letters of Lorimer Fison and A. W. Howitt to Lewis Henry Morgan," *American Anthropologist* 32 (1930): 257–79.

"ethnologists of the study" because Morgan clearly was one of them, and yet Howitt and Fison used his theory to establish the chronology of the Australian tribes. His appeal in general lay in his support of evolution and Marxist-like social theories in which he construed ordinary social conventions, such as the authority of government, private property, and monogamous marriage, as late inventions in human history. Howitt and Fison would have been attracted to his writings all the more because he frequently illustrated his theories with examples from Australia, though we must remind ourselves that these examples obviously go back prior to the thorough discoveries undertaken later by Howitt, Langloh Parker, and others.

Since Howitt was not just a government employee but a competent self-taught anthropologist, there must have been some reasons that enabled him to see Morgan's theory in his data. What was the evidence that he could associate with Morgan's ideas?

1. There were some peculiar marriage habits among the aforementioned Dieri and Urabunna, those whom Howitt considered to be representative of the earliest Australian cultures, who did not show any evidence of belief in a supreme being. Among the Dieri, the normal pattern of marriage was that a man would take one wife. This relationship was called *tippa malku*, and so the man was the *tippa malku* husband of the woman. Subsequently, he might receive permission from the clan to enter the arrangement called *pirrauru*. This meant that if he received it, he would be allowed to engage in sexual relations with other women, subject to the convenience of their own *tippa malku* husbands. The Urabunna had a similar institution called *piraiungaru* but dispensed with having a particular term for the usual marriage (I would think because it was the normal pattern and didn't need any further designation).

    This practice certainly does not meet the straightforward understanding of monogamy, but, contra Howitt, it seems to presuppose monogamy, and it is a far cry from the idea of free group marriage with only the phratry as boundary. Without having committed oneself to Morgan's imaginative speculation, there does not seem to be anything in this system that should lead one to think that *pirrauru*, a modification on a basically monogamous arrangement, was preceded by a practice of group marriage with fewer restraints.

2. Designations of familial relationships in traditional cultures are often complex and misleading. Even in contemporary modern societies, words indicating family relationships often serve more than one function. In English-speaking countries Roman Catholic Christians address their priest as "Father." Growing up in a Baptist congregation in Germany, my parents referred to the various members as "Brother" and "Sister" while I was expected to refer to them all as "Uncle" or "Aunt." In some Asian countries the expectation goes beyond religious association; all children are expected to address adults as "Uncle" or "Aunt." This practice also moves up the age ladder so that I, long past youth, will still address an older South Asian woman who is in a position of respect as "Auntie." My point is simply that often such designations go beyond their literal biological meaning and become terms of honor. We saw earlier that Howitt chastised Lang for not recognizing that distinction when it came to the use of the term "Father," as applied to the headman and the supreme god.

Terms for relatives in some societies get extremely complex. In Hindi, there are different words for uncles and aunts on the mother's side than on the father's side. In many languages a boy and his sister will use different words to address the same relative. In his article responding to Lang, Howitt gave a number of instances of how this fact works out in different tribes; and, on first reading it one is likely to get dizzy. Entire generations of one phratry may be addressed as the "father" or "mother" of the next generation.[36]

---

[36] Howitt, "Native Tribes of South-Central Australia," 177–83.

For example, Howitt documented the difficulty he had to extract from a boy the identity of his biological father because the child addressed two brothers equally as *mungan*, "father." Howitt finally found out which one was the real *mungan*. The other man, the boy's uncle by our terminology, was then designated as the *breppa mungan*, the "other father." Howitt intended to use this experience to illustrate that in this group every man of the father's generation was considered to be the boy's biological father (*mungan*).

Thus, Howitt's case was that given the origin of these terms at the time of group marriage (the point he is trying to prove), the local people did not mean the familial terms as honorifics or functional titles but as expressing the actual physical relationship. Thus, despite the eventual success in finding out who was the biological father of the boy in the above example, the everyday language does not make that distinction. Consequently, according to Howitt, the people of the group actually did think of each man in that generation as the father of the boy in the same sense as in our culture we think of each person having just one father, our male biological parent. We Western outsiders may think the real father has to be one man only, but Howitt insisted that the local people did not think that way. Going back to the time when, according to this theory, group marriage was the norm, the entire preceding generation would be addressed as "father" in a literal sense.

This assertion by Howitt is puzzling in light of the fact that he had earlier gone to great lengths to emphasize the ceremonial and societal use of the term "father" as a matter of courtesy for elders and chiefs and the supreme being. Now he insists that we must understand the term in its full biological meaning, just as we understand it in English at home, except to refer to an entire generation. It seems that Howitt's examples count against his theory. In the case of the boy mentioned, if Howitt's interpretation had really been true, then he never should have been able to find out, as he did, who was the real *mungan* and who was the *breppa mungan*. In the language of the clan, the term *mungan* may have been used for everyone of a generation on an everyday basis, but that fact apparently did not entail that the actual biological relationships had been totally swept under the eucalyptus leaves. It simply was not a part of normal discourse to refer to the reality of the formalities of custom, though it would have been known. There is no question that the systems of address in many cultures are extremely complex, but that need not force us to think that either the people in those cultures were ignorant of the biological relationships, regardless of terminology, or that the terminology is a survival from a hypothetical time when the biological relationships were irrelevant. The better explanation seems to be that the same principle that demands the use of "father" for chieftains and the supreme being obtains with regard to other expressions of relationships as well.

At this point Howitt came down hard on Lang. Let me now give the larger version of an earlier quotation:

> Mr. Lang's position really bears out what I have said, that most white men, like himself, brought up in our views of individual marriage and descent, seem quite unable to place themselves mentally in the position of these aborigines who use the classificatory system of relationships. This is one of the unfortunate circumstances which attend the studies of those who, to use Mr. Lang's own words, are "ethnologists of the study," and who are not willing, like some others, to take the opinion of men who have first-hand knowledge of the natives. Mr. Lang's explanations of the origin and meaning of the Australian terms of relationship are merely

guesses, without the support of any direct
evidence, and do not, I think, require any
further notice here.[37]

This outburst is rather confusing, and maybe a little further notice
would have helped us make more sense out of what Howitt was saying. He, who had earlier insisted that relationship terms needed to be
understood in the same literal, biological way as we would in ordinary
conversation at home, is now saying that Lang is too tied to the categories of home because he is not applying the categories of home.
Granted that Lang was not in the presence of the Australian people
when they used the terminology, Howitt had already pointed him into
the direction one should go with one's interpretations, namely as honorific appellations, but then Howitt dramatically reversed himself. For
that matter we must ask: Had Howitt really personally *observed* that
the Australian people meant the terms for relatives in our accustomed
biological sense? This question is not easy to answer, but it is certainly
clear that he did not observe the historical development of which
he assured us. Furthermore, the discussion on the use of the word
father and the anecdote of identifying the boy's biological father seem
to show that his insistence on his theory was inconsistent with his
actual observations. It appears more likely that Howitt was grasping
at straws to support the group marriage theory, and it strikes me that
the bizarre nature of his outburst against Lang underscores that fact.

The point is, then, that Howitt's work in the services of the
anthropology of religion would have been even more productive if
he had not tied himself from the beginning to the thought of L. H.
Morgan. Morgan presented his theory as basic principles, specifically
that all cultures began with group marriage. That is a thesis that can
be tested if we can establish a sequence of cultures in time. And at
this point in the book, we are almost ready to do so. One last hurdle
remains: We need to get a clearer delineation of totemism than I have
provided so far.

---

[37] Ibid., 183–84.

Clarifying Totemism

Much of the discussion of this chapter has made reference to the various subgroups into which a larger population may be divided. We can simply call them subgroups, classes, or clans. In many parts of the world, such subgroups are associated with an animal or a plant. In this case we may call this institution totemism, and the item with which a subgroup is associated is known as their totem. The subgroups can be called totem-classes, phratries, and sometimes moieties. There is no absolute standard of vocabulary, and this is good because there are no standard arrangements.[38]

Totemism became a large red herring in the discussion on the origin of religion because it was misunderstood and universalized beyond all reality. It will ultimately play a fairly small role in our conclusion, namely as an indicator of how long a culture had been developing; but because it does run interference so often,[39] we cannot dispense with taking a few moments to understand it properly.

For our purposes now, I'm going to assume that L. H. Morgan was wrong and that human culture did not begin with "group marriage" across two phratries as he described it but that it began with a society in which there were no intrinsic divisions, where monogamy was the rule, and descent was reckoned through the father. I have not yet given evidence for that claim, and I will do so at the proper point. In the meantime, it is to our advantage to get more acquainted with the idea of totemism first, and it will make our progress a little more efficient if we ignore the fantasies of repressed Victorian gentlemen. In short, I will leave the alleged bestiality of early human beings to low-budget science fiction films.

---

[38] For further discussions on totemism on my part, please see Winfried Corduan, *Neighboring Faiths: A Christian Introduction to World Religions*, 2nd ed. (Downers Grove, IL: InterVarsity Press, 2012), 212–15, 248–52.

[39] E.g., eventually we need to take a closer look at Émile Durkheim, *The Elementary Forms of Religious Life*, trans. Carol Cosman (1912; repr., New York: Oxford, 2001).

The word *totem* is derived from the language of the Native American Ojibway tribe, where it was called a *doodem*, an object indicating one's relationship to a part of the natural world. Although for our purposes totemism is most significant as a social institution, we must mention that there is also such a thing as an individual totem, like an animal, plant, rock, or the like that brings spiritual power to an individual. Individual totemism was important among the tribes of the Great Plains. Our focus will be on totemism as an element within a society.

Let any population group get large enough, and some subdivisions will occur. There are several criteria by which the subgroups can be delineated. Among the observed possibilities are: (1) geographic locations, (2) hierarchical arrangements (ranging from a system of nobility and commoners all the way to a caste system), and (3) parallel associations (clans or subtribes with or without totemism). All three possibilities can be combined in different, sometimes surprising, ways. The more we back off from establishing fundamental rules for totemism, and the more we can avoid using that term at all, the less likely we are to commit mistakes of overgeneralization. The nineteenth-century scholars, with their penchant for finding "laws" of human cultural evolution, created blueprints using single explanations where multiple explanations, varying from case to case, would have been more appropriate.

Keeping the above *caveat* in mind at all times, let me now draw up some general schemes so we can clarify the terminology. We will have to accommodate ourselves to the traditional ambiguous word *tribe* for the largest social unit but leave ourselves the privilege to resort to various words for the subdivisions.[40] The best term to use in

---

[40] A good introduction to the basic forms of totemism on the Australian continent, at least as far as it was known in his time, was provided by Andrew Lang in his rather polemical introduction to Parker's book (K. Langloh Parker, "Introduction," *The Euahlayi Tribe*). See also his *The Secret of the Totem* (London: Longmans, Green, 1904).

general is *phratry*. But then what do you call the subdivisions underneath a phratry? Let's be as flexible as necessary.[41]

We can begin by stipulating a tribe with two phratries; let us unimaginatively call them A and B. Almost invariably marriages must be exogamous, meaning that marriage partners must come from different phratries. To which of the two phratries the children belong depends on the culture; the rule can be either patrilineal or matrilineal.

Presumably, totemism began as a way of preventing the genetic consequences of inbreeding and incest, and this side is definitely emphasized in the long run. However, in many cases it is also a method of regulating the food supply. The phratries are frequently named after particular animals, and in numerous cultures it is strictly forbidden for someone to kill, let alone eat, their totem animal. Thus, if there were two totem groups, which we can arbitrarily call the Lizards and the Kangaroos, members of the Lizard clan could eat kangaroos but not lizards, while kangaroos would be off the menu for the Kangaroo phratry though they could eat all the lizards they desired. Now, if there were a shortage of lizards one year, it would not affect the Lizard clan at all, since they could not eat them anyway, and since the entire tribe does not depend on lizards for its sustenance, there may still be enough for the Kangaroos. To what extent the rules for apportioning food contributed to the persistence of totemism[42] we cannot know, but it can be a definite benefit in addition to the provision for exogamy.

From here on, until I indicate differently, we will assume exogamy and that, at least in theory, any system can be either patrilineal

---

[41] The following descriptions, insofar as they are not general knowledge, are primarily based on my own observations. I wish to acknowledge the support of Taylor University for several research trips, including one specifically to study the culture of the Tlingit nation in the summer of 2008.

[42] I know of cultures classified as totemic who have exogamy but no food taboos, but I'm not aware of any that have food taboos but do not practice exogamy. Whether any significance can be inferred from this observation is hard to say.

		Total Population (Tribe)	
		Phratry A	Phratry B
Patrilineal	Marriage	♂ ◯◯	♀
	Offspring	♂ ♀	
	Marriage	♀ ◯◯	♂
	Offspring		♂ ♀
Matrilineal	Marriage	♂ ◯◯	♀
	Offspring		♂ ♀
	Marriage	♀ ◯◯	♂
	Offspring	♂ ♀	

Figure 5.2. A society with two phratries. Marriages must cross phratry lines. The affiliation of the children depends on whether the society is matrilineal or patrilineal.

or matrilineal. There are a number of ways in which the totemic system can become more complex.

The system was undoubedtly used to prevent accidental incest. But setting up the phratries would not completely seal off that possibility. In a matrilineal system a young woman and, say, her paternal uncle would be in different phratries, so it would still be possible for her to have relations with him, who would be a close relative. The resulting child could suffer the consequences. In a patrilineal system the same possibility could occur with a young man and a woman closely related to his mother with the child, again, possibly reaping the genetic results of incest. As a measure against this eventuality, many cultures divided each phratry into two classes: "old" and "young." One of these was the Euahlayi, as investigated by Langloh Parker. Leaving out all of the details and contingencies of figure 5.2, following is a simple diagram (fig. 5.3) of how this innovation worked.

Not every totemic group system has such a straightforward generational rule built in, but we'll stipulate that with few exceptions they have some device to prevent incest.

Another way in which the systems get complicated is by adding more phratries. As we mentioned above, this can happen on an entirely parallel level. There are no "typical" numbers where this development has occurred. For example, the present-day Cherokee of North Carolina recognize seven clans: Long Hair, Wolf, Deer, Wild Potato, Bird, Paint, and Blue. The marriage rule is, of course, exogamous; and, in this case, for the members of any clan, any of the other six groups present an option for marriage. Descent is reckoned in matrilineal fashion. There are no food taboos. In other groups multiple parallel clans may have further rules restricting intermarriage and other regulations based on clan membership.

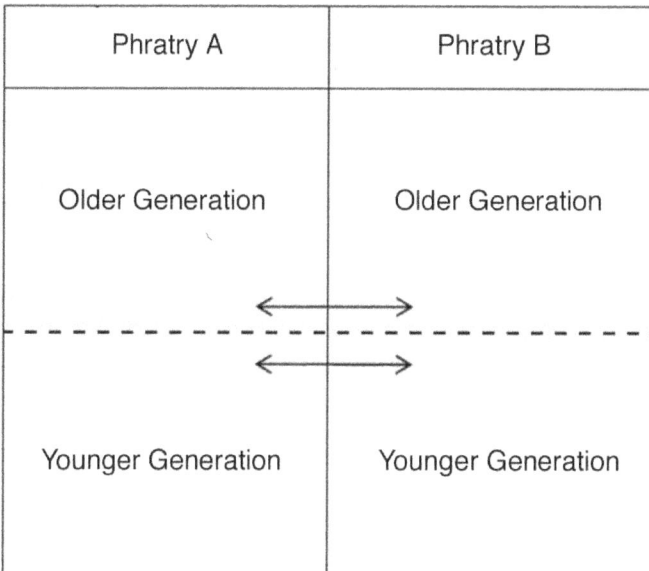

Phratry A	Phratry B
Older Generation	Older Generation
Younger Generation	Younger Generation

Figure 5.3. In addition to the provisos shown in figure 5.2, a society may also separate its phratries by age groups, and a marriage may not cross generations.

Total Population (Tribe)						
Phratries	A	B	C	D	E	F	G

Figure 5.4. A population with seven clans of equal standing. There may not be any restrictions beyond marrying inside one's own phratry.

In the tribal lore of cultures that fit this pattern, phratries often wound up being associated with certain skills or other marks of distinctions, regardless of whether such associations had a genuine basis in fact. All members wanted to see their clan as excelling in something.

It is also possible to have each phratry divided into two subgroups of equal standing. So we might have A_1 and A_2 on one side and B_1 and B_2 on the other. The two groups on each side will have their own totems and, consequently, different food taboos. Since exogamy prevails, someone belonging to one A group could not marry someone in the other A group; but either of the two B groups would be open to him. The reverse would be true for someone among the B groups who would be limited to finding his mate among the A's.

Neither this diagram nor the next one implies a hierarchy of clans.

As one observes cultures that extend beyond the previous arrangements, it becomes necessary to add an overarching term for each side that is not the name for a specific totemic group. Let us call the two big umbrella groups *moieties* and then apply the term *phratry* to the totem classes underneath them, which are the actual social associations of the people. Let us assume a typical case in which we have the two moieties and a number of phratries of essentially equal standing underneath.

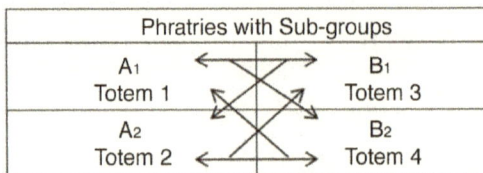

Phratries with Sub-groups	
A_1 Totem 1	B_1 Totem 3
A_2 Totem 2	B_2 Totem 4

Figure 5.5. Phratries may become subdivided, in which case the marriage taboo will include the subdivisions of one's own phratry. This system could also apply to tribes where there are more than two phratries. We would merely have to lengthen the arrows and make sure that there were no directly vertical ones.

Now, as always assuming exogamy, it could be that for anyone in the A moiety anyone in any of the B phratries could be a potential spouse. Sometimes, however, matters get trickier; people on either side may be limited in their range of possible marriage partners due to their phratries. The reasons for such limitations could be pragmatic or shrouded in the mists of mythology. We can imagine a culture in which someone in phratry A_1 may marry someone from phratries B_2, B_3, or B_4 but not from B_1 or B_5.

The above scenario leads us to the next obvious possibility, namely the case in which the phratries are arranged hierarchically underneath the moieties. This scenario is most likely found in fairly advanced cultures in which there are two moieties whose phratries have degrees of social standing associated with them. There is no normative number of phratries.

Under this scheme A_1 has higher standing than A_2, A_2 higher than A_3, and so forth. The degree of standing would be closely mirrored in moiety B. So this scheme combines totemism with a caste system.

Total Population (Tribe)										
Moiety	Moiety A						Moiety B				
Phratry	A_1	A_2	A_3	A_4	A_5		B_1	B_2	B_3	B_4	B_5

Figure 5.6. A tribe with two moieties, each of which has five phratries of equal standing. A person must marry outside his or her moiety, and there may be further restrictions, depending on the culture.

Total Population (Tribe)	
Moiety A	Moiety B
Phratry 1: A_1	Phratry 1: B_1
Phratry 2: A_2	Phratry 2: B_2
Phratry 3: A_3	Phratry 3: B_3
Phratry 4: A_4	Phratry 4: B_4
Phratry 5: A_5	Phratry 5: B_5

Figure 5.7. Tribe with hierarchical phratries under two moieties.

A setup of this nature is illustrated by the Tlingit people of Northwest America. They have two moieties, the Ravens and the Eagles. Underneath the Ravens one finds phratries such as the Dog, Salmon, and the Frogs, while the Eagles include Killer Whales and Bears among their phratries. The phratries are ranked so that as one selects a marriage partner across the moiety boundary, one is also restricted to phratries that are roughly on an equal level. Someone of the higher phratries of the Ravens, for example, should not marry someone toward the bottom phratries of the Eagles.[43]

After looking at all of these configurations, we hesitantly establish the following general "rules" for totemic social systems.

1. They are usually exogamous. One must marry outside of one's phratry and, where the larger classification exists, outside of one's moiety.

2. In a majority of cases, the animal or plant after which a phratry is named is sacred. Consequently, eating or killing it is forbidden.

3. Membership in a phratry is almost always determined by either patrilineal or matrilineal descent, dependent on the particular culture's tradition.

*A Unique Australian Instance

The Aranda of Australia have found a unique way of determining the phratry of one's offspring, rather than either patrilinealism or matrilinealism,[44] that is found nowhere else around the globe. It is connected to their belief that even though sexual relations are a necessary prerequisite for the birth of a child, the infant is not really con-

---

[43] Thus, this "caste" system is not nearly as rigid as the one we associate with Hinduism. Of course, Hindu culture is not totemic, and it is endogamous in that one must marry within one's caste. Consequently, since mother and father both belong to the same caste, the question of whether the descent is patrilineal or matrilineal is moot in this regard.

[44] This description is based on Lang, "Introduction," in Parker, The Euahlayi Tribe.

ceived until the spirit of the child has entered the mother's womb. According to the Aranda, children have been in existence ever since the creation of the world (in the *Alcheringa* or "Dreamtime") but have been in a state of preparation until now. When they are ready, their prebirth spirits are tied to specially marked stones in certain areas of the wilderness. These places are known as the locations where the totem beings had died after they had founded their phratries. The stones are called *churinga nanja*, and the marks confirm the totemic affiliation of the location. Consequently, a preborn child already belongs to the totem of that area.

Let us say, using fictional totem names, that an impending mother belongs to the Lizard phratry while her husband, the father, is from the Kangaroo phratry, which are classified underneath the Eagle Hawk and Black Swan moieties respectively. Let us diagram the scenario as we move along.

Let us continue to suppose that as this particular band makes its annual trek through the bush, they have made camp for a short while in the location associated with the Cockatoo totem. Right about then, the pregnant woman feels the first movement of the child inside her. This sensation indicates that the spirit of the child has entered the woman and is now going to spend several months in her womb prior to birth. When the child is born, even though coming from Lizard and Kangaroo parents, his or her totem will be the Cockatoo. The couple searches for the proper *churinga* stone to confirm this affiliation. If it cannot be found, a quickly carved replica takes its place. The *churinga* is kept securely.

Aranda Population of a Large Geographical Area	
Moiety A: Eagle Hawk	Moiety B: Black Swan
Phratry A_1: Lizard	Phratry B_1: Kangaroo
More Phratries	

Figure 5.8. Aranda totemism: The initial set-up in which the mother belongs to the fictional Lizard phratry underneath the fictional Eagle Hawk moiety, and the father belongs to the Kangaroo phratry underneath the Black Swan moiety.

The first question one might want to ask is under which moiety this child with the Cockatoo totem will be classified.

One might think (I know I would) that there would already be a fixed moiety to which the Cockatoo phratry belongs. But that is not the case. The child's moiety will be that of the father. Since the father in our imagined scenario belongs to the Kangaroo phratry underneath the Black Swan moiety, the child will belong to the Cockatoo phratry underneath the same Black Swan moiety. So patrilineal descent does play a role in determining one's moiety, though not one's phratry.

Now another question presents itself: Isn't it just as likely that in due time another couple would camp in the same area and the woman would become host to a child of the Cockatoo totem, but this time the affiliation of the parents would be reversed? In this second case the mother would belong to the Kangaroos of the Black Swan moiety, and the father would be a Lizard under the moiety of the Eagle Hawk. Then wouldn't the child belong to the Cockatoo phratry but be on the Eagle Hawk side of the moiety ledger this

Aranda Population of a Large Geographical Area	
Moiety A: Eagle Hawk	Moiety B: Black Swan
Phratry A_1: Lizard	Phratry B_1: Kangaroo
Cockatoo—???	

Figure 5.9. Aranda totemism: To which moiety does the child born as a Cockatoo belong?

Aranda Population of a Large Geographical Area	
Moiety A: Eagle Hawk	Moiety B: Black Swan
Phratry A_1: Lizard	Phratry B_1: Kangaroo
	Phratry B_2: Cockatoo (in this case)

Figure 5.10. Aranda totemism: The moiety of the child, who does not belong to the phratry of either parent, is determined by the father's moiety.

Aranda Population of a Large Geographical Area	
Moiety A: Eagle Hawk	Moiety B: Black Swan
Phratry A_1: Lizard	Phratry B_1: Kangaroo
Phratry A_2: Cockatoo (in the new case)	Phratry B_2: Cockatoo (from the previous case)

Figure 5.11. Aranda totemism: If the father belongs to the Eagle Hawk moiety, the child in the Cockatoo phratry still belongs to the father's moiety. Thus the same phratry can exist under either moiety.

time? The answer is simply yes. In this unique situation, you can have the same phratry exist under both moieties.

The bottom line is that in this society any phratry can be housed in both moieties at the same time. This phenomenon is unheard of among any other totemic societies.

Given the above phenomenon, a new question seems to be unavoidable. What happens to exogamy in this strange case? It remains strictly intact; one may still marry only outside of one's own moiety. But here we have a case that pushes the rule to the limit. Let us say that the two hypothetical children, both born into the phratry of Cockatoos, are of opposite sex. Eventually they meet and want to get married. Once again we may be in for a surprise. In all other cases marrying inside of one's own phratry is as unthinkable as marrying within one's moiety. However, even though these two Cockatoos share the same phratry, they do not share moieties, and the difference in moieties wins out. Cockatoos of the Black Swan moiety and Cockatoos of the Eagle Hawk moiety may get married. It's the moiety that counts.

The Origin of the Totem Being

One of the items with regard to totems on which it is best to say as little universally or normatively as possible is the origin of the totem being. A long-standing theory is that each phratry considers itself to be descended from the totem being and that its members, therefore, actually think of themselves as identical with their totem entity. Thus, assuming there might be somewhere a totem group called the

Tigers, the initiated persons in that phratry would believe they are all descended from some remote ancestral heroic tiger of the past and share the same essence "tigerness" with their totem tiger. I cannot rule out that this belief in totemic ancestry might occur somewhere in some totemic societies, but we should not accept it as a standard explanation. The stories vary. We may stipulate that more often than not there is some intimate relationship between the phratry and the totem being, but beyond that basic generality we face massive diversity in the mythologies that explain the relationships.

We must emphasize that the totem beings are not gods and in most cases do not receive veneration. Sometimes the totem is considered to be a living spirit, but whether it receives attention and how depends on specific cases. As we saw in the case of the Aranda above, they believe the original totem beings have died; there is no reason to think this particular aspect of their otherwise unusual system is unique.

Andrew Lang, trying to fight the unsubstantiated claims concerning totems made by some people, came up with a theory of his own, which, alas, remains unsubstantiated as well.[45] He made the case that the names of the phratries were essentially nothing more than ways of clans to distinguish one another and frequently originated as derogatory terms given to them by their rivals. Due to constant repetition the words lost their bitter meaning, and the people of the phratry started to refer to themselves by those terms as well. Consequently there would initially be no organic relationship between the people of a phratry and their totem being, but the mythology about such relatedness might eventually come about. The idea of a pejorative term eventually becoming a word that members of a group use of themselves is not at all unusual (e.g., "Methodists"). But that this scenario would be the origin of the designations for totemic groups all over the world stretches one's credulity, particularly since whether it's a good theory or not, there is no evidence for it.

---

[45] Lang, *Secret of the Totem*.

The Totem Feast

Out of the many hundreds of totemic cultures, there are few—four, to be exact—that actually observe an occasional ceremony when they break the strict rules about their totem animal, engage in a ritual that removes the taboo connected to it, and consume it.[46] Where it happens, the phratry seeks to ingest the powers of the totem being. Even though this practice is a highly unusual aspect of totemism, found only among four Australian tribes (one of them being the Aranda), it has become attached to most standard descriptions. Furthermore, once the idea of a "totem feast" had become known in the nineteenth century, it was found to be suitable for the vivid imaginations of various scholars. Robertson Smith particularly distinguished himself in this respect.[47] His creativity knew few bounds; he ascribed totemism to the ancient Hebrews and then interpreted the Levitical sacrifices as totem feasts. For the record, neither the theory of totemism in ancient Israel nor the notion of sacrifices as related to totemic animals is in any way sustainable.

However, this illusion had a future in the writings of Freud, who included it in his depiction of the early human beings to which we alluded. I mentioned that in Freud's creative mind the earliest humans lived in hordes in which only the oldest male had the prerogative of approaching any of the females. Let us now complete the story.[48] After many generations of waiting on the sidelines for their turn, the young men conspired to kill their father. They followed through on their plan but shortly thereafter had regrets; further they refused to touch the women after all, thereby completing all that was necessary for a full-blown Freudian Oedipus complex. Since all early humans were cannibals, or so Freud presumed, they honored the father whom they had just killed by consuming him and thereby absorbing his

---

[46] Wilhelm Schmidt, *The Origin and Growth of Religion: Facts and Theories*, trans. H. J. Rose (1931; repr., London: Methuen, 1935), 114.

[47] W. Robertson Smith, *Lectures on the Religion of the Semites*, 2nd ed. (London: Adam and Charles Black, 1894).

[48] Freud, *Totem and Taboo*.

attributes. Furthermore, they continued to assuage their consciences by repeating this ceremony once a year. According to Freud, this custom continued to be adapted and practiced around the world and became the origin of the Christian practice of Communion. Since this pseudo-narrative lacks facticity, I cannot provide factual answers to factual questions.

It is amazing, even before Freud's psychoanalytical theories were discredited as such, that this idea was ever accepted as anything but an utterly groundless fabrication. As I mentioned above, only four instances of totem feasts are known at all, and there is no evidence anywhere of a cannibalistic totem feast.

Totem Poles

Even though we should now know enough about totemism to make progress in later chapters, I dare not leave the topic yet. We will need to return to totemism, but before we let it rest for a bit, let me clarify the nature of totem poles. They have virtually nothing to do with the social institution of totemism. For example, they are not a pictorial inventory of the totemic groups of a tribe. Their origin lies with the Tlingit and Haida nations of northwestern North America, and, even though some other Native Americans have adopted them to a limited extent, they are not found in the overwhelming majority of totemic (or, for that matter, nontotemic) people. It so happens that at times they bear the clan or moiety emblems, but that is only the case because the story depicted on such a pole happens to be about the clan or moiety animal. They are illustrations of stories. In fact, the analogy gets even closer when we think of a book for small children that is richly illustrated. I am not implying childishness on the part of the Tlingit people or making light of their tradition; I'm just using an analogy. If you look at the pictures in a children's book, you may be able to figure out much of what is happening in the story. Nevertheless, you won't know the whole plot, and you may even miss out on some important parts unless you also read the words. Similarly, a totem pole illustrates a story, perhaps a new story that someone has created for a special occasion. If one knows a little bit about the patterns of Tlingit art, one can identify certain standard characters on various levels of the totem pole and to some extent get a feel for what the story must be about; however, one must hear the entire story to understand fully the meaning of the various depictions. The fact that totemic figures are found on many totem poles is due to the fact that many of their stories are about totemic figures.

In short, totem poles have no necessary connection to totemism. They just happened to become popular in some strongly totemic societies. They are not idols; they are not a message in the form of pictographs (that is, writing by means of pictures); they are definitely not pictorial genealogies. They are illustrations of mythology, history, and even current events.

Conclusion

So, where does totemism fit into Andrew Lang's theory of an original monotheism among some Australian people? As we noted, the groups among whom the idea of a supreme being was developed the most strongly did not have a totemic system, and we can even say that the more developed the totem system, the less developed the idea of a supreme god. Sir J. G. Frazer, who supported numerous theories on totemism, adopted Morgan's theory of primitive group marriage and then described how this rudimentary arrangement eventually gave way to totemism, first in matrilineal form, then into patrilinealism (or vice versa, Frazer was prone to reverse himself on the matter within pages[49]). Finally the abandonment of totemism was a great leap forward, and thus, the belief in a single god would have been tied to this cultural advance.[50]

---

[49] See Lang, "Introduction," in Parker, *The Euahlayi Tribe*.
[50] Sir J. G. Frazer, *Totemism and Exogamy*, 4 vols. (1910; repr., New York: Cosimo Books 2009).

So this discussion on totemism was not just an excursus away from our plotline. Frazer saw totemism as an early exercise in tribal magic, preceding animism and ancestor worship with monotheism a far distance away. Others saw totemism as the origin of religion, as we shall discuss later. Once again it comes down to the question of whether there is a way of distinguishing the relative ages of various cultures. We shall begin with this point immediately in the next chapter.

CHAPTER 6

Wilhelm Schmidt
and Culture Circles

This chapter will look at a method that will help us answer the question of how one can possibly write a chronology of preliterate cultures. Our main advocate will be Wilhelm Schmidt,[1] who built particularly on the work of Fritz Graebner.[2] These writers and their colleagues considered themselves as being a part of the

---

[1] Wilhelm Schmidt, *The Culture Historical Method of Ethnology: The Scientific Approach to the Racial Question*, trans. S. A. Siebert (New York: Fortuny's, 1939).

[2] The fundamental idea of tracing the history of cultures by analyzing their traits was due to the geographer Friedrich Ratzel (1844–1904), whose largest work is *Völkerkunde*, 2 vols. (Leipzig: Bibliographisches Institute, 1885–88). The method was employed subsequently for a time by Leo Frobenius (1873–1938), *Der Ursprung der afrikanischen Kulturen* (Berlin: Bornträger, 1898). Frobenius, however, waffled back and forth between a historical method and Darwinism. However, W. Foy, who was curator of the ethnological museum in Cologne and who did not publish much, clearly expressed in his guidebook to the holdings of the museum the idea that cultures need to be seen as historical. *Führer durch das Kölner Museum für Völkerkunde* (*Guidebook to the Ethnological Museum of Cologne*), 1910. B. Ankerman defended a historical approach in his works, e.g., "Kulturkreise und Kulturschichten in Afrika" *Zeitschrift für Ethnologie*, 1905. Foy's successor at the Cologne museum and subsequent professor in Berlin was Fritz Graebner (1877–1934), who gave the method its definitive form in his *Methode der Ethnologie* (repr., Ann Arbor: University of Michigan orig., Heidelberg: Carl Winter's Universitätsbuchhandlung, 1911).

"culture-historical school," which we will describe presently. Schmidt, the school's most important representative, spent much of his career in Vienna, Austria, where he taught at the university and founded the Anthropos Institute. Consequently, even though many writers associated with this group were not living in Austria—including Graebner and his predecessors—,they became widely known as the Vienna School.[3]

The basic difference between these scholars and the previously dominant schools is that they denied the idea that human cultures progress according to fundamental laws of development, as theorized by Tylor, Frazer, and Morgan. Instead, they claimed that the story of nonliterate people is ultimately not dissimilar from the story of literate people, except that they left no written records. However, their cultures contain many unwritten records, if one knows how to read them. Thus, just as the people who constitute the subject matter of the usual written histories, nonliterate cultures also have a genuine history. The social units studied by the ethnologist consisted of individuals who lived in the same dimensions of space and time as the ones treated by historians. They, too, made their own decisions, and their lives consisted of work, suffering, joy, and sorrows. These people also experienced successes and failures as they came up with both good and bad ideas. They created cultural innovations for various reasons, sometimes to alleviate stresses imposed upon the group (say, some man somewhere conceived of the idea of a shield to protect himself against the enemy's spears), or because they were bright and creative and thought of a way to make life a little easier (say, a woman figured out how helpful it would be to carry a large vessel if the potter installed handles on its side).

The point is that these were real people who occupied a certain amount of the same space as any other person, including ourselves.

---

[3] Not to be confused with the Vienna Circle, an association of Logical Positivist thinkers, such as Moritz Schlick and Rudolf Carnap, who met on a weekly basis to discuss the need for language to follow the principles of the scientific method.

They just lived a little earlier in time. In every aspect in which we would consider ourselves unique, they were unique; in every aspect in which we can come up with new ideas and inventions, some people in "prehistoric" cultures were able to come up with unique ideas and inventions. They did not leave their names, but they left their legacies. Thus, the defenders of the culture-historical method insisted that ethnology is a science of human beings and the human spirit, and neither a study in artifacts per se, the products of the human spirit, nor a natural science where events are perceived as the necessary result of the principles of inevitable processes.

Simultaneously, other anthropologists reached similar conclusions but ruled out to varying degrees the possibility of constructing a history of large geographical areas or even of a tribe. In contrast, the culture-historical school held that one could compile sufficient data concerning cultures all over the world in order to write a fundamental "history" without historical documents. For the sake of the story below, I need to mention that this idea received the coolest reception in Great Britain, the country that had supplied the greatest number of leading figures in anthropological theory so far. An important point is concealed in this observation, which has nothing to do with nationalism. With the evolutionary/developmental schools losing credibility, the culture-historical school became the only one willing to put forward a reasonable and scholarly theory of global applicability. With a few noteworthy exceptions, by the 1930s the choice was between either some version of the culture-historical method or some means of analysis that ignored altogether the questions concerning historical development on a worldwide basis.[4]

---

[4] Paul Radin, as well as Arthur J. Vidich, the author of the lengthy introduction to his book, did not think anthropology had become sufficiently particularist but approved of the decline of a global anthropology. Paul Radin, *The Method and Theory of Ethnology* (New York: Basic Books, 1933). Arthur J. Vidich, "Introduction" to the reprint, 1966.

Wilhelm Schmidt

Wilhelm Schmidt was born to a working class family in an industrial region of Germany in 1868. They were devout Catholics. Around age fifteen, Wilhelm joined a religious order, the Society of the Divine Word (*Societas Verbi Divini, SVD*), to study for the priesthood, a goal not necessarily entailed in joining a Catholic order. He was fully ordained in 1892. The Society's main purpose was to send out and support missionaries to foreign lands. Schmidt became a part of the support team at home. For a year or so after ordination, he taught at a high school. Then his order sent him to the University of Berlin with the freedom to take whatever courses he thought would be necessary for his future ministry. He was neither required to major in one particular field nor to obtain a doctorate. His main interest had been in philosophy, following St. Thomas Aquinas, but he became increasingly interested in linguistics. Even though Schmidt had not studied ethnology directly, due to his focus on linguistics, particularly the languages of Oceania, Australia, and Southeast Asia, his study was deeply integrated with the anthropological discoveries and debates of his day.

Schmidt was a genius. Unfortunately, such an evaluation often carries the unspoken (or, at times, even spoken) implication that, therefore, he did not need to work hard on his subject or, in contemporary parlance, "everything was handed to him." Such a description certainly did not fit Wilhelm Schmidt. He was extremely self-demanding, assuming he needed to have studied a subject exhaustively before he felt free to express an opinion on it, whether in teaching or in writing. Few people would be able to master the languages of Australia in just a few months, but few people would stay up late into the night in an effort to do so. Always driven and never content with anything but virtual perfection, he earned himself several episodes of enforced rest after physical breakdowns.

Schmidt moved to Vienna in 1895 to teach at the order's school, called St. Gabriel's Institute. He also started to teach at the University of Vienna. His assignments included a number of subjects at first, each of which demanded a lot of preparation. Nevertheless, he also made time to devote himself to research and writing. His first publication in 1904 concerned the Oceanic, Australian, and Southeast Asian languages, which immediately earned him a solid reputation as a scholar. Two years later he took on the project of publishing a journal called *Anthropos*, whose initial target audience was missionaries around the world, providing them with cutting-edge information on developments in anthropology, as well as giving them a forum to record their discoveries. It soon became a publishing outlet for numerous highly ranked scholars. Contributors were not required to promote Schmidt's point of view; however, if their articles were polemical and ran contrary to Schmidt's theories, they could expect a hard-hitting rebuttal from Schmidt in a subsequent issue.

From 1908 until 1910, *Anthropos* ran a series of articles by Schmidt that expounded a critical history of anthropological theories. In these publications Schmidt also threw his weight of support behind Andrew Lang's thesis of an original monotheism. Schmidt wrote the articles in German and then translated them into French because the majority of the missionaries who would benefit from these studies would likely be more at home in French than in German. In 1910, he published this series as a book under the title of *L'origin de l'idee de Dieu* (*The Origin of the Idea of God*). Then, in 1912, he issued a German edition (*Der Ursprung der Gottesidee*[5]), with the clear understanding that this was the first volume of two and that the second, concluding volume, would come out shortly. It turned out that a second volume was not sufficient for everything Schmidt needed to say. The twelfth and final volume was published in 1955, shortly after Schmidt passed away.

---

[5] Wilhelm Schmidt, *Der Ursprung der Gottesidee*, 12 vols. (Münster: Aschendorff, 1912–54, 1955).

At the same time Schmidt wrote numerous articles and reviews; founded the Anthropos Society;[6] served as lecturer and professor at the University of Fribourg, Switzerland; established a museum on missions and ethnology at the Vatican at the request of the pope; and wrote several more books and uncountable articles, including the one on methodology, which is the subject of this chapter.

He expected the same conscientiousness that was his standard from his students and other writers. In scholarly discussions he never pretended to be neutral in his worldview but believed that having a worldview and scientific objectivity were compatible. Much like Lang and Hartland, his critiques of the views of others often were masterful displays of rhetorical irony, though his facts were always thoroughly documented. He would be disappointed when his "opponents" did not respond with substantive arguments from which he could learn.

There was one particular "criticism" that came up over and over again and still is prevalent today. That is the accusation that Schmidt's conclusions were predetermined by the fact that he was a Catholic priest. This is not really a criticism; it is bigotry. Schmidt was Catholic, and he never tried to hide that fact or pretend that being so did not affect his thinking. However, he pointed out many times that the people who voiced this notion were simply blind to the fact that their worldview was coloring their thinking as well. Furthermore, since they did not want to admit that fact, they were more likely to allow their background philosophy to skew their scholarship. He could get sarcastic when critics used terms such as "Catholic," "priest," "Christian," or "missionary" merely as an epithet or as an immediate disqualification of his scholarship. If, other than just "name-calling," he was criticized for letting his religious beliefs slant his use of the evidence, he would request his opponents to point out where exactly

---

[6] A center of anthropological learning, which also had missionary activity in view. Schmidt, along with the institute, had to move to Fribourg, Switzerland, when the Nazis took over Austria. It is now at home in Germany, in Sankt Augustin, not far from Bonn.

in his writings this occurred. Then, even if they zeroed in on an aspect of his system on which they disagreed, it was clear that there was no connection between this matter and his status as a Catholic priest.

Allow me to present one example of Schmidt's efforts to squelch the habit of declaring the field reports of religious people as inadmissible. The context happens to be a discussion by Ling H. Roth on reports concerning the religion of the by-then-extinct Tasmanians. Among his sources was a description by a man named Leigh (to whom we have no direct reference) to the effect that these people believed in a good spirit and an evil spirit and that they prayed to the good spirit for protection and a safe return on trips. Schmidt states in his summary: "Ling Roth remarked concerning this report: 'This assertion of a belief in good and evil spirits clearly resembles an imported religion.' His proof? 'Mr. Leigh was a missionary.' This nonsense of declaring as worthless the testimony of an author concerning higher forms of religion simply because he was a missionary has got to stop!"[7]

The Need for a Clear Book on Ethnological Methodology

In 1911, Fritz Graebner wrote a definitive book on the method of the culture-historical method. It was compact and contained a good number of illustrations. Its most significant flaw was that Graebner's use of language was so confusing that even native German speakers had a difficult time following it, and some statements were downright unintelligible. Thus, it was easy for a number of writers belonging to Graebner's school to believe that some of the British reluctance in going along with this new approach was due to the fact that they simply did not understand it. What was needed, they believed, was a clear and readable text on the culture-historical method, hopefully thereby recruiting further English-speaking adherents. A good English translation of the same book would be an additional advantage.

---

[7] Schmidt, *Ursprung*, vol. 1, 212.

Schmidt steadfastly refused to write a book that would compete with Graebner's until the latter had died. Then he produced what he intended to be a clearer manual, but he built it around Graebner's statements, frequently verbatim, so as not to lose continuity with the originator of the method. By sticking that closely to Graebner's own language, he reincorporated some of the same ambiguities. Still, a good translation of the book into English might have done wonders. But when A. Siebert, the young, inexperienced translator was finished, even he was not satisfied with the final product.[8] Between having to render Graebner's frequently opaque German statements into English (How do you translate a sentence you don't understand?), having to coin neologisms to represent the nuances of various technical words, and not feeling free to depart too much from the German syntax of the original, Siebert graciously but pointedly lamented that he was not able to produce the translation he had hoped to produce.

The Narrative Behind the Method

Let me venture to provide my own general description of the culture-historical method as I understand it. I shall introduce technical terms as gently as I can and slowly try to transfer us back to the discussion of a hundred years ago as smoothly as possible. Hopefully, as I attempt to do so, the ideas will become more comprehensible, some of the more simplistic criticisms will be answered automatically in the process of this description, and—if I may be forgiven for my optimism—some of the readers of this book will find the theory more plausible than it has been allowed to be in many contemporary summaries. Of course, I cannot do so without including some of Schmidt's basic assumptions concerning human beings and human culture in general.

---

[8] S. A. Siebert, "Translator's Preface" in Schmidt, *The Culture Historical Method,* xxvii–xxx.

People Migrate

As stated in the first chapter, when I say "people," I mean true human beings, *Homo sapiens sapiens*. I am not concerned with *Homo erectus* or *Homo neanderthalis*, not even if you call him *Homo sapiens neanderthalis*. The only point of focus here is genuine human beings, not their alleged ancestors or supposed cousins or uncles.[9] Our starting point, as we clarified earlier, is with the first humans already on earth. It is not unimportant from a larger standpoint whether they arrived here by direct creation (as I believe) or by physical evolution, but that is not the issue we are considering at this point. We are stipulating, as most anthropologists do today, that there was one initial small population meeting all of our criteria for *Homo sapiens sapiens*. To that extent we are ahead of the time of Wilhelm Schmidt when many people (though not he) still thought human beings (again, the single species and subspecies *Homo sapiens sapiens*) evolved separately, though simultaneously, at different locations throughout the world—a theory that flies in the face of common sense as well as commonly accepted principles of biological evolution. The majority of anthropologists today have reached agreement that human beings, as we know them, originated in one place where they multiplied and from whence they migrated in various shifts across the world.

Why do people migrate? There are many reasons: They want more space; someone else encroaches on their space; the conditions of their space have changed and no longer suit their preferred way of living (e.g., too little water or too much water); hostile groups have moved into their neighborhood; they want to subdue neighboring groups and spread themselves out in their territory; or, believing that their present environment has become home to some disease, they may set out for healthier air. The list could go on for a long time. The migrations could include relatively small trickles of clans over time

---

[9] For a solid discussion of this issue, see Fazale Rana and Hugh Ross, *Who Was Adam? A Creation Model of the Origin of Man* (Colorado Springs: NavPress, 2005).

or an entire nation or tribe all at once. The reasons are many, but the end result is unequivocal. The history of humans is to a large extent the history of the migrations of people groups. And that is why the advocates of the culture-historical method asserted that, writings or not, all cultures have a history.

Since people carry their cultures along as they migrate, cultures migrate with them. For example, when Europeans migrated to the Americas, they brought European cultures along. Furthermore, as shown by this example, the group with the more sophisticated material culture is more likely to gain ascendancy over the simpler one. The people with guns are likely to take the land from the people with bows and arrows, and the people with flint heads mounted on their spears are possibly going to displace the people with sharpened sticks. To make it a little more realistic, since such items are usually bundled into cultural complexes, the people who have spears with flint heads, pottery in which to carry water, a way of sheltering themselves from bad weather (such as huts or tents), and a method of nurturing the bushes from which they eat the berries, are likely to get the upper hand over the people whose territory they have invaded, who may have nothing but sharpened sticks for weapons, rely only on those shelters that are provided by nature, and are tied to the presence of springs since they have no vessels with which to carry water, and hope that the bushes will provide many berries again this year. At that point, the less developed people may either retreat into an area less hospitable than the present one, or they may also find themselves being assimilated into the new culture, while most of their older material culture simply dies out. However, the stories, songs, and rituals of the older culture may persist and be performed a long time after the material side of the older culture has, for all practical purposes, disappeared. What I have described here is a "horticultural" group establishing ascendancy over a "hunter-gatherer" group.

Elements of Cultures Diffuse

For our purposes I would like to maintain a verbal distinction between *migration* and *diffusion*. Both of them are ways in which the features of a culture can spread. In migrations people actually carry the items with them. By the term *diffusion*, I mean the distribution of cultural items apart from people changing their place of residence, e.g., by trade or by imitation. A somewhat silly, but applicable, example would be the hula-hoop craze of the late 1950s. It started in the United States, but before too long people in Germany (and presumably in many other countries) bought and used this toy without leaving their areas of residence to do so. Once the idea had caught on, the object was either imported or produced locally. On the more serious side, we see the global spread of cell phones. An even more significant example is the adoption of European business culture all over the world, which has included standard forms of dress (European-style "business suits" and ties), acceptance of common (or at least convertible) standards of measure (calendar, time, volumes, and weights), a protocol regulating standards of courtesy, sharing "business cards," deference to authority, and the manner in which negotiations are carried out, as well as some tacit agreements on what is and what is not legitimate business practice. Here we see how cultural traits are bundled together as they cross cultural lines. Of course, to a certain extent, some of the specific features have also adapted themselves to their newer non-European cultures.

Cultures Manifest Specific "Forms"

Above I talked about "items," "traits," and "features" of a culture. The term Schmidt used was "cultural forms," and I need to clarify it. To do so I will start with an informal working definition of *culture*.[10]

---

[10] It might seem odd that in this book in which we have talked about "cultures" right from the beginning, we should only now provide a definition of culture. The

There are many ways in which the word *culture* can be and has been defined, and anyone intending to create a red herring can pick apart the definition I'm about to use and thereby miss the point of my explanation. For our purposes I shall give the word the most minimalistic definition I can. Your "culture" includes all the stuff in your life that humans have created, which is not truly essential to your survival. Theoretically, a person could live without clothes in natural caves, eat whatever is accessible to him or her with bare hands, have the capacity for speech (which is a part of being human), but lack a shared set of vocal symbols for regular communication with others. Neither stories, nor music, nor any form of visual art is essential for life.

I seriously doubt that such humans have ever existed,[11] but once the first stone has been sharpened, the first loincloth has been donned, or the first standard greeting has been uttered, we already have a rudimentary culture, according to this definition. (If you take a biblical view, Adam and Eve were both created with actual language, not just a capacity for speech, so by my definition they already came into the world with a culture.)

Cultures display numerous forms. A form is some attribute ascribed to a particular article or activity that exceeds the bare essentials for it to meet its purpose. On that basis, people may use some objects that may not actually qualify as a cultural form. Let's say that our hypothetical uncultured person finds a rock with a sharp edge, which enables her to cut roots so that they will be easier to eat. We're probably best off *not* to include simply finding and using a rock

---

reason is simply that we haven't needed any before now because only now, at least for the moment, we're dealing with some formal matters. Definitions are never as exact as we like to think, and they open up areas for oblique critiques that direct us away from the main point of discussion. I doubt anyone has misunderstood the discussion in the previous chapters because I held out on a definition of *culture*. If they were unused to the term, a quick look at a dictionary would have been sufficient.

[11] Particularly with regard to language, all the known evidence goes counter to human speech evolving from primitive grunts and pointing to complex form; wherever we encounter evidence of language, it is fully developed.

under the heading of culture, since even animals use rocks or sticks to achieve a purpose at times.

However, there are many rocks about, so let us say that this woman keeps losing track of her cutting rock among all of the others. So she uses some other rocks and chisels an X on her special cutting rock. Other people in her group see what she did and make similar marks on their special cutting rocks. Now we have a cultural form.

Perhaps in a group not too far away, someone else goes in a different direction in treating his rock. He grinds away at the side opposite to the cutting edge and gives his rock a nice, smooth handling surface. People in his clan are impressed and copy his technique. Because these rocks now have been modified by humans, the addition of a handle would constitute a cultural form.

In a third area people also use stones to cut things, but they do not modify them. However, we find that whenever a woman sits down and cuts up a number of roots for her family to eat, she chants a little melody thanking the earth for providing the roots. Pretty soon other people pick up this practice. This, too, is a cultural form.

So a form is a feature of a particular culture. It is an element of an object over and above what is needed for the simple utility of the object.

To use another example, let us say that a culture uses the bow. In order to have a functioning bow, you need to have a curved stick and a string that connects the two ends. We encounter a lot of variety when we consider the particular properties of the bow. Of what material (or, in many cases, combinations of materials) does it consist? How large is it? What is its shape, both strung and unstrung? What is the string made of, and how is it attached to the bow? Do the ends of the bow extend beyond the string attachment, and if so, do those protruding lengths have a particular shape? Is there a grip on the bow, and is the grip constructed merely for handling, or does it also guide the arrows and perhaps even protect the archer's hands from the friction of the arrows? Are there decorations or other marks on the bow? And we haven't even begun to address the arrows. All of such factors are forms.

As already intimated by the example of the spread of business culture or the woman chanting while using her cutting rock, forms are not confined to firm objects. Forms include customs, beliefs, societal arrangements, religious mythology, language, and manners of personal interaction. It seems virtually impossible to exhaust all areas in which cultural forms show up.

In certain cases, a single form may be so distinctive for a group of people that for today's anthropologists the form becomes a label for handy reference to that group or the larger culture of which they are a part. For example, a number of the cultures of our recent acquaintances in Southeast Australia are sometimes referred to as the "boomerang culture."

Human Beings Migrated Across the Earth

Regardless of how they came into existence (creation or evolution; I favor the former, but I don't want to beg the question), or where they started (Africa, outside of Eden, after the flood, or at the Tower of Babel), as human beings multiplied, they started to move into various directions, carrying their culture with them and making innovations as time and creativity permitted and as circumstances necessitated. Clearly, this exodus did not happen all at once, as though someone had opened a gate and everyone started marching as fast and as far as they could. Different people found places to their suiting; their bodily structures and physiologies adapted to their surroundings; their language underwent changes; they established a material culture, as well as the immaterial aspects that went with it; and when it appeared that they had settled in for good, they moved again for one of many known or unknown reasons.

For illustrative purposes, let us imagine a simplified story of the first group leaving humanity's home area. They would have been at the barest level of material culture, resembling the hunter-gatherers among the Australian tribes. Since they were the first to leave, they would have had their choice as to where they wanted to settle, which, we can safely assume, would have been the most productive areas for the sustenance of their lives. If presented with options, people are going to live in an area where all the necessities of life are easily accessible rather than in a desert, where they are confronted with the need for water and food on a daily basis. But they could not remain. Eventually, a group with a more powerful culture would come along, and they would have to give way, either by moving or by absorption. And this displacement would continue. As we said above, the groups with more complex cultures would have the advantage over the less developed ones. Thus, the groups representing the earliest migrating groups, carrying the simplest cultures, must have spent much of their history on the run, as it were, as new and more sophisticated cultures moved in. They would have been pushed and pushed until they wound up where modern anthropologists found them: in remote deserts, deep jungles, isolated islands, or barely habitable climates. In other words, they had to go where no other people wanted to live, and there they maintained the only way of life they knew, one of bare subsistence.

Why did these vulnerable groups not adapt their material cultures on their own initiative or adopt the cultures of those who were displacing them? Who says they did not? Many of them did. My simplification obviously carries with it the danger of oversimplification. Sometimes invading people were held off by the people occupying the territory; sometimes they wound up living side by side with the original residents of the area; sometimes during or shortly after such an encounter, a third, even more powerful culture moved in and overran both, leaving again a number of possible outcomes. So my hypothetical analysis is not intended to describe an invariable scenario but one out of many possible ones. Still, it is one whose results we can visibly observe in the distribution of cultures around the world. The least developed cultures wound up having to live in the least desirable areas, there subsisting according to the ways they had carried with them from the earliest times.

Of course, these groups manifesting the vestiges of an original human culture underwent changes as well, and it becomes necessary for us to distinguish between forms that are close to the heart of a culture and forms that can be picked up easily and discarded easily. The hula hoop of the 1950s is an example of a highly adoptable but also highly disposable form. A religious belief or practice would be on the other end of the spectrum. This distinction is true of the original cultures as well. Simple material forms are easily picked up and modified. One group finds the boomerang a useful instrument; another group adopts clothing suitable to their frigid environment. Also, the various groups will observe their neighbors and attempt to copy their superficial material innovations, though some things are impossible to make once people have been pushed too far into barren regions. One needs clay, plenty of water, and a lot of burnable material to make pottery; making metal implements requires the proper ores and certain facilities (again including a lot of wood or brush for fires); you cannot make baskets where there is nothing to weave; and, perhaps worst of all, trade with other populations is not going to work well if the group is isolated and does not produce anything trade worthy. So, apart from some essential regional adaptations, the material level remains where it was, and, even more significantly, so do the immaterial forms of the culture.

We need to keep in mind an important and simple point, though it is one that frequently does not occur to the people in an invading culture,[12] namely, that the original-culture people do not see themselves as primitive savages on the lowest rungs of humanity (as they should not). In their view they are God's children, and they may receive their greatest strength in hard times of conflict by consoling themselves with the nonmaterial forms of their culture. Maintaining the intangible aspects of their culture has given them cohesiveness in the face of physical and material challenges. So the things they

---

[12] As exemplified by, say, W. H. Willshire, *The Aborigines of Central Australia* (Adelaide: C. E. Bristow, 1891).

would be least likely to change would be their religious beliefs and ritual practices.

We can think of the migrations of various people groups as occurring in waves of people whose cultures resembled one another to a certain extent. As they expanded, they came across the people of previous migrations in different geographical areas. Such encounters would have been particularly significant if the newcomer culture stood in contrast to the older culture by more than a few minor differences. It might carry along an entirely new package of cultural forms that usually come clustered together, including, as a hypothetical example, such items as decorated pottery, more powerful weapons, a more detailed arrangement of clans, or expanded patterns of mythology and religious rituals. In other words, it would be a fairly tight bundle of the many material and immaterial forms we mentioned earlier. These well-integrated and coherent cultural complexes are what the culture-historical school called culture circles (*Kulturkreise*), and so, such an encounter would be a meeting between two cultures from different culture circles.

According to the view of the culture-historical school, by a careful study of ethnic cultures, we can come up with patterns of interconnectedness beyond immediate geographical patterns. Due to any number of possible reasons, the specific members of a culture circle may become distanced from one another. A simple case in point is one in which a new arrival cuts through the territory of an already settled culture. The two separated groups may display independent changes from now on but are still a part of the same culture circle.

We have, then, a pattern of waves of migration, where the later comers usually belong to newer culture circles. They move into areas where they displace, assimilate, or, in a few cases settle alongside people of previous culture circles. As we said above, the groups derived from the original culture circle were oftentimes the first to arrive in a new area because they were being pushed from behind by culturally younger, more powerful people. Frequently, they wound up on the margins of inhabitable territory. In the process the groups carrying

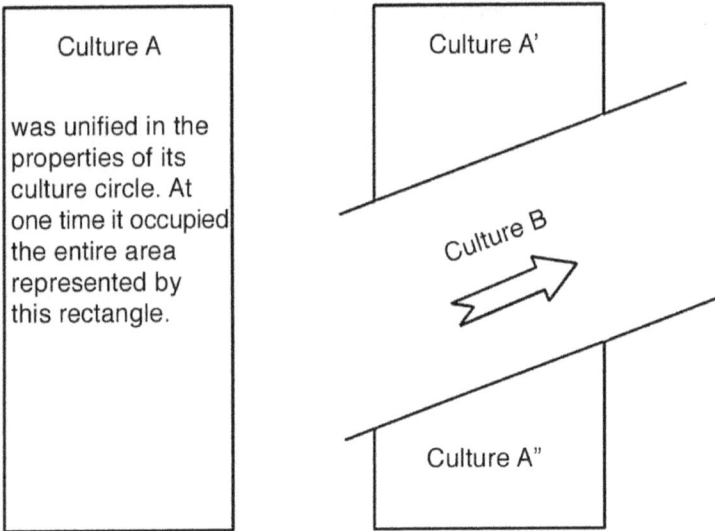

Figure 6.1. As Culture B, representing a more recent culture circle, moves into the area, it splits up the geography of Culture A. Culture A divides into A' and A", both of which are still members of their original culture circle.

the original culture became separated from each other, as did members of other culture circles.

Now let me ask a rhetorical question: Is there a good reason to think there may be a geographical limit to the distance of these migrations? Clearly not, since human beings are found in all habitable areas of the earth. So it is evident that the same process repeated itself, including migrations to new continents when conditions permitted it. The pattern continued, with the people of less complex cultures arriving first and then being displaced by later comers. The crucial point is to recognize that separation between groups of different culture circles is not due to cultures leapfrogging but to numerous waves of displacement. Thus, after thousands of years, there are bound to be people groups all over the world bearing an adapted version of the culture of the first migrants. The fact that they have ended up separated by continents is to be expected because they will have always been pushed to the margins of habitability.

Numerous critics of the culture-historical method have insisted on a limit along geographic lines. Sure, they agree, we can picture cultural connections across large areas, maybe even stretching across an entire continent. However, the idea of a culture circle that includes utterly separated groups in Southern Africa, the Philippines, and North America seems to be incredible. But did not people migrate to all of those areas, and would not the same dynamic of putting pressure on other cultures to move in reaction remain in effect?

If you've followed my description so far, it should be clear that the consequence of original-migration cultures winding up all over the world in highly inhospitable areas is an expanded logical consequence. If people migrated in waves from a roughly shared area of origin, if each wave pushed the people of previous waves ahead of itself and thereby separated them from one another farther and farther, and if the migrations included crossing over into other continents, then the same pattern had to continue on those new continents as well. I will go so far as to say that this result is not a law but follows directly from the principles of culture-historical theory. To the extent to which humans have populated the earth, it is a tautology that they have migrated there, have taken their cultures there, and have been subject to cultural diffusion. The migrating people did not allow theoretical barriers to the geographic distribution of cultures to stand in their way.

Going on the basis of my description of Schmidt's method, not to understand that the culture-historical method must lead to finding original-migration cultures in widely separated areas on different continents is not to understand the method at all. I did not say that one must agree with this theory, which is different from understanding its logical results. Furthermore, I have yet to present the actual method and its application. It would certainly make things easier if we had written travelogues of all of the various migrating groups, but, in their absence, applying the culture-historical method can take us much further than one might expect initially.

Cultural Diffusion Accounts for Developments
on a Smaller Level

Cultural diffusion, you will recall, refers to the distribution of cultural forms apart from being tied directly to the migration of people groups, at least in my usage. It occurs by many different means, including trade, informal interaction between neighboring groups, and perhaps just because of the reputation of an innovation. Remember that cultural forms are not just material things but also such features as stories, songs, vocabulary, or methods of work and play.

At this point the supposed dictum of the Vienna school, that each innovation in culture may occur only once, rears its head. R. B. Dixon wrote concerning some extreme diffusionists in contrast with some other, unnamed and unclarified option: "The [diffusionist] grasping at similarities, tries to establish thereby links in a chain connecting the widely separated areas and insists that, whether or not such links can be found, diffusion alone can explain the facts. In their opinion a trait can only have been invented once; and multiple invention, even of the simplest trait, is unthinkable."[13]

Schmidt comments that this description, if meant to be directed at him and his colleagues, is misapplied: "Are there or have there been such extreme diffusionists? At any rate, if this criticism is meant for the culture historical school, I must declare this characterization a gross caricature, as it has never set forth such extreme views."[14]

Such distortions aside, the culture-historical school does insist on the *uniqueness* of each invention. For one thing, one should abide by the principle of scientific parsimony. The less specific a hypothesis is, the stronger it is. If I say that "someone invented the wheel," that statement would be easier to defend than saying "exactly one and only one person invented the wheel," or even "the wheel was invented an indeterminate number of times." The first alternative sentence

---

[13] R. B. Dixon, *The Building of Cultures*, 182, cited in Schmidt, *Culture Historical Method*, 50.
[14] Ibid.

assumes that "someone" could only have been a single person, while the second one, though not closing the door on a one-time invention, pretty much assumes several inventions, imitating the evolutionary notion of "convergence." "Someone" is a nicely open word, asserting that the wheel has been invented at least once by a person, but it doesn't eliminate logically that the process may have been repeated somewhere else by another "someone." The members of the culture-historical school were willing to accept multiple origins for cultural forms insofar as the data supported that notion.

However, the more important point in this regard is that since we are looking at history, each invention was a creative act by a human being at a particular time and location and is, therefore, unique. Should it be the case that somewhere someone else made the same discovery, this event, too, was a unique, never-to-be-duplicated, historical occurrence. The emphasis is not on the innovation but on the individual who made the innovation. There never will be another person just like him doing the same thing he did. All human beings have led their own lives; and insofar as they made a contribution to humanity, the particular act(s) unique to individuals are not repeatable.

An important historical aspect to this contention was to get away from the notion of "laws" governing human development, which was so much a part of earlier anthropology. We should remember that E. B. Tylor's understanding of human culture included a set of immutable (though not necessarily yet known) laws governing the development of virtually uncountable cultures around the world. This is the reason, whenever he brought up the mountains of data in support of his scheme, that he considered it to be a benefit when he found allegedly similar situations in two or more cultures, which were widely separated in time and place. This method would fit in well with the rules of inductive logic, as practiced properly in the natural sciences.[15] As we saw, in Tylor's hands it turned into

---

[15] Specifically, the benefit of a large amount of negative analogy in the general sample. For example, if we want to defend the hypothesis that probably people all

unregulated picking and choosing of what was relevant for his theory, but he was hoping to isolate genuine laws on this basis. Thus, in
his system, the same cultural innovation could occur thousands of
times as each individual culture followed the path prescribed by his
evolutionary road map.

Similar ideas were behind the ideologies of Morgan, Frazer, and
many others. Cultural innovations were determined by evolutionary
laws and not—and this is the important point—by significant human
creativity. When their adherents claimed that Andrew Lang's theory
of monotheism violated the laws of development, the evolutionists
were really thinking in terms of normative laws. The Vienna school
protested against this mechanical understanding of what it means to
be human. Does it make sense that thousands of times around the
world, whenever a culture was ready, the unseen hand of evolutionary principles led someone to invent pottery?

In the last chapter, in the case of A. W. Howitt's understanding
of the development of Australian indigenous cultures, we see this
approach along with the problems it is bound to create. We recall
that Howitt, following L. H. Morgan, believed human society began
with "group marriages," of which he claimed there were vestiges
among the Dieri and Urabunna. Thus, strictly following the laws laid
out by Morgan, he declared that these two tribes represented the
earliest culture of Australia, manifesting a simple form of totemism,
matrilineal descent, and no known belief in a supreme deity. This is a
typical case of alleged laws determining one's chronological conclusions. But this cultural determinism immediately broke down when
Howitt argued that the next step of development from the stage of
the Dieri went in two directions. One moved toward the cultures of
the North Central tribes, such as the Aranda with a more complex
totem system, more demanding initiation ceremonies, an increased
move into the direction of patrilinealism, and no known (at the time)

---

over the world enjoy French cuisine, that hypothesis is strengthened if the people
sample came from different continents rather than, say, only from Paris and Marseille.

belief in a supreme being.[16] The other direction of advance, according to Howitt, was toward the culture of the Southeastern coastal tribes who had clans without totemism, strict monogamy, relatively simple initiations, patrilineal reckoning, and a clear monotheism at the expense of ancestor veneration and animism. One cannot help but wonder: If there are laws of development at work, how can a supposed advance go in two such different, opposed directions?

By contrast, the Vienna school posited that you couldn't invent laws of development and that innovations were made by human beings on the basis of their abilities. By means of migration and diffusion, they were then propagated. The point was not at all that an innovation could not be made more than once. It opposed the absurd idea of the same innovation being made over and over again on the basis of unsubstantiated evolutionary laws.

The Method

Let us then examine what the ethnologist of the culture-historical school sets himself to do. He is looking at a geographical area, which will ultimately be the entire world, though one might want to start with more limited coordinates. In this area there are various people groups, some of them obviously related in the sense of biological kinship, judging by language and appearance, some of them most likely not related in an obvious way. They may or may not appear to have similar cultures. So the ethnologist is attempting to establish a sequence in time for the cultures of these groups, at least relative to one another.

We have already posited the frequent waves of migration by humans. We would not be out of line if we inferred that all other things being equal, the people who traveled the farthest took the longest amount of time and, thus, represent the oldest culture in the region. The extreme alternative would be the ridiculous notion that

---

[16] As I pointed out, Strehlow's observations that the Aranda did, in fact, have a supreme being were not widely distributed at the time.

all cultures departed the place of origin at the same time and that the people who traveled the furthest walked faster than the others. Regardless, since migrations occurred with many stops and starts, it would be going far past what we can establish with accuracy to decide who traveled for the longest time without applying criteria.

We must be careful to distinguish between the criteria the ethnologist uses and the idea of laws, which, according to Tylor and others, would be discovered by the ethnologist. When we state that by means of one of the criteria we can draw an inference, what we are saying is no more than precisely that: we have drawn an inference for this particular situation. We are not saying, since we have been able to make an inference, we have, therefore, discovered a law of human development.

The criteria by themselves are logical and perhaps even what one would expect on the basis of common sense. However, the application of these criteria to various forms and their cultures requires a lot of intensive labor and commitment. There are two fundamental criteria and two auxiliary ones, the latter of which arbitrate the application of the first two.

1. *The Criterion of Quality (or Form)*. This criterion uses the idea that where two cultures manifest the same or closely similar forms, the two cultures have probably been in contact with each other. This criterion cannot stand alone, and certainly a single similarity would not account for a cultural transference. One must make the case for a common connection carefully, taking into account all available data. Furthermore, the appearance of similarities does not by itself yield a time sequence.

One issue Schmidt lists under the criterion of quality could also appear under the criterion of quantity, which we will describe next. This is the phenomenon of the absence of a form in a particular culture. Now we cannot necessarily draw a significant direct inference from the fact that a certain culture does not have a particular form. It is not of great interest to ethnologists that, for example, the army of the United States does not use boomerangs; nor, for that matter, would be the fact in and of itself that North American Indians did not use boomerangs. There are good reasons in both cases not to expect them. However, if among the various Australian tribes, one of them did not know of boomerangs, then this negative fact might hold a lot of interest.

Similarly, we can picture a set of cultures that surround one particular culture where all of the surrounding cultures share a particular religious chant, while the culture in the center appears to be totally unaware of it. This absence is definitely an important issue for the ethnologist. A third example: In the previous chapter we mentioned that the Australian tribe of the Dieri did not have an apparent belief in a supreme being although almost all of the neighboring tribes had one, even the Aranda. Therefore, the fact that no such god has been discovered among the Dieri must be a major clue for the relationships between the tribes, though in and of itself we cannot say in which direction the clue points us.

2. *The Criterion of Quantity.* This second criterion serves to confirm whatever tentative conclusions one may have attained on the basis of the first one. This criterion works in two ways. For one thing, if we are looking at a particular form and if it occurs frequently in one culture but is scarcely evident in the other culture, we begin to get a good reason to believe the item in question originated in the first culture and then was picked up to some extent by the second culture. However, such an antithetical approach can never decide a case by itself. The other aspect of this criterion addresses a collection of numerous forms that tend to appear together. The more similarities there are between two cultures, the more likely it is that there was some connection between them. And this is, of course, what happens in the real world; many forms are usually linked together. That is the reason Schmidt ultimately was able to demonstrate interdependent circles of cultures (*Kulturkreise*) rather than having to trace particular forms separately.

3. *The Criterion of Continuity.* The possibility of influence of one culture on another one has to be premised on the possibility of some kind of physical connection between the two. Now it may be possible that two cultures manifesting a high degree of similarity are presently

separated from each other geographically by a large distance. Figure 6.1 above illustrated such a possibility. In fact, this is a common occurrence. Nevertheless, if the possibility of physical continuity between the two groups can be demonstrated, then the probability of a connection has been strengthened. To make it even stronger, if there are two cultures, call them A' and A", which are culturally similar but are geographically separated by culture B, and there is the possibility that at one time both A' and A" were conjoined, it becomes likely that culture B is a later accretion or invasion that separated what at one time was a unified cultural region. But we cannot just make a blanket assertion to this end. The case has no feet unless we are able to show that there are traces of the original culture A still visible within B; they could be obvious, or they could be highly subtle survivals, but if no historical continuity between A' and A" through region B can be shown, we cannot simply assume a connection. Contrary to another one of the many misrepresentations of the culture-historical method, cultures cannot leapfrog.

4. *The Criterion of Degree of Relationship.* This criterion measures the extent to which a particular cultural form is distributed in a wider geographic area. If we can discover that a specific cultural item is strongly represented in one specific area and then radiates out from this dense location with less and less representation toward the circumference, then most likely the item originated in the area of greatest density and spread out from there. Furthermore, let us say that as the forms of a specific group radiate outward into various directions, we observe that there are minor changes in the form, where the last culture on the radius differs the most from what appears to be the culture of origin, it appears that the cultures furthest on the outside of this group have a lesser degree of relationship than the ones closer in and are, therefore, probably younger in time. Let us imagine the following situation, and please keep in mind that this diagram only shows connections. It is not a map. To come even just a little closer to a realistic, map-like diagram, we would have to draw things in such

a way that influence and overlap between the cultural "arms" is possible. Reality is a much better artist than I could be.

Let us say that there is a cluster of cultures, called A, B, C, D, and E in a large area. Each of whom decorates their pottery with a flower design.

Culture A shows the flower design and nothing more.

In **Culture B**, we have the identical flower design, except with a slightly different color of glaze. As we move outward to the closely related Culture B', each pot shows two such flowers, and the most outlying culture B East manifests the more demanding techniques of two flowers, still of identical design, intertwined with each other.

Culture C picked up the identical flower design, but as the distance from Culture A increases, the design becomes circumscribed by a circle which, by the time we reach Culture C South, has little curls at each corner.

Culture D moves from a fairly close copy of Culture A's flower to giving the flower a human face in D West, while keeping its shape and positioning in other respects.

Finally, **Culture E**, again starting with the original flower design, multiplies the petals on the flower so that by the time we look at E North, there are twice as many petals. To summarize:

When we look at this pattern, it seems fairly clear that Culture A originated the design and that this is a case of cultural diffusion. Each of the four others copied the design but then continued to make changes and, since I think simple examples make for greater clarity, in each case we can detect a clear line of development. The point here is merely to illustrate the criterion of degrees of relationship, with each of the most distant cultures showing less obvious connections than the closer ones.

Nevertheless, it is not yet time for celebrations and cartwheels. The most we can learn in this particular case is that this specific form originated with Culture A. But that fact by itself does not mean the people of Culture A were in that location prior to the others. It could just as easily be the case that Culture A moved in and settled in that

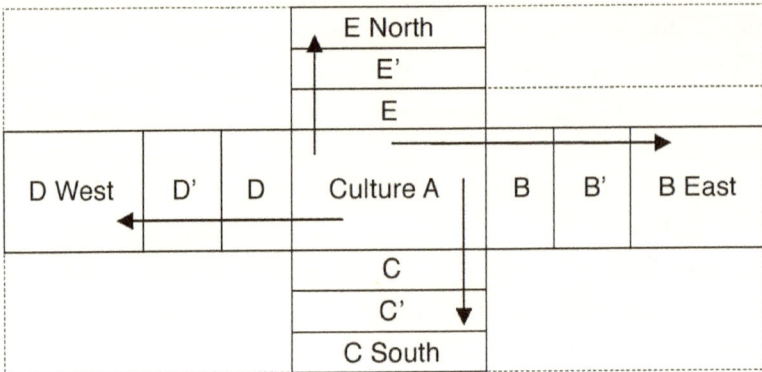

Figure 6.2. The criterion of the degree of relationship.

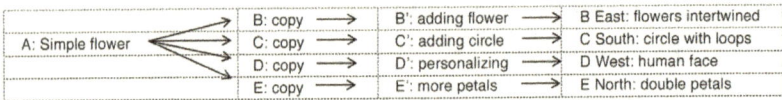

Figure 6.3

spot after the four other cultures, who then picked up A's pottery design and embellished it. Further, even though the sequence of the design's diffusion clearly gives A priority, the order in which the five cultures arrived in the area cannot be deduced from this single form.

Hypothetical Examples to Establish Priority

Let us look at some more thought experiments in order to grasp how straightforward the criteria actually are, although their application in the actual world may not be easy. Imagine that there are four adjacent cultures, each of whom includes a certain narrative in their lore. We want to find out if it is possible to identify which of these cultures—as always, known as A, B, C, and D—may have been the culture that first told the story from which the others learned it.

A: A girl went to the garden to pick some berries.
B: A girl went to the garden to pick some flowers.
C: A girl went to the meadow to pick some flowers.
D: A boy went to the garden to pick some flowers.

All four stories are different, but they only differ in one element. B has all three elements, for which one is exchanged in each of the other three cultures, and thus is probably the original version.

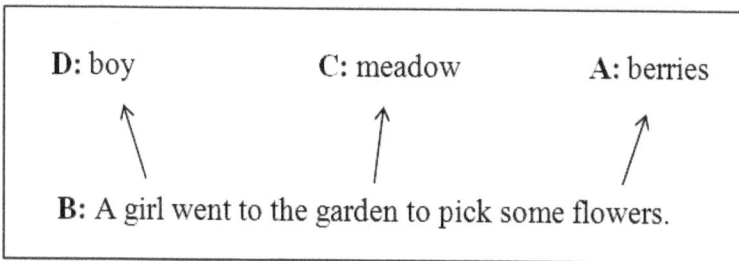

Figure 6.4 Four Variations on One Story

Again I must emphasize that reality is not that easy. A more realistic collection might be:

A: A girl went to the garden to pick some berries.
B: A little girl ran to the garden to pick some berries and flowers.
C: The angry seagull went to the forest to find some mushrooms.
D: The ancestors told about a girl.

Here we see a more realistic example of cases where it is not possible to sequence cultures on the basis of just one form, but neither would one need to do so. The identification of the origin of one form may be helpful, but the correlation of entire populations on the basis of the totality of their forms is what we are after.

To the best of my knowledge, there is nothing we could tell from these four examples, supposedly representing four different cultures, about which culture originated the myth and which copied it and adapted it. Now that does not mean we are out of options for determining the answer. We can look for further clues within the case or in the total cultures that surround each instance. Since we are dealing with a hypothetical example, we can give ourselves some latitude and invent some further facts that might be accessible to an anthropologist or ethnologist.

So, what additional information might help us solve the puzzle (without invoking omniscience, time travel, revelation, magic, miraculous writings, or anything else out of the grasp of a "normal" twenty-first-century scholar)?

A legitimate place to look would be the languages used in each culture, and we could make up enough additional data in this direction so a solution would become possible. So, what follows is totally ad hoc and is purely intended to illustrate a possible solution should the facts present themselves in a favorable manner. Of course, there are clear counterparts in reality, but looking at relatively familiar languages will probably help our understanding more than my trying to find workable examples in Australian dialects, for example.

Let us then suppose (rather unrealistically) that the languages of the four cultures are French, Lithuanian, Latin, and English, although the areas for these countries are not necessarily France, Lithuania, Rome, or England. They just happen to speak those languages. I'm adding just a few further details, which will help us construct a scenario under which it would be possible to find the original source. The four sentences in the languages I have assigned to them are as follows.

A: A girl went to the garden to pick some berries.
<u>French</u>: *Une jeune fille, allée dans le jardin pour cueillir des baies.*
<u>I am adding</u>: **Mergaitė**, *une jeune fille, allé dans le jardin pour cueillir des baies.*

B: A little girl ran to the garden to pick some berries and flowers.
<u>Lithuanian</u>: **Mergaitė** *nubėgo į sodą pasirinkti tam tikras uogas ir gėlės.*
<u>I am not adding anything.</u>

C: The angry seagull went to the forest to pick some mushrooms.
<u>Latin</u>: **Mergus iratus** *vadebat ad silvam ut invenire fungos.*
<u>I am not adding anything.</u>

D: The ancestors told about a girl.
<u>I'm adding</u>: *The ancestors told about* **Mergaitė**, *a girl.*

As you can see, I have added *Mergaitė* to A and D, where the word seems to be functioning as a name, assuming the story originally came with that word. Presumably it could also be a name in B, Lithuanian, but it isn't; it is actually the word for "girl" or "little girl." So the term is entirely at home in that language, whereas it is not in A and D. So the most likely reconstruction is that the culture of origin is the Lithuanian-speaking culture B and that the initial transmission of the story included the Lithuanian word *mergaitė*, which cultures A and D misinterpreted as a name.

The fact that the sentence in B is longer than in A plays no role; it could go the other way as well. Cultures may expand or contract a story. (Goethe expanded the medieval legend of Dr. Faustus; Shakespeare shortened the life of Caesar as recorded in Plutarch's *Lives*.) Furthermore, the fact that culture D only makes a brief reference to the ancestors and this girl by itself does not prove anything else either. In this case the linguistic clue would take precedence in establishing probability over the details conveyed. Since a girl named *Mergaitė* is otherwise unknown to the mythologies of A and D, it is not surprising that her name would frequently not be mentioned and the story often just refers to "a girl." In that respect other scenarios are both likely and common.

A big question is why we would even put culture C's myth into the same cycle. The idea of an angry seagull rushing into the forest to discover mushrooms seems to be rather distant from a girl heading for the garden to pick berries and flowers. The connection is admittedly rather tenuous. However, there is an explanation that would both make sense of the unexpected distortion and give a reason for why C's version of the story is included in the cycle.

We posited that cultures A and D, not understanding the word *mergaitė*, simply accepted it as a name without looking for further meaning. There are many instances in which a culture substitutes a word that has meaning in its own language, though the myth or story will receive a strange twist in the process. So let us say that the Latin-speaking culture C interpreted *mergaitė* as *mercus iratus*, the angry seagull. This possibility would gain in strength considerably if (a) there were some kind of a mushroom-oriented cultus in culture C, and (b) a seagull of any disposition or temperament were never mentioned anywhere else in connection with this cultus, except in this myth.

This is one possible scenario in which we are inventing a number of facts, which, once in place, would make it possible to identify the culture of origin with some plausibility. The idea is, of course, that this "invention" is, in fact, a scenario that is replicated in many real situations. An advantage of this particular example is that the main reconstruction occurs right on the level of the data, i.e., the languages used, and we wouldn't have to look for many external changes. As it turns out, the language connections of verbal cultural forms are often helpful clues in establishing reconstructions of cultural interactions.

Earlier I provided a hypothetical example of three Paleolithic cultures endowing their cutting stones with cultural forms: marking them with an X, smoothing out handles, and chanting a melody when using them. Let us add the hypothetical proposition that these three cultures were adjacent to one another. There are going to be areas of overlap and "nodes," by which I mean areas where more than two cultures intersect. These places are going to be of particular interest to us. Let us make a Venn diagram of the hypothetical situation, calling the cultures by our customary names: A, B, and C.

In contrast to the previous diagram, which only indicated logical relationships, in this case we may look at it as a stylized map of a rather large area. It should be large enough that the overlap areas (AB, AC, BC) and the node (ABC) contain populations with distinctive cultures engendered by the interactions. Including the different forms we had assigned to the cultures, the diagram could theoretically look like this:

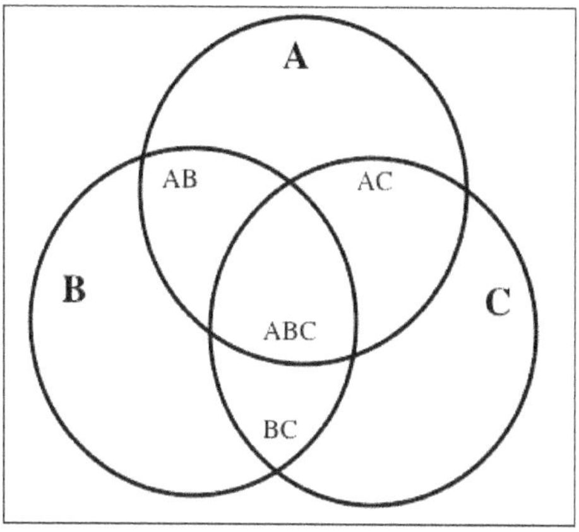

Figure 6.5. Alignment of Three Cultures

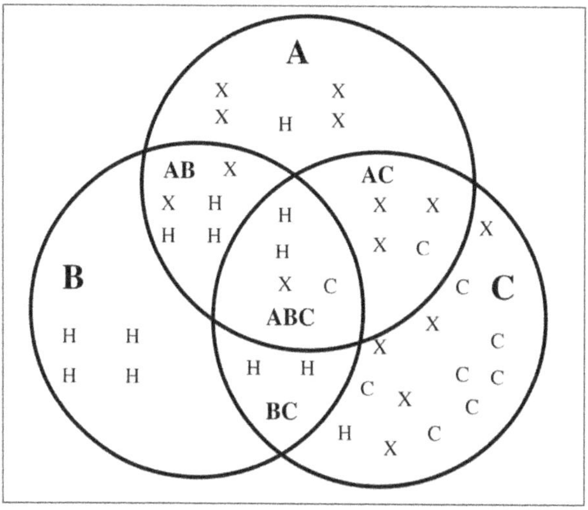

Figure 6.6. Distribution of Cultural Forms Across Three Cultures;
Form X originated with Culture A; form H stems from Culture B;
and form C belongs originally to Culture C.

X refers to the marking of an X on the stone; H refers to giving the stone a handle, and C stands for doing a little chant while cutting. This diagram is totally idealized, showing a regularity in the relationship between the three cultures that we are never blessed with in reality. Each main culture (A, B, and C) has only elements pertaining to itself, the overlaps show exactly half the forms of each culture, and in the central node (ABC) each culture contributes exactly a third. We never see this kind of neat arrangement in reality, which is good because if that's all we had, we would not be able to learn from it. Here is a more realistic representation:

Smaller-sized letters refer to the forms originating in each culture. B is clearly dominating the entire central overlap, including the node for all three cultures. There are some survivals of culture C in both the overlap and the node, and some survivals of A in the node as well, but that entire crossover section has been pretty much taken over by the culture of area B. B's strength is also shown in that some of its forms are found in both A and C. Culture C is the one that has been "contaminated" the most. It still has some strong forms of its own, but A has become dominant to the point where some of C's original forms now exist only as survivals in its own territory, and C only appears in the overlap in the form of survivals. As mentioned already, B is also showing up in C's territory. Now we can draw some inferences.

First, any overlap areas must be younger than the cultures themselves. Or, to put it the other way around, the cultures themselves are obviously older than the overlaps, otherwise there could not have been any overlaps.

Culture C appears to be older than either A or B. Many forms out of A and a few out of B have replaced some of C's original forms. In the overlap areas remnants of C are found exclusively as survivals. C looks a lot like a cultural colony of A at this point.

Culture B is by far the most prevailing one and is most likely the youngest. We find it represented in every field of our diagram except in the AC overlap area. Apparently, in that area, which would have been crucial for A to establish itself as dominant over C, its people emphasized cultural purity to such an extent as not to leave any room for forms out of B. B is clearly the most important culture, having claimed three out of the overlap areas and leaving its marks in the other two cultures as well.

Thus my analysis on the basis of these assumptions is this: If the rest of reality does not forbid the inference for some other reasons, culture C is the oldest of the three. Somewhere along the line, culture A came around and in some manner diffused its forms into the territory that was once the confines of C alone. However, B, a later arrival yet, is in the process of creating major changes in A and B. It controls, so to speak, both of its overlap areas and has already taken hold to some extent in the actual cultures. Therefore, my conclusion is that going from oldest to youngest, we have C, followed by A, and both of them are older than B in that area.

Applying the Criteria

In addition to the formalized criteria, there are some straightforward applications.

Before proceeding with this part of the description, I might just mention that we have another advantage over the days of Wilhelm Schmidt. Modern science matured under the aegis of Newtonian physics, where supposedly all the data could be quantified, and laws and theorems could be expressed with equations providing the certainty of mathematical calculations. Thus, in order to be recognized as a true science, many disciplines attempted to emulate if not the methods then at least the assurance of their conclusions. This approach appeared not to be too problematic with the natural sciences but was far more difficult to attain in the social sciences, not to mention the humanities. We saw earlier, for example, the fruitless quest for laws in language and cultural development, and, even in the absence of laws, it seems as though there was an expectation of

Newtonian certitude. Thus, at the same time as new developments in physics, particularly quantum mechanics, were doing away with the absolute precision of Newtonian physics, ethnologists were still striving for the unattainable goal of indubitability for their conclusions.

Since then we have come to greater terms with the idea that having a method for attaining some knowledge with a great amount of confidence still does not confer omniscience on the scholar. Back in Schmidt's day, the use of the term *probably* was often equated with expressing a degree of uncertainty, which could then be raised rhetorically to a manifestation of doubtfulness. Even statements made dogmatically, but not with absolute a priori certainty, could be seen as implying insufficient decisiveness. Thus, when someone wrote that he or she was convinced in all probability, say, culture A arrived earlier in time at a location than culture B, our natural reading of this statement would be that the author felt certain about this conclusion and was simply allowing for the slight probability of human error or some presently inconceivable change in the data. Back then a polemically minded critic would possibly jump on the expression "in all probability" and claim that probability was not sufficient for a conclusion in science and that the author clearly showed signs of waffling on the topic.

Fortunately, we have become wiser than that and hopefully have recognized the evident weakness in reading unwarranted doubtfulness into statements concerning the term *probable*. In what follows I will often attach some variation on "probability" to my statements for the above-mentioned reasons: Omniscience is beyond our capacity; no scientist *qua* scientist can ever rule out a revolution in the availability of new and better data; we must, at least theoretically, allow for the fact of human fallibility. But let me add another important point along this line: If I state a conclusion in terms of a high probability, the fact that I am expressing a conclusion in terms of scientific probability does not therefore confer status of viability to a competing theory of negligible probability. For example, if I say that event X has a probability of 99.997 percent and that event Y has a probability of .003 percent, the fact that I have not endowed event X with 100 percent certainty in no way means that Y is as likely to happen as X or that Y is ever going to happen. Probability is never more than probability, to be sure; however, the number assigned to a probability is significant and does not level the chances of both events to happen to the mathematical probability of 50 percent each. So, if I say that the moon in all probability consists of rocks similar to those of the earth, I am not implicitly opening the door to the hypothesis that it is made of cheese. Please remember that these are conclusions that arise from criteria, not laws.

Here are some conclusions we can draw in general when the various criteria are applied to a specific geographical area or, possibly, to the comparison of two areas.

1. The culture in the overlap between two adjacent cultures is always younger than either of the two constituent cultures. You could not have an overlap until you had the two overlapping cultures first.

2. In a given area the culture that shows strong signs of diffusion from an adjacent area is younger in those respects than the culture from which the forms are diffused. If the forms that have migrated are a part of a large bundle and appear to have replaced a similar bundle present in the "receiving" culture, the "diffusing" culture is probably younger.

   a. For the most part such a picture is highly strengthened if the diffused forms appear to be more complex than the previous ones.

   b. It is difficult to apply this criterion to mythology or folklore per se, but such specific forms can be pinned down in sequence more if there are further forms associated with the verbal material.

   c. This conclusion is particularly likely when it occurs in connection with rituals and worship practices.

3. A simple culture occupying a fringe territory that is generally inhospitable to human beings is probably one of the oldest cultures.

4. If within a certain area a complex culture is dominant and there are survivals of forms belonging to simpler cultures, the complex culture is younger.

5. "Foreign" words in a local language or dialect are probably imported; thus, their originating cultures are probably younger in the area.

After having applied the criteria, Schmidt came to the conclusion that three (or four) culture circles came close to representing (though not being)[17] the culture of the original migrants. I shall explain the entire larger picture after I have made this one more methodological point. There was the question if it was possible to distinguish which of these three (or four) could be considered the oldest. The two likely candidates were the Southeast Australians and another circle that included both African and Asiatic pygmies. Schmidt used the following additional reasoning. In general, it is safe to assume that those forms that add something to the natural state in which human beings are born, particularly those that are not necessary for subsistence, appear later in time than the more "natural" state. For the most part I am quoting from the summary provided by Brandewie:[18]

a. "Those who have no, or less, by way of bodily mutilation are older.

b. "The simpler way of making fire—by rubbing one stick in a groove on another (fire plow)—indicates great age. . . . Indeed, one group of central pygmies, the Andamanese, does not even know how to make fire.

---

[17] We would be jettisoning all of our intention to taking a historical view if we didn't allow for the fact that even the most primordial culture circle has thousands of years of history and that change in it must have happened. However, change in basic cultures is extremely slow.

[18] Ernest Brandewie, *Wilhelm Schmidt and the Origin of the Idea of God* (Lanham, MD: University Press of America, 1983), 50–51.

c. "Those groups which have no stone tool industry are older."

d. Absence or utter simplicity in musical instruments, except in cases of evident borrowing, indicate greater age.[19]

e. The same with art: the less, or the simpler, the earlier.

f. "Where totemism, even individual[20] or sex-related totemism, is absent, we have older and earlier.

g. "Funerals also differ and are indicative. Where there is no eating of flesh, or where accusations of witchcraft are absent, there again we have a simpler kind of culture. Therefore, this is earlier and older."

Combine all of these observations, and the culture circle that comes out as probably most closely resembling that of the earliest migration culture is the "central circle" of pygmies and pygmoid people.[21]

The *Primitive* Culture Circles[22]

There is no need for us to go through all of Schmidt's reconstruction of the history of humanity. The important point for us is to identify the cultures that most likely most closely resemble the original human culture; thereby, we don't need to engage with a number of criticisms of Schmidt's work, which does not affect the outcome.

---

[19] I am paraphrasing a paragraph overloaded with unnecessary qualifying clauses.

[20] "Individual totemism" refers to the idea that an individual person in a culture is expected to have a specific item (animal or plant perhaps) that is personally holy to him or her. This practice is well illustrated among some Native American tribes, e.g., the Lakota of the Plains. There, for a young man going on a vision quest to let his totem reveal itself to him is a part of the rite of passage into adulthood.

[21] People groups who are *somewhat* taller than those whom we would usually identify as pygmies but otherwise resemble them greatly in appearance and cultures.

[22] Any readers who want to pursue the following ideas would only get confused if I used different vocabulary from Schmidt's own terminology in English translations, although they are not commonly used today. I shall designate them as technical terms in Schmidt's sense by capitalizing and italicizing them. His three main groupings of the culture circles are the *Primitive* the *Primary*; the *Secondary*, and the *Tertiary*.

Ernest Brandewie gave Schmidt's work a rather thorough inspection, and he concluded,

> Schmidt's factual investigations led him to conclude that the oldest groups of people often (always?) had a notion of a high god and often expressed very little animistic thinking. Therefore animism could not have been original or first, but had to be later. And this, as an aside, is a point, I think, which can be accepted without having to accept the rest of Schmidt's elaborate methodology.[23]

To undertake this identification of the least altered cultures, Schmidt invoked both geographic isolation and a lack of socioeconomic complexity. By this time, having looked at all of the hypothetical examples above, some of his actual cases ought not to be too hard to follow. Let us be more specific.

Geographically, just as we had predicted, the cultures that come under consideration as Schmidt's *Primitive* cultures are all located at the extreme edges of their geographical areas. Their history is one of displacement, and so they find themselves in the Arctic and at the tip of South America (Tierra del Fuego). They subsist in the bush and in the desert. They occupy distant, isolated islands and craggy valleys in mountains that are hard to access.

Then, alongside the evidence of the fact that these cultures had been pushed to the margins of habitable land, their economic ways of life show little growth, and there is no evidence of any earlier stage from which they may have reverted. They are hunter-gatherers. Men find and kill animals for food while women collect edible plant material wherever it grows. Neither sex does anything to increase the food supply, but the people trust for conditions to be good so that nature will produce its bounty.

These are what Schmidt calls the *Primitive* cultures. They are as close as we are going to get to a link to the original culture (*Urkultur*) of human beings; however, they, themselves, are no longer

---

[23] Brandewie, *Wilhelm Schmidt and the Origin*, 49.

the original culture because all cultures have changed. These cultures are patrilineal; they may recognize clans but do not have totems; their marriage pattern is monogamy; and, in contrast to the people whom one might call "primitive" because of their self-immolations and deviant sexual practices, Schmidt's *Primitive* cultures live by a solid moral code. Schmidt recognized three divisions among the *Primitive* culture circles.[24]

- *The Central Primitive Circle.* Even in comparison to the other *Primitive* cultures, they have the simplest material cultures, but the monotheism is clear and, in contrast to what we saw among the Southeastern Australians, a single Supreme Being receives definite worship practices. For groups in this circle who hold to this Supreme Being, I shall quote Schmidt: "To begin with Africa, we find him among the Boni Negrillos of the east, the Anongo and Nkule of the west, the Batwa in Urundi, the Bgielli of the Cameroons, the Batwa of Ruanda, and the Bambutti (Efe and Bakango) of the Ituri."[25] Furthermore, there are the Andamanese, the Semang, and the Negritos of the Philippine Islands.

- *The Southern Primitive Culture.* Members of this circle are the San people ("Bushmen") of Africa, the inhabitants of Tierra del Fuego, and the southeastern Australian indigenous people. As we saw, in some of these cultures, monotheism is becoming a little faded so that the Supreme Being does not receive regular worship.

- *The Arctic Primitive Culture.* There is a lot of interaction with surrounding animistic cultures, but, according to Schmidt, monotheism is strongly represented among the Samoyeds, the Koryaks, most of the Eskimos (though fairly vestigial in

---

[24] Wilhelm Schmidt, *The Origin and Growth of Religion: Facts and Theories* (New York: Humanities Press, 1931), 237.

[25] Ibid., 258.

many cases), and—also under quite a bit of animistic influence—the Ainu.

- *The Boomerang Culture (maybe)*. These are the Australian cultures just north of the Guain and others. They included the Kamilaroi. Fritz Graebner had flattened most of the Southeastern Australian indigenous people into one chronological layer; and at first Schmidt went along with him, but he eventually changed his mind. The problem was that even though these people were on about the same cultural level as the coastal ones, they had become totemic and matrilineal, definitely a step away from the more likely earlier pattern. There are certain counterparts to this group in Africa. They are not sufficiently complex in their cultures to qualify under the next category (*Primary* cultures), but they are just a step ahead of Schmidt's category of *Primitive* cultures.

Further Culture Circles[26]

Many anthropologists today insist that, in theory at least, one should not make generalizations across cultures.[27] In practice, doing so becomes unavoidable, and then the question becomes to what extent the generalization is meaningful because it is based on an intentional differentiation of the cultures that are of different kinds and ages. Many scholars today continue the precedent set by E. B. Tylor of making generalizations on the basis of data drawn from various cultures, regardless of their age and relationship to one another. For example, anthropologist Annemarie de Waal Malefijt seeks to rebut Schmidt by pointing out that "some preliterate cultures are polytheistic."[28] However, even though for purposes of our discussion

---

[26] Ibid., 240–41 for a small diagram.

[27] See our discussion in a later chapter of Radin, *Method and Theory*.

[28] Annemarie de Waal Malefijt, *Religion and Culture: An Introduction to Anthropology of Religion* (Long Grove, IL: Waveland, 1968), 66–67.

we have focused on the *Primitive* cultures, this identification becomes far more meaningful if we analyze the more complex cultures with which we contrast them.

Schmidt found that the *Primitive* culture circles yielded to what he called three *Primary* culture circles. Please keep in mind again that these are not laws that govern the development of cultures but are a description of three popular results of decisions made by humans (sometimes under duress, to be sure) concerning the nature of their societies. Schmidt makes the distinction between the *Primitive* cultures and the *Primary* ones by calling the former "food-gatherers" and the latter "food-producers." Still the "production" of food in these *Primary* cultures can be minimal. The three *Primary* culture circles include:

1. *Hunting Economies.* The fundamental way of living in these cultures is not all that different from the *Primitive* cultures, but hunting has become more sophisticated. The weapons are better, and, due to new tools, the methods of processing the animals are more efficient. These cultures are usually totemic; marriage is exogamous; and the descent is reckoned patrilineally.

2. *Horticultural Cultures.* In the case of these cultures, the distinction is based on the greater sophistication demonstrated by the woman's side of the original hunter-gatherer culture. Whereas before the gathering was merely a matter of finding edible material, she now nurtures the various plants that yield the food. For example, if a bush produces good berries, she may plant some shoots and make sure all the bushes get water so they will grow and give her many berries. These cultures are matrilineal, and marriage is exogamous in so far as there are clans, which may or may not be totemic.

3. *Pastoral Nomadic Cultures.* In this third culture circle, the people realized that it may be more efficient, rather than to hunt animals, to collect and domesticate certain animals that

lend themselves to this purpose: cattle, sheep, goats, camels, or llamas. This different approach to life also has clear implications for the nature of the society. They are patrilineal in assessing one's heritage, but, other than that, there are going to be few, if any, subgroupings of a particular band. Whereas the first two *Primary* cultures speedily turned toward animism, ancestor veneration, and magic, the pastoral nomads tended to retain the original monotheism more clearly.

Again speaking descriptively and not normatively, the *Primary* cultures eventually led to two circles of *Secondary* cultures. Both of these are "free," which means there are no marriage restrictions except for the common ones against incest, but they are not exogamous or restrictive about clans. The only difference between them is a matter of whether the descent and family affiliation is patrilineal or matrilineal. Secondary cultures are at least to some extent agricultural.

Finally, there are the *Tertiary* cultures. Schmidt calls these the "oldest civilizations of Asia, Europe, and America." He uses the term "civilization" here in the technical sense of a culture that builds cities, not in the implicitly offensive sense in which we find it used so often in the nineteenth century where *civilized* was used as a contrast to *barbarian*.

Conclusion

I have attempted to provide a description of Schmidt's method that is clear and faithful to his intentions. Needless to say, the century or so between his writing and mine has left its mark. There are things we can assume now, and Schmidt did not, and vice versa. If my attempt at explaining the method was successful, then hopefully Schmidt's results will also look more plausible than they are often portrayed many times. In the next chapter we will take a closer look at exactly what he found, and then we cannot escape the need to deal with his critics.

CHAPTER 7

Wilhelm Schmidt: The Results

In the previous chapter we attempted to clarify Wilhelm Schmidt's use of the culture-historical method of ethnology, which led him to the recognition of a number of culture circles around the globe. These integrated complexes of cultures were due to the migrations of people groups as well as other means of diffusion of cultural forms such as trade or imitation. The most common pattern was that when a later culture arrived in an area occupied by an earlier culture, it would either absorb or displace the older culture, oftentimes including the people who held it. By a careful analysis of the forms of culture manifested by different groups in different areas, Schmidt constructed chronological sequences, with the least sophisticated cultures (those whom Schmidt called "*Primitive*"[1]) as the ones most likely to resemble the original culture of human beings. His conclusion was that the people in the lowest position with regard to their

---

[1] As in the previous chapter, I shall italicize Schmidt's terms and capitalize them because these are the terms readers will encounter in his translated works. I hope that by using this style I will be making clear that I do not intend any of the potentially derogatory meanings associated with some of the terms today. Furthermore, as Schmidt showed, the cultures he designated as "*Primitive*" in his technical, material sense frequently manifested the highest state of spiritual and moral culture.

material culture occupied the highest level of spiritual culture if one were to apply an evolutionist's hierarchy. They were monotheists. In this chapter we shall look more closely at some of the cultures whom Schmidt included in this group so as to get a better understanding of what he actually meant by "original monotheism."

Some Clarifications on Monotheism

I have refrained (so far) from the unnecessary waste of the reader's time by making a show of wrestling with a definition of *monotheism*. The concept seems to be, and actually is, clear: the recognition of a single supreme being and worship of him alone. In conjunction with Andrew Lang's theory, we listed among the attributes of the supreme being as found among, say, Australian indigenous people, that he is not just a highly developed spirit arising out of animism, nor just the presiding deity in a council of gods, nor a glorified ancestor, chief, or culture hero. He is the good creator of the world, omnipotent, omniscient, and eternal, the author of moral obligations, who expects human beings to live by them.[2]

God and Other Spirits

However, some issues need to be clarified. For one thing, we should not think that monotheism must exclude recognizing the reality of other spiritual beings. If the meaning of monotheism were the belief that God is the only spiritual being in the universe, that would be a seriously wrong definition out of keeping with normal usage of the word. There would be no actual monotheistic religions either in the past or present, which would definitely be out of harmony with common usage of the term, assuming we correctly identify at least Judaism, Christianity, Islam, as well as some phases of Zoroastrianism as

---

[2] See particularly Andrew Lang's summary in his *The Making of Religion* (repr., Charleston, SC: Bibliobazaar, 1968; orig., New York: Longmans Green, 1898), 182–88.

monotheistic. In all of these religions, the spiritual world is populated by angels as well as evil spirits under various descriptions. We even find an evil being (Satan) more powerful than most of the other spirits. So, if the total absence of all spiritual beings were a requirement for true monotheism, the historical existence of monotheism as a belief would be in serious doubt, and the entire discussion would be about nothing.

A profitable way of approaching this topic is by asking whether the beings who are subordinate to God were dependent spirits or independent gods. I trust that it is not entirely arbitrary with the common use of terms to think that a god should be considered uncreated (though perhaps born of other gods) and be able to make free decisions.[3] Such is not at all the case for the spirits one finds in connection with monotheistic religions. Whether they are angels or demons, they are creatures dependent for their existence on God, who created them and who sustains them in existence as long as it pleases him. Furthermore, despite what some of the evil spirits may think, according to the scriptures of these religions, they are weak in power, their decisions are predetermined, and they are headed for ultimate destruction. This point is clear, for example, for both the *daevas* of Zoroastrianism and the *jinn* of Islam. They have limited power now, and the clock for them to have any power at all is running out. The good spirits of the religions, the angels in Christianity, for example, recognize the fact of their limitations, and, consequently, are comfortable in their role of obeying God's decrees.[4]

One should not forget that humans are spiritual beings as well. Without taking recourse to the Tylorian notion of souls having

---

[3] Perhaps that minimal definition is too minimal; it would definitely rule out various "gods" in the mythologies of various cultures because there were many stories about them as acting under various compulsions. But, then again, it is not at all clear, as Max Müller taught, that even the people of those cultures took their mythologies all that seriously. See F. Max Müller, "Comparative Mythology" in *Chips from a German Workshop*, vol. 2 (New York: Charles Scribner, 1871), 1–141.

[4] As demonstrated, for example, in Rev 22:8–10, where an angel refused worship from John.

separate existences from the bodies they inhabit, and without getting into the sometimes complicated questions of the nature of the soul and its interaction with the body,[5] the more familiar monotheistic religions clearly teach that an important aspect of being human is to have a non-material side, to which we can refer as soul or spirit. The terminology is not as important here as the reality of this belief and the fact that it is not thought of as compromising the monotheistic nature of the religion in context.

In fact, if we wanted to define monotheism as meaning that God is the only spiritual being in the world and yet wanted to accommodate the reality of human souls or angels, the result would be pantheism, which—though it may be "mono-theistic" in an all-too-literal sense—is not what we normally call monotheism, where the "theism" part refers to a transcendent as well as immanent being. It would be a matter of forcing terms in a direction that does not fit with the meaning of words as we usually understand them. Thus the idea that the one and only God created spiritual beings as well as material objects is a normal part of monotheism.

Still another question arises in this connection. It is one thing to recognize the reality of other spirits besides God; it is another to worship the spirits as well as God. To what extent is spirit-worship in a culture compatible with still calling it monotheism?

This question I am raising is one of terminology, not of correct worship practices. Let me begin with an example out of Islam, a religion that is surely monotheistic. At various times and in various places, reformers in Islam were fiercely opposed to certain practices they considered to be animistic. A significant person in that role was Muhammad-ibn-Abd-al-Wahhab, who in the eighteenth century condemned various common practices as idolatrous. His teachings eventually became mandatory in Saudi Arabia and, for a time, in Afghanistan under the Taliban. My point is that believers within a

---

[5] See my summary discussion on some of the issues involved in this regard in Winfried Corduan, *Handmaid to Theology: An Essay in Philosophical Prolegomena* (Eugene, OR: Wipf & Stock, 2009; orig., 1981), 41–59.

monotheistic religion may vehemently disagree on how much attention may be paid to inferior spirits, but it would take a lot more than finding syncretistic practices in certain Islamic locations to say that Islam is not monotheistic. The same thing would be true in other monotheistic contexts, as well.

Furthermore, consider an important verbal distinction I have deliberately overlooked in the previous two paragraphs. Many cultures have different terms for their actions directed to God in contrast to those directed to lesser beings. For example, Jomo Kenyatta emphasized such a distinction for his own people, the Kikuyu tribe of Kenya.[6] The Kikuyu have traditionally believed in Ngai, a single supreme god, who does not usually interfere with human affairs but whom they beseech in times of crisis. When the entire community (including the ancestor spirits) gathers under a large tree to beg for Ngai's help, the expression is *gothaithaya Ngai*, "to worship" Ngai. Kenyatta insists this term is never applied to the ancestors, where the correct phrase is *gointangera ngoma njohi*, "to pour out or to sprinkle beer for spirits";[7] less colorfully one might say that they make offerings to the spirits. Given this terminology, the traditional Kikuyu culture displays monotheism, but on the whole it is clearly animistic because it includes "making offerings" on a regular basis, whereas one would have to say they hardly ever "worshipped."[8]

Many other religions maintain a similar distinction, including Roman Catholic Christianity, which we need to bring up because Schmidt himself relies on that distinction at times.[9] Catholicism includes the practice of believers calling on the saints as well as on God. But English-speaking Catholic theologians will also point out

---

[6] Jomo Kenyatta, *Facing Mt. Kenya* (1938; repr., New York: Vintage, 1965), 222–31.

[7] Ibid., 223.

[8] Of course, the reference here is to the traditional Kikuyu culture. Today most Kikuyus are Christians, but the word for God in Kikuyu language continues to be *Ngai*.

[9] E.g., Wilhelm Schmidt, *High Gods in North America: Upton Lectures in Religion* (Oxford: Clarendon, 1933), 78.

an important difference in the language used: Catholics "worship" God and "venerate" (or "honor") the saints. The Greek words that stand behind that distinction are *latria* and *dulia* respectively. Therefore, Schmidt, for one, does not believe Catholic Christianity's monotheism is compromised by the veneration of saints since saints are only honored and not worshipped.[10] Thus the monotheistic nature of Catholic Christianity would not be lessened.

Somewhere one needs to be able to draw a line to distinguish between when we are looking at monotheism alongside spirit veneration and when we are really observing animism with a part-time god in the background. That judgment has to be based on the importance of the supreme being and the spirits within the lived culture. To some extent it comes down to a judgment call of whether the god or the spirits are dominant. It appears to me that if the spirits receive all of the day-to-day attention, and the god is only brought out of storage from time to time, we can safely describe such a religious culture as animistic. Let me stress again that this issue is about the application of terminology; it is neither about right belief nor correct practice, let alone about salvation. No one's eternal destiny is decided by whether I or anyone else calls their religion monotheistic.

The Description of God

So, are we supposed to recognize a divine being with dog's feet as God? Well, I'm not ready to put Altjira of the Aranda on a par with Yahweh, the God of the Bible. Still again, that is not the issue. If we are setting out to find the Christian God in other cultures, we're going to be disappointed, although it is all-too-easy to make the leap from identifying correctly the origin of the belief in a supreme god with

---

[10] Thus, as a Protestant, since I do not want to ascribe something to people they specifically repudiate, I should not object to the "worship" of the saints because Catholics state that they do not "worship" them. Of course, I am still free to object to the "veneration" of the saints (and I do); however, in that case I have acknowledged that Catholicism is monotheistic (which I also do), and that is the point of this discussion.

God himself to identifying the supreme god, described under the concepts of that culture with God as described in the Bible. Once more I need to stress that the anthropologist's interest is different from that of the Christian theologian or evangelist (though, eventually there will be a payoff in the area of apologetics). In this case the important issue is whether the being in question deserves to be called "God." If a god is described theriomorphically, as we may ascribe eagle's wings to God, but is also considered to be eternal, omnipotent, and omniscient, he is already more of a God than the one described by various theologians today. We need to be careful, though, to make sure such theriomorphic descriptions are simply that and not an actual instance of an animal people have exalted.

They Come to America[11]

We cannot possibly do justice to all of the cultures Schmidt discussed in depth in the twelve volumes of *Der Ursprung der Gottesidee*. Let us focus on one geographical area that is representative of Schmidt's methods and conclusions, and let us choose one that will not be totally undiscovered territory for most readers of this book, namely the American Indian cultures of North America.

The majority opinion among scholars today is that those we now call "Native Americans" came to this continent by migrating across the so-called Bering Land Bridge, which in earlier times formed a direct connection between Siberia and Alaska. More specifically, it would have been during one or more episodes of glaciation, the ice ages, that the sea level was low enough that this wide area of land, dubbed "Beringia," was open to animals and the people who hunted them. In fact, even though this was an ice age, the glacial masses would have been blocked by Beringia and thereby also have served as windbreak from the polar winds that otherwise would have hit eastern Siberia, Beringia, and western Alaska. Thus, these newcomers

---

[11] In this discussion we are going to rely to a large extent on Schmidt, *High Gods*.

may have found the climate in the new area hospitable. However, once they reached British Columbia, they may have found their way barricaded for a while, and they might not have been able to proceed farther onto the continent until the glaciers receded.

To the best of my knowledge, there has never been a time since this issue has been treated academically that there has not been a counterproposal or, more likely, a supplementary proposal, by someone advocating further migrations of people from other areas of the world onto this continent by some other means.[12] For example, Wilhelm Schmidt reported as something acknowledged in his day by "all competent Americanists" that tribes with a matrilineal totemism arrived in Central America and Mexico later than the people who had crossed the Bering Bridge, having traveled by boat from Indonesia and Southeast Asia.[13] Their culture was supposedly more advanced so that they were capable of such navigation.

The theory of Indonesian sea-travelers arriving in Central America cannot be maintained today, but some well-credentialed archaeologists, such as Thomas D. Dillehay, are trying to get a hearing for some plausible revisions concerning theories of settlement.[14] Schmidt, as we will see shortly, wrote at a time when serious archaeology in America was just beginning, and he could not have known of what was just being found and only partially reported. He was justified in saying at the time that "the majority of scholars are even of opinion [sic] that no true palaeolithic discovery has ever been made in America."[15] Right at the time when he was writing these words, the situation was changing with the discovery of the so-called Clovis culture, dated around 10,000–9,000 BC,[16] and the Folsom

---

[12] I am *not* including here ungrounded mythology, such as the notion that the American Indians are the supposed ten lost tribes of Israel.

[13] Schmidt, *High Gods*, 18.

[14] Thomas D. Dillehay, *The Settlement of the Americas: A New Prehistory* (New York: Basic Books, 2000).

[15] Schmidt, *High Gods*, 14.

[16] Robert F. Spencer, Jesse D. Jennings, et al., *The Native Americans: Ethnology and Backgrounds of the North American Indians*, 2nd ed. (New York: Harper & Row,

culture, enjoying dominance for the subsequent millennium, c. 9,000 to 8,000 BC. However, a fascinating phenomenon is that on the whole, archaeological data document few fundamental changes in North American cultures over the last several thousand years, except within the Mississippi valley. The basic economy of a hunter-gatherer society seems to have been the rule for over 10,000 years with few exceptions. Even the distinctive Adena and Hopewell mound-building cultures still were hunter-gatherers.[17] New discoveries added good information to the knowledge pool but also spawned a lot of offspring in the sea of speculations. Interestingly, as of this writing, some of the theories long held as firmly established by archaeologists are now being put to question, and some of the latest ideas line up much more closely with Schmidt's analysis, though some differences remain. In the interest of minimizing confusion, it will be best to stick with Schmidt's views in this chapter and bring up the alternatives in the next chapter. There we will direct ourselves to criticisms and corrections of Schmidt.

This discussion assumes a correlation between a people's language and its further ethnic connections, a way of identification often used by Native Americans themselves. To draw up a simplified scheme, Schmidt believed that among the tribes crossing the Bering Bridge was a contingent that moved to California, one that settled in the Northwest (the Salish), and one that turned into the widespread Algonquins, who moved farther east. Somewhat later the Athabascan (Dené) peoples entered the lower mainland. The tribes associated

---

1977), 10. For our purposes I'm going to stick with traditional (BC/AD) dates, rather than the system frequently used by archaeologists of expressing ages of artifacts in terms of B.P. ("Before Present"). The reason for this usage simply lies in the fact that radio-carbon (C_{14}) dating does not recognize the calendar distinction and gives dates from the time of measurement. That means that if it had greater precision, the B.P. dates would constantly have to be changed or expressed as "Before Measurement," in which case one would still need to know the calendar date to make sense of the information. So I'm reporting all the dating numbers in terms of BC and AD by deducting 2,000 years from each B.P. report. Technically that is not entirely accurate, but it certainly suffices for us here.

[17] Ibid., 24–36.

with this group formed a fairly unbroken chain from the center of
Alaska to the Apache and Navajo in the Southwest. Then followed a
mass migration north by the groups that had entered the continent
from Central America and Mexico, named again for the most part
according to language affiliation: The Siouan people, the Iroquois,
the Cherokee (actually a part of the Iroquoian group), the Muskogeans
(Southeastern tribes), the Pueblo groups, the Pawnee, and the
Shoshone (whose language is closely related to that of the Aztecs).[18]
The arrival of these groups put pressure on the groups already present to move and thus contributed to the separation of related groups
from one another. After being isolated, subgroups of such large entities as the Athabascans and Algonquins often underwent fairly rapid
changes in their languages and cultures.

This scenario is questionable today. However, the issues raised
about Schmidt's geography of later migrations do not detract from
his conclusions because the layers of cultures are still there even if we
now do not necessarily accept in which direction the later cultures
moved. Schmidt based his conclusions on the empirical information
as it was conveyed to him, placing data ahead of theory as much as
possible. His conclusions are not dependent on whether the Siouan
people, for example, traveled up from Mexico. They did move into the
Southwest and the Great Plains, causing unrest among other tribes
as a consequence. Whether the Iroquoian peoples walked across the
Bering Bridge or cruised into Acapulco in canoes does not matter as
much as that they represented a culture that is significantly different
from that of the Algonquins, with whom they came into conflict and
whom they superseded in certain territories.

Furthermore, Schmidt's view contributes an important realism
to the depiction of Native American migrations. Specifically, it cuts
away at the common portrayal of the immigration into North and
South America as exploration tours, motivated by some unexplained
inner drive. Even books that do not conform to the "Beringia-only"

---

[18] Schmidt, *High Gods*, 17–18.

theory still wind up creating the impression of the incoming people as being out on an adventure to see what may be across the next hill, always moving, always hoping to find more interesting places to reside, and only coming to a halt once they reached Tierra del Fuego with no further place left to go.

This mind-set originated with the notion that the economy of the earliest immigrants was almost exclusively based on big-game hunting, where "big" stands for mammoths, mastodons, giant sloths, prehistoric species of bison, and anything else huge and meaty. According to this stereotypical picture, the incoming people chased the animals at a rapid speed, causing their extinction wherever they went. They supposedly covered the entire range from the Yukon to Tierra Fuego in record time because they had to keep up with the animals. Only after the large fauna was eliminated did they settle down to live as more conventional foragers, adding more plant material to their diets and settling for smaller animals to hunt. This commonly accepted mental picture is still with us.[19]

Neither the big-game hunter model nor the subsequent quasi-tourist model make sense in the light of how and why people groups migrate. One does not uproot one's entire tribe just to go out on an adventure or in the hope that a little farther south the mammoth meat will be less stringy. Common sense dictates that people eat what they can get, and the idea that they will hunt mammoths while ignoring any other edible small mammals or vegetation lacks both persuasiveness and a sense for good nutrition. Until recently, archaeologists had found arrow and spear points in the skeletons of large mammals but no evidence for plant collecting, thus giving rise to this rather skewed account. They did not really come to terms with the fact that whereas projectile blades will survive, roots and berries, once digested, leave few permanent traces. Moreover, whatever minimal processes the people may have performed on the vegetative side of their cuisine did not necessarily require either stone or bone

---

[19] It appears to be the view assumed in Spencer, Jennings, et al., *Native Americans*.

utensils. Thus, the presence of projectile points and the absence of other objects in the archaeological record dictated the theory.

What is one to make of statements such as this conclusion concerning a group of humans in prehistoric California? "A noticeable absence of seed-grinding implements suggests that the early hunters did not avail themselves of the abundant and diversified edible plants."[20] It appears to me that the absence of seed-grinding implements in the present archaeological record indicates nothing more than that so far archaeologists have not found anything they would recognize as a seed-grinding implement in the area. To jump from there to a generalization that the group in question eschewed vegetative nourishment is an unwarranted leap.

An excavation at a site called Monte Verde in Chile, more specifically the level called *Monte Verde II*, excavated under the direction of Thomas Dillehay, has provided evidence of how tenuous the theory of a purely carnivorous diet of the early inhabitants of America has been. This site, which has evoked its share of a priori skepticism, was situated in a peat bog in such a way that not only bone and stone artifacts were preserved but also wooden implements and other organic remnants. Dated around 10,500 BC (a date that is significant by itself because it antedates the more commonly accepted time for cultural artifacts in North America), it shows that its occupants did partake of a mixed diet of meat and plant material. The find even included *wooden* mortars, which would not usually have survived and which could be used with stones manifesting little or no human alteration, thereby not leaving recognizable residue in more usual locations.[21]

But simply dropping the big-mammal hunt as an all-explanatory factor and leaving the people racing south to the end of the continent without serious motivation is not convincing either. People groups do

---

[20] See Spencer, Jennings, et al., *Native Americans*, 203. Since Jesse Jennings is credited with the exposition of the prehistorical material in the book, we can probably attribute this statement to him, and, unsurprisingly, his career was clearly more focused on the shovel than on the field ethnographer's diary.

[21] Dillehay, *Settlement*, 160–68.

not migrate merely because they are awestruck by all of the new territory (how could they know how much there was?) or travel at an accelerated pace so as not to miss out on all of the new opportunities. Even Dillehay, who is trying to balance established dogma with a more flexible vision, has not been able to purge himself entirely of this view. He comments in a congratulatory tone toward the Paleo-Indians (in the context of remarking on some oddities in the archaeological record):

> [The apparent anomalies] may also be explained by the first Americans' different experience. They achieved something never done before by modern humans (except for the Australians)—they conquered a previously uninhabited landscape. Surely, the demands of this unique adventure accelerated invention and socialization, as well as cause the abandonment or suspension of certain cultural practices.[22]

This is a confusing statement because (a) it is strictly a speculative ad hoc hypothesis with little plausibility; the "suspension" of cultural practices in the excitement of migration is not a convincing idea; and (b) there was nothing all that unusual in the American situation for *Homo sapiens* on the whole. Assuming a single origin of human beings in some specific geographic location, perhaps in Africa, as numerous anthropologists believe today,[23] the rest of the world would have been a "previously uninhabited landscape," including most of Africa, Europe, and Asia as well Australia and America. Dillehay could not rationally ascribe the settlement of the Old World to prehuman hominids, such as the Neanderthals, since by definition they were not "modern humans." Still, even if he were to commit such a "tour-de-force" and, contrary to all rationality, counted them

---

[22] Ibid., 234. The matter in question is not a minor one. For some reason, archaeologists have not found skeletons or alleged burial sites pertaining to this early period. Dillehay allows for numerous factors for this phenomenon, including—as shown in this statement—the idea that Paleo-Indians just either did not practice burial at all or disposed of their dead in a totally unique manner.

[23] See Rana and Ross, *Who Was Adam? A Creation Model of the Origin of Man* (Colorado Springs: NavPress, 2005), esp. 125.

among "modern humans," his statement would still make no sense because then the honor of pioneering unsettled areas by "modern humans as redefined" would be shared by *Homo neanderthalis* for the Old World and *Homo sapiens* for America and Australia.

In America, as anywhere else, people migrated because there was pressure to leave their present area and they needed to find a new territory in which to establish themselves and maintain their way of life (though adaptation often became necessary). It is hard to imagine the majority of migrations without a great deal of agony (note that I said, "imagine"), and there certainly is evidence that the nonmaterial forms of cultures played a significant role in maintaining the unity of the social units in such situations. Schmidt's scheme saves us from the picture of the Paleo-Indian running south with a spear in one hand and a packed suitcase in the other.

In keeping with the culture-historical method, as Schmidt surveyed the reports on the American Indian tribes, he identified three culture complexes, each a part of three different culture circles, that qualified as *Primitive*, all three of them having entered the continent by way of the Bering passage. These are several tribes of North Central California, a number of Algonquin tribes, and the inland Salish. They are pursuing a hunter-gatherer economy, and they have a pronounced monotheistic religion.

The Creator

We will first look at how the Creator is described in these cultures and then at how people in each case relate to him. Each description will begin with a quick identification of what we may know of their antecedent geographical origins.

North Central California

The Yuki. Let us imagine a likely scenario for the Yuki people of North Central California. They are a group with a rather unique language, who found their way out of Alaska, which was becoming highly over-populated (at least in relative terms) early in the migrations. Presumably they navigated the passage through the Yukon Territory, which would still have been treacherous, and were now looking for a comfortable and resource-rich area to settle down. A far larger group of people, united by the Penuti language, came a short time behind the Yuki. By the time they were in coastal Washington and Oregon, the Yukis' wildest hopes might have been fulfilled. It is a mere guess that they took a break from their migration in that area, but it is based on the conviction I expressed earlier that people would not leave an area once they found what they had probably been looking for. In this ecological niche, obtaining food seemed as simple as stretching out their hands and grasping for it. So it is possible that they might have decided that this was the end of their journey and that it was time to occupy this area for their hunting and gathering purposes.

If the Yuki did stop north of California, it was only temporary, based on a scale where time is measured in centuries. Other people groups were coming their way, perhaps proceeding at a faster pace than had been possible for the Yuki, now that the ice sheets were receding further. I already mentioned the Penuti peoples, whose migration came shortly after that of the Yuki. After this time the Algonquin as well as the Salish were entering the lower forty-eight states, one right after the other (so to speak—we should, of course, posit multiple generations between their arrivals). Eventually, the Athabascans, who had already established themselves firmly in Alaska over thousands of years, stretched out a chain of tribes all the way down from Alaska to the Southwest. Their cultures were more advanced than previous ones; they built permanent dwellings wherever their clans set up. The Yuki would have had no choice but to move farther down the coast into California, and at first they may have found conditions there even better than farther north.

Geographically, a cross section through the topology of California at that latitude yields west to east: (1) an extremely narrow coastline, which may have still been in the process of receding as the glaciers from the last ice age were melting, (2) the coastal mountain range, (3) the Sacramento Valley, and (4) the much taller mountains of the Sierra Nevada. Northern California does not have a wide coastline, and the mountains pretty much come right up to the edge of the ocean.

The Yuki settled down primarily in the coastal region north of where eventually San Francisco would be built, which gave them sufficient room, particularly because a large contingent of them moved inland, across the coastal mountains, right into the Sacramento Valley. But pressures from other incoming tribes continued to mount, and Yuki territory also started to shrink. The Penuti-speaking tribes took over the Sacramento Valley. Those Yuki who moved inland needed to head back into the mountainous area and were also increasingly adopting elements of other people's culture and religion in place of their own heritage. Still more tribes squeezed into California (perhaps some of them coming from the south as well as the north and the northwest or perhaps even along the coastline by boat), and the Yuki faced the same dilemma now that had confronted so many people before: In order to survive, they must either assimilate with the more powerful newcomers or retreat as much as possible and hope they could preserve their identity, living adjacent to people with different cultures and religions. Only a few bands of Yuki managed to remain true to their original culture.

Similar things were happening to certain bands of the Patwin tribe, who belonged to the Penuti language family. Apparently they displaced the Yuki from the Sacramento Valley, but then they, too, wound up being surrounded by intrusive and hostile cultures that threatened to eliminate them and their culture. The Maidu group became a case in point.

California became a multicultural, multilingual complex, partially because it became the last refuge for some tribes who were being pushed as far as they could go and partially because it was attractive to every new invading group. Some of the languages spoken by the tribes there included small representations of the well-known Algonquin and Athabascan families, and the lesser known Penuti, Hoca, and Yuki groups.[24] Hoca is related to Iroquois, which is, of course, a major language family in North America. Out of this mosaic Schmidt isolated the two partial tribes as belonging to the oldest inhabitants and showing the least deviation from their original cultural patterns, the coastal Yuki and the Maidu.

The coastal Yuki population was already virtually extinct by the time that A. L. Kroeber published his results.[25] It was only due to the corroboration by the Algonquin Kato, who had thoroughly absorbed Yuki culture (as evidenced by incorporation of Yuki terminology and some clearly Yuki practices), that a solid description was possible. On the whole it is crucial that we observe the distinction between the coastal Yuki-as-mediated-by-the-Kato and the inland Yuki, who had syncretized their religion and culture. Descendants of the latter group have survived into the present.

*Excursus on the Fate of the Inland Yuki

Stephen Powers provided a description of the inland Yuki after they had been deported to a reservation.[26] His article falls into the all-too-large group of negative descriptions of a people whose tribe has just been decimated, who have been quarantined on their reservation, and who have been deprived of their way of life. They would not cooperate with Powers's apparently rather forceful interrogation, and he concluded that they were by nature utterly immoral, defiant, and liars. He concluded that they were liars because when he asked them even the simplest questions involving numbers, they did not come up with the right answer. Apparently, he decided, they were incapable of making any true utterances. But Powers clearly had no idea that the Yuki number system worked on a base of four, rather than on a base

---

[24] Schmidt, *High Gods*, 25.

[25] A. L. Kroeber, "Yuki Myths," *Anthropos* 27 (1932), 914.

[26] Stephen Powers, "The Northern California Indians," *Overland Monthly and Out West Magazine* 5 (October 1872): 305–13.

of ten, our common decimal system. Also, in line with the common view of his day, Powers observed that the Yuki, a hunter-gatherer culture to the core, demonstrated their depraved nature by their unwillingness to improve their lots by taking up agriculture. This idea was applied to many Native Americans, who had no concept of agriculture until they were shoved onto a reservation and handed seed corn by those in charge of looking out for their welfare.

Studies that have similarly ignored obvious factors while passing negative judgment on the people who were being studied have continued to be perpetrated in other times and places. Arthur Vidich gave a good assessment of the work of Cora Dubois,[27] who blamed the poor self-image and malaise of the people in the village she studied on bad child-rearing practices, while ignoring the fact that these people had been forced from their original homes by the agents of a colonial government. They were being brutalized, tortured, imprisoned, depersonalized, and robbed on the pretext of taxation—even at the time when she was administering her Rorschach tests.[28]

The Patwin-Maidu. The other group is the Maidu band of the Patwin tribe, which belongs to the Penuti language group. Schmidt describes them as surrounded by a circle of Hoca groups, interrupted occasionally by a Shoshone branch, though they were not totally isolated from other Patwins or other members of the Penuti group. Again it is necessary to draw a line between the more eastern contingent resident in the Sacramento River valley and on the verge of extinction, and those Patwin groups living further west in the next mountain range, who did not preserve the culture as well and accommodated themselves to the cultures of later comers.

These two surrounded and beleaguered groups, the coastal Yuki and the eastern Patwin, show the clearest evidence of a truly monotheistic religion. Not only do they recognize a single God, but they

---

[27] Cora Dubois, *The People of Alor*, 2nd ed. (1944; repr., New York: Harper Torchbooks, 1961).

[28] Arthur J. Vidich, "Introduction," in Paul Radin, *The Method and Theory of Ethnology* (New York: Basic Books, 1966), xcii–cx.

pray to him and worship him regularly. Schmidt summarizes their cultures as follows:

> In their oldest pure forms they know neither totemism nor mother-right; they do not practice agriculture, but acquire their food by hunting, fishing, and collecting wild vegetables. Their simple social constitution is founded on the natural family, and their little village communities exhibit rudimentary chieftainship. Now, it is precisely among these three oldest primitive peoples of North America that we find a clear and firmly established belief in a High God, a belief which . . . is of quite a particular character by virtue of the high importance attributed to the idea of creation. . . . Quite a number of them have reached the highest summit of the idea of creation, denied even to Aristotle, viz. the belief in *creatio ex nihilo*, only by the will of the all-powerful Creator.[29]

As we saw, of the two California cultures, Schmidt held the Yuki to be older than the Patwin, having been displaced from the Sacramento Valley by Penuti-affiliated groups. There are a number of variations of the Yuki creation story. In some of them the Creator is clearly the supreme being, who is called *Tsenes*, which means "thunder" or "thunder man." In some he is accompanied by the original ancestor or culture hero, who goes by the name of Nagaico or Taikomol, which mean "great wanderer" and "solitary wanderer" respectively;[30] however, this great human was unable to create anything. In yet others "Taikomol" is used as the name for the Creator.[31] It does not appear to me, as Schmidt hypothesizes, that here is a case of the ancestral hero taking over for the supreme being but that the supreme being here had the name of the person who served as ancestral hero in other versions. His attributes are clearly divine. The situation seems similar

---

[29] Schmidt, *High Gods*, 19.

[30] Ibid., 29.

[31] Edward S. Curtis, *North American Indian: The Indians of the United States, The Dominion of Canada, and Alaska*, vol. 14 (Norwood, MA: Plimpton Press, 1924), 169–70.

to the one we found in Australia, where *Dhuramullan* is definitely the high god for some tribes, even though he appears as a secondary figure in others where Baiame is the name of the Supreme Being. The most important line in the Yuki story is reminiscent of Genesis: "He spoke a word, and the earth appeared."[32] In those versions in which Taikomol is the name of the glorious ancestor, he accompanies God and assists him in implementing God's divine commands in creation. God also creates a wife for him *ex nihilo* and then other human beings out of clay. After a flood destroyed all people and animals, God created them once more.

The Maidu creation story, given its setting in a somewhat later culture, is a little more complex.[33] At first there was nothing but water and darkness (which, in the absence of abstract terms, is frequently used as a description of chaos, which in turn represents the inconceivable state of nothingness). When I say "nothing," I am not including the Creator, who lived in the sky. One of his names is Wonomi, "without death."

Then Turtle and a human-like figure called Peheipe came into view, riding on a raft. You may be wondering where these two raft-riders came from if nothing had been created yet. The answer lies in the fact that these two beings are spiritual, not material, in nature. Peheipe is considered to be Wonomi's herald, the one who often speaks for him. We would most likely call him an angel. Turtle routinely represents the earth, and we are justified in thinking of him as the spirit of the earth, though he obviously suffered from the deficit of an earth at this point. So even though we cannot attribute such a Western conceptual answer to the people, the point is that they may not even have felt they needed to raise a question.

After a time Wonomi came down to the raft by climbing down a rope of feathers, and he sat together with Turtle in silence for a long time. After some time Turtle asked Wonomi of his origin and

---

[32] Ibid.

[33] R. B. Dixon, "Maidu Texts," *Publications of the American Ethnological Society* 4 (1912): 39ff, cited in Schmidt, *High Gods*, 33.

found out that he came from the sky. Some more time elapsed, and Turtle had another question. Couldn't Wonomi make dry land (i.e., the physical earth)? Wonomi said that he could, but he would use Turtle as his agent. Wonomi commissioned him to dive to the floor of the ocean and bring back some sand.

Turtle's expedition took six years, and when he finally surfaced again, covered with green algae and slime, the only sand he managed to bring back was what got caught under his fingernails. However, that was enough for Wonomi to transform the little bit of grit into the entire earth. Subsequently, at Turtle's request, he opened the shutters for Sun and Moon to illuminate the world he had made, and then he made human beings, many of whom had the shape of animals at first. Coyote alone, of all the people and animals, was allowed to see the Creator's face.

Wonomi wanted people to live a life without hardship, but Coyote, who was his adversary, intended for people's lives to be difficult, and Wonomi gave him permission to cause trouble for others.

*More on Coyote's Role

More accurately, Coyote was being a "trickster," which was a role played by various figures in many cultures. He is usually smart, sometimes too smart for his own good. Although he is not usually thought of as innately morally evil, he loves to stir up trouble, sometimes to achieve a good end, sometimes just for the fun of creating mischief. In many cultures people give recognition to him before they worship their other gods under the theory that once the trickster has been placated, there is a better chance of the petitions reaching the ears of the gods. At times, such as with the god Esu, who plays the role of trickster among the Yoruba people, the worshippers believe he intercedes with the gods on their behalf once he has been given veneration.[34] The cartoonish spooky spirit Twanyirika of the Aranda people in Australia

---

[34] E. Thomas Lawson, *Religions of Africa* (San Francisco: Harper and Row, 1985), 60–61, 65. Paul Radin, *The Trickster: A Study in American Indian Mythology* (New York: Glennwood, 1956).

would come under this heading, and so might Dhuramullan in some of the Australian groups where Baiame is the name of the supreme god. There Dhuramullan is considered his trouble-making relative.

In many cases it became customary to make regular offerings to the trickster in order to keep him on the good side of the people, while the Supreme Being, who was already good, did not need any further incentives to make them well disposed. Thus, the trickster eventually displaced the Supreme Being completely in some cultures; therefore, we find Coyote heading up the spirit world in a number of Native American tribes.

The Maidu Creation Story Continued. Still, Wonomi had planned that his creatures should live forever. When the first man, *Kuksu*, was ready to die, Wonomi gathered everyone together at the lake and demonstrated that *Kuksu*, after having been immersed in the water for a period of time, emerged again young and strong. The same opportunity was there for anyone else; no one ever needed to die permanently. But Coyote brought up a lot of arguments against such an idea. People would take their lives for granted; the earth would become overpopulated; people needed to learn to accept tragedy without complaining, and so forth. Wonomi, the Creator, let himself be persuaded by Coyote, but he set up events so that shortly thereafter, Coyote's son died. Coyote was in inconsolable grief. He tried to revive his son by dumping his corpse into the lake water, and he appealed pathetically to the Creator to bring him back to life. Apparently Coyote had figured that he would be an exception to the rule for which he had lobbied with Wonomi. But Wonomi said that he had done precisely what Coyote had wanted and that he could not be an exception. With his selfishness and lack of concern for anyone but himself exposed, Coyote disappeared in shame.

This myth reveals far more depth than one is used to in many preliterate societies where cleverness often outruns wisdom. The description of creation is not *ex nihilo*, to be sure, though a case could be made that once one interprets the symbols of the grains of sand brought up by Wonomi's agent out of the depths of "nothingness," it could be its equivalent in poetic expression. The finely tuned approach to evil in the world is extremely impressive. Coyote had "outfoxed" himself and suffered for it; consequently, human beings will suffer and die. But we see here neither a god with an evil side nor fatalistic resignation nor a simplistic dualism. This account also does not display simplistic emotions. Wonomi is not delighting in having outsmarted Coyote but is pained by the suffering of his creatures. He did not want them to have difficult lives and then to die, but he gave in to Coyote because he saw that Coyote, himself a creature, was right. Human beings need difficulties and the reality of death to make their lives worthwhile; otherwise, they will simply carelessly waste away their days.

It is fascinating to compare the versions of this story as recounted by those tribes who had absorbed elements of the surrounding cultures. For some (under influence from the Pomo tribe, a Hoca group) Coyote became the creator. For others, due to an amalgamation with other Penuti-affiliated groups, Eagle fulfilled this role. In yet others, the two of them cooperated or competed.

The Algonquins

As you may remember from chapter 5, E. B. Tylor had first dismissed the idea that the supreme beings in simple cultures were derived from Christian missionary influence. Later on, however, he conjured up its ghost again, using the same arguments against it, which he had protested earlier. Lang, Schmidt, and most other anthropologists came right back against him with his own earlier arguments, which had been strengthened in the meantime. Nonetheless, since the history of anthropological thought is apparently not studied thoroughly by American archaeologists, who, rather than ethnologists, have developed the theories for the past of Native American people in this country, one can read in more contemporary books paragraphs such as the following:

Some ideas out of the European cultural sphere reached many
native cultures indirectly. The Woodlands, especially among
the Western Algonkins, had the concept of the "Great Spirit,"
and some developed a notion of a "Happy Hunting Ground."
Neither concept, that of a supreme being or that of life after
death seems compatible with cultures possessing ceremonial
associations, curing, or hunting and fertility rituals. Christian
ideas had evidently spread from tribe to tribe in advance of the
missionaries and were incorporated somewhat vaguely into a
native world view.[35]

Once again we are encountering a purely a priori declaration and
a rather bizarre one at that. The idea of a "happy hunting ground"
can be overstated since it is not necessarily a part of all Algonquin
tribal lore, but it cannot be ignored since it is present in some of the
Algonquin tribes that show the least amount of outside influence.
Why should the idea of a supreme God and an afterlife be incompatible with ceremonial societies (the "Freemasons" or "Shriners" of the
tribes, if I may stretch the point a bit for clarification) or with various
rituals for healing, for success in hunting, or for fertility? It appears to
be an obvious non sequitur in light of the fact that such practices are
frequently found in religions that are undoubtedly monotheistic and
have a strong belief in an afterlife. (I'm thinking here of various practices in Judaism, Christianity, and Islam—particularly on the popular
or "folk" level.) The notion that the belief in a single supreme being
spread lightning fast, ahead of the missionaries, can only be characterized as Tylor's bad story made worse. If these supreme beings
were inconsistent with the rest of these cultures, if in some tribes
they never received any worship, and if they were not associated with
any benefits from believing in them, it makes no sense that all of
these tribes picked them up instantaneously. It is utterly implausible,
which may just be the reason there is no evidence for it.

---

[35] Spencer, Jennings, et al., *Native Americans*, 366. Again, given the placement
of this statement, it was most likely supplied by Jennings, the archaeology specialist.

According to Schmidt's reconstruction, the original area of settlement for the Algonquin tribes was north of the Great Lakes, which
is certainly true if we start with the Bering passage. This changes
nothing with regard to their distribution as encountered in historical times, even if there were a number of subsequent meanderings
from which many returned to the northern vicinity of the Great
Lakes. Migrating further south from that territory, they would of
necessity wind up either on the East Coast or at the edge of the
Great Plains area. Given this understanding of their "itinerary," it is
clear that any Algonquin tribes directly south of the Great Lakes,
such as the Miami, the Potawatomi, or the Shawnee, had more complex paths of migration. It appears that the westward extension by
the Algonquin Cheyenne and Arapaho into the northern area of the
Great Plains all the way to Colorado was a relatively new development. Their more mobile cultures were self-contained; thus, they
remained more closely related to their original culture than those
who moved toward the center and settled among tribes of different
heritages. Similarly, the Lenape (Delaware) on the East Coast managed to maintain their cultural independence to a larger degree than
other Algonquin peoples.

Given the number and geographic diversity of the many
Algonquin tribes, it may be surprising how closely they have clung
to their cultures, as well as the affinity of their beliefs to other older
Native American cultures, namely the North Central Californians.
We do, however, also have to address certain Algonquin distinctives
when we speak of their monotheism.

The usual Algonquin name of god is *Gitche Manitou* or some
variation thereof. The word *manitou* simply means "spirit," and we
have already shown that this fact does not mean that under the influence of Christian missionaries the Algonquin tribes merely elevated
one of their animistic beings to the status of supremacy in order to
please the white people, should they happen to come by later. Nevertheless, we are looking here at one of the situations we mentioned

at the outset of this chapter, where there are many active subordinate spirits. Gitche Manitou is clearly not the only spiritual being. In fact, some of the others manitous, to use the earlier vocabulary, certainly receive veneration.

When discussing this issue previously, I clarified that it is a reasonable expectation that a being should be uncreated and capable of making free, autonomous decisions to qualify as a god. That is not the case with the lower manitous. They are definitely created by Gitche Manitou, and they are bound to carry out his will. It is also clear that given their absence in some Algonquin tribes, and given the different mythologies that surround the manitous in various Algonquin cultures, they are later accretions subsequent to a time when a single Great Manitou was the only recognized divine spirit. Furthermore, in this case (which is not to say that the same is not true in others), only Gitche Manitou receives genuine worship, as we shall see below.

Schmidt chose to use the far Western Arapahos and the Eastern Lenape as his representatives for the Algonquins. The creation story as told by the Arapahos will sound familiar. It begins with a Man with a Great Pipe, who is the supreme being, Gitche Manitou, walking on a vast expanse of water. Contemplating the establishment of the earth, Pipe-man calls together all the waterfowl and reptiles, who exist already since they are a part of the water system. He asks them where they might find the earth. Only Turtle knows and informs everyone that the Earth lies at the bottom of the sea. Now every fowl and reptile attempts to dive down far enough in order to find the earth. Each one, and eventually each group, takes longer than the previous one, but none of them is able to complete the task. Finally, Pipe-man turns himself into Red-headed Duck, and he, along with Turtle, attains the bottom of the sea. They return with just a single muddy tuft of grass each. Pipe-man, having returned to his original form, makes clay out of the tufts, which he places upon his pipe. Then the clay turns into the entire earth.

The general outline of the story is, of course, similar to that of the Maidu Indians, and the continuation also parallels it—except that the role played by Coyote in the ongoing scenario is taken over by Bitter-man.

As before, this is hardly the case of the creator speaking the world into existence, but it is still the case that only the supreme being, disclosed in the form of Pipe-man, is able to create the earth.

By way of contrast, the Lenape creation account is straightforward. First, there was nothing except for fog occupying what we might call the space-time continuum. The Great Manitou dwelt in this amorphous medium. He was everywhere, and then, if one wanted to settle for a brief summary, he made everything. If one wished to be more specific, a common recitation gives a more specific list. It enumerates the land, the sky, the moon, and the stars. After pausing for a moment to coordinate the movement of these heavenly bodies, Gitche Manitou went on to cause a strong wind to bring islands to the surface of the water. He then created the other manitous and human beings, to whom he also gave a Great Mother. He made fishes, turtles, animals, and birds. One of the lower manitous tried his hand at creation but was only able to produce some evil beings such as mosquitoes, flies, and gnats. All (other) beings, including the manitous, were helpful and kind. They made sure the newly created men had wives. Everyone was content. Unfortunately, the harmony of the world was eventually disrupted by the appearance of an evil magician who brought strife, natural disasters, sickness, and death to all people. The recitation ends with a note to the effect that all of this happened prior to the flood, referring to this inundation as though it were an event with which everyone was familiar.

There are clearly enough differences to the biblical account that there can be no serious question of borrowing from Christians, unless one subscribes to the popular dogma that all things are the same as long as one ignores the differences. Nevertheless, it is certainly an example of creation *ex nihilo*.

The Inland Salish

Once again it is essential to make proper distinctions so as to arrive at the most original version of a culture. The Salish people are generally divided into their coastal (Pacific) tribes and their interior tribes. The coastal culture carries an obvious overlay of the Northwest Athabascan cultures, such as that of the Tlingit. The interior tribes, occupying an area from Montana to British Columbia, provide us with a better look at the *"Primitive"* (i.e., "original," not "backward") expression of Salish culture. But even here, broad regions manifest cultural cross-overs including some mixing with Shoshone culture. According to Schmidt,[36] the tribes located in the southeastern range of the Salish have retained the purest form of their original culture and religion. These include Okanagon, Pend d'Oreilles, Kallispel, Spokan, Coeur d'Alène, and the undeservedly misnamed Flatheads.[37]

The Salish culture emphasizes living in harmony with nature and the spirits that indwell other living beings. However, the stress is laid on maintaining the positive relationship, and actual animistic practices or magical rituals are minimal. As we shall see, in these tribes religious practices are directed to the creator of nature.

In the case of these people, missionary influence had indeed made it difficult to identify genuine Salish culture, as Schmidt himself

---

[36] Schmidt, *High Gods*, 33.

[37] Most of the names we use for American Indian tribes are based on what early Europeans called them, oftentimes based on the misunderstanding of a native term. The fact of the matter is that in most cases people groups do not call themselves anything except generically "people" or "real people," and much of the time they refer to anyone not associated with them with the generic term of "enemies" or something else dismissive. The idea of each tribe having a unique name is a European convention, driven by the necessity to distinguish between many distinct groups, and the popular name is often of highly dubious meaning. In the case of the Flatheads, the reason for the appellation is not only unknown but paradoxical as well. Many, if not most, Native Americans carry their infants in cradle boards onto which the forehead of the child is bound with a leather strap. After spending much of the time on this contraption for a year or more, the consequent flattening of the bones of the forehead remains as a permanent part of a person's appearance. However, the Inland Salish, including the Flatheads, do not use the cradle board.

recounts. Several Iroquois (the tribe was not specified) had converted to Catholic Christianity and subsequently married Salish people. They were wishing the other Salish would also become Christians; and on their recommendation, the Salish sent a delegation of the tribe's people all the way from Montana to St. Louis to invite Jesuit missionaries to come to them. They expected them to come and teach them more about the one God and how to worship him, which the Jesuits did. However, they also took on an authoritarian position and tied their religious message to Europeanizing the culture of these tribes and suppressing all of their heritage. What was reported to Schmidt as a brilliant success was nothing of the kind to the Salish, who eventually wound up on a reservation, physically removed from most of the land of their culture as well.

Thus, here was a culture with monotheistic beliefs and practices in which heavy Christian influences were evident. If ever there was a case that appeared to support the borrowing hypothesis, this was it. However, precisely due to the clear knowledge that there was strong orthodox Christian teaching, the situation was not hopeless for an anthropologist.[38] Think about three different situations: (1) a group that shows clear monotheism as a part of its total culture prior to significant European missionary contact, (2) a monotheistic tribe that has existed for some time in the shadow of a Christianized culture, though without documented missionary efforts, and (3) a tribe for which we have highly probable knowledge that it had been monotheistic and then received Christian teachings, knowledge of the content of that teaching, and knowledge that there were conversions. For the first group, rather than positing unknown missionary teachings that would not fit into Christianity or assuming mental waves dispersed over thousands of miles and induced people to tape a pointless form of monotheism to their culture, the most

---

[38] A thorough analysis that attempted to isolate what was originally a part of Salish culture was undertaken by James A. Teit, *A Mythology of the Thompson River Indians* (New York: Leiden, 1913). Schmidt relies heavily on Teit in *High Gods*, 123–28.

plausible inference is that the monotheism was indigenous. The second case would be the most ambiguous, and it would be difficult to know which aspects of the culture came from outside influence and which ones were truly indigenous. However, the situation in the third case, where it is clear which cultural forms came from outside and where we have enough information about roughly similar cultures that were not subjected to the same Christian influence, it is possible to isolate with high probability what was indigenous and what was imported. Anything that bears the clear stamp of Jesuit teaching we can ascribe to missionary influence. Anything that looks like it could be a superficial adaptation of Jesuit teaching, we must treat with great care and are probably best off leaving to the side as undecided. However, any items that are inconsistent with what the Jesuits likely would have taught and bear the stamp of the surrounding culture are with high probability ("certainty" in early twentieth-century parlance) of native origin. Such sifting has been applied to the Salish, and the result has been that one can piece together a good number of their previous beliefs and practices, including which of their current beliefs and practices were most likely not imported.

We already mentioned that the Salish emphasized a close relationship to the spirits of nature. They respect them (I wonder whether even "venerate" is putting matters too strongly), and they communicate with them as Creature to creature. But there seems to be no question that the creator, *Amotken* by name, stands behind the entire world, both spiritual and physical, and directs it.

We do not have a coherent creation myth for the Salish, but the fact that Amotken created everything is included in all the various fragments that have been put together. Tellingly, the native American nature of the various partial accounts available to us is brought out by the fact that such stories as we do have usually begin with a desert of water and Amotken bringing the earth up out from this water.

Schmidt draws the following picture of Amotken:

He has always been and always will be. He is everywhere solitary and alone, without wife or children. He is of never-changing kindness, making all that men need grow for them; he helps in sickness and provides for making life easy. . . . His power is the highest, and there is no other being whose power could be even remotely compared with his. On him depends the order and prosperity of the world. He is the source of life everywhere on earth. The North-East group says frankly: "he has unlimited power."[39]

Let me emphasize again that these cultures not only recognize a supreme being in the background but that in their original form an active cultus (all cultural forms surrounding his recognition and worship) of the supreme being is also included in these cultures. This phenomenon, coupled with a lesser development of material culture, sets apart the people of Schmidt's *Primitive* culture circle wherever they appear, whereas in the *Primary* cultures, even if there is a strong memory of God, there is usually little interaction with him. Thus, we should now look at the practices of these three American Indian tribes as they are directed to the supreme being.

Worship

Schmidt makes the argument that the truly monotheistic nature of these religions is brought out not just by their creation stories and other mythologies but by the worship practices of these people. The point is similar to the one Lang made against Hartland but stands on much easier ground in the case of these groups. In other words, there is no embarrassing mythology to sweep away; the mythology of a good creator god with his standards of righteousness and the worship practices are consistent with each other. Once again we will look at the three groups and point out some of their main practices that illustrate this fact.

---

[39] Schmidt, *High Gods*, 114.

North-Central California

In the case of the Yuki and the Maidu, as was the case with the
Australian tribes, the clearest place to find the focus on one and only
one God is in the initiation ceremonies.[40] Now, when we refer to
initiation ceremonies, most likely our minds will start turning in the
direction of tests of strength, endurance, pain, and physical immola-
tion. Whether what the North-Central Californian tribes practiced is
better or worse than the stereotypical actions, I will leave up to the
reader to decide. In their case, the initiation ordeal consisted of a class
in tribal catechism that lasted an entire winter season. With certain
variations the young people on the verge of becoming adult members
of the tribe were instructed day after day by their chief in knowledge about their god, how to relate to him, and the ethical require-
ments that originated with him. For the first month or so, they were
expected to sit still without moving a muscle while the chief spoke
to them. The ideal that was conveyed in the instruction was that all
people should live their entire lives in the light of god's presence.

There are some records of prayers directed to the supreme being.[41]
Another characteristic mark for the worship of the supreme being in
cultures such as these is the practice of making symbolic offerings.
At the risk of creating some temporary confusion, I shall add that the
emphasis in this observation is that these offerings were not sacrifices.

Let me explain this somewhat artificial but helpful terminologi-
cal distinction, which applies to all of the cultures under consideration. Animistic cultures typically make abundant sacrifices to the
spirits; frequently, they speak of "the spirits being fed." If I may take
an example from a highly developed culture, it is an important part
of Chinese religion to present food to the ancestor spirits. The spirits, if they are so inclined, will consume the "essence" of this food
and leave behind its material remnant, which can then be eaten by
human beings. Sacrifices, in this sense, are ways of negotiating with

---

[40] Ibid., 42–59.
[41] Ibid., 45.

the gods and spirits. The spiritual beings profit from what is being given them, and the human being hopes that his sacrifices will generate particular help from the spirits or gods. This attitude underlies much of the motivation in animism.

For our purposes in this context, we will make this distinction in order to bring out two different attitudes. We will speak of "symbolic offerings" when they are essentially gestures acknowledging gratitude toward God and all that he has provided as Creator. They are neither feedings nor objects given to God as a part of a spiritual bargain. Typical for cultures on the *Primitive* level, under the heading of "symbolic offerings," are what Schmidt calls "primitial" offerings. These are offerings of firstfruits. A hunter, having slain an animal, may take a small part of it and lay it to the side of the fire on which he is cooking the animal, while expressing his thanks to the Creator for having provided this source of food. Similarly, on the plant side of the menu, after a large amount of edible vegetation has accumulated, there may be a ceremony of thanks in which a small, symbolic portion is devoted to God, strictly as a way of acknowledging that all the people have really belongs to God and that they are grateful to him for allowing them to share some of it. There is no question here of feeding God or of winning his favor. Presumably, if that were the motivation for the people to carry out such a rite, they would increase his portion and give him food at other times than these special occasions, which is precisely what happens when monotheism is replaced by animism and polytheism. But in the case of the *Primary* cultures, these offerings are merely expressions of gratitude. As we said, ultimately everything belongs to the Creator already anyway, and human beings cannot do anything for him. Still, they can demonstrate their gratitude to him with these gestures.

The Algonquins

In the case of the Algonquin tribes, the fact of regular prayer to and worship of Gitche Manitou is beyond doubt. From the abundance of examples, let me choose one prayer as a good illustration. This one comes from John Tanner.[42] He reported on being a part of a dangerous sea voyage with the Ottawa Indians who had raised him.

> We were passed on . . . into the sea about 200 yards, when all the boats halted together, and the chief with very loud voice addressed a prayer to the Great Spirit, in which he implored him to conduct us safely through the sea. He said, "Thou hast made the sea, and thou hast made us thy children. Thou canst also arrange that the sea remains smooth, whilst we pass on in safety." In this manner he continued to pray for five or [ten] min. Then he threw into the sea a small handful of tobacco, and all the canoes followed him. They then all continued their voyage and the old chief began a song of a religious nature.[43]

The Algonquins also practiced an offering of firstfruits. In acknowledgment of Gitche Manitou as the provider of all food, a number of tribes maintained the practice that no food may be wasted. The implication was that if someone were to kill an animal accidentally, he would have to eat it.

The West Algonquins, such as the Arapaho and the Cheyenne, practiced the Sun Dance,[44] but we need to sort through some of the dances that were similar in either name or form before this statement becomes meaningful. The most famous versions of the Sun Dance are those practiced by the Lakota tribes (Oglala, Teton, etc.), who are members of the larger Siouan family of tribes that include the Dakota as well as the Mandan. As a matter of fact, the Sun Dance is probably a late adoption for the Lakota. They probably combined elements from two major sources. The famous, tortuous elements

---

[42] Ibid., 82–83. Tanner was the son of European-originated parents. He had been captured by the Ottawa as a child and grew up with them and lived with them for several decades.

[43] Ibid.

[44] G. A. Dorsey, "The Arapahoan Sun Dance," *Field Columbian Museum Publications, Anthropological Series* 4 (1903): 39. Dorsey's observations are the basis for Schmidt in his description of the creation myth and, later on, of the description of the Sun Dance, which narrates it.

probably come from the Mandan, while much of the rest of its ritual content is based on Algonquin practice. The Mandan, who had been settled in the Great Plains for quite a while, observed the *Okipa* ceremony.[45] Okipa refers to a collection ("bundle") of items intended to ensure agricultural fertility and success in bison hunting. Over four days various members of the village would act out Mandan mythology, while the central participants, the dancers, would spend the last three days of the occasion undergoing grueling torture. They would be raised to the top of the ceremonial lodge by means of leather straps that were attached to their bodies with wooden skewers. While they were gyrating from the ceiling, the Buffalo Bulls, a warrior society, performed a dance underneath. For the dancers the day would end once they had passed into unconsciousness.

When the Lakota Indians came to the Plains, they started to dominate the Mandan and other settled groups, such as the Omaha, but they adopted the tortuous elements of the Mandan dance. They added it to the last day of a lengthy ceremony, much of which they had apparently picked up from the Algonquin Arapaho and Cheyenne. However, whereas for these Algonquin tribes, whose ultimate target of worship was the Great Spirit, the Lakota directed their activity to the sun, their supreme deity, hence the name "Sun Dance." Thus, the great dance ceremonies of the Lakota and the Arapaho are similar; but for the Siouan group, torture became an essential part of it, whereas for the Algonquins it was unthinkable.

Schmidt suggests that the Arapaho dance ceremony was essentially a dramatization of the mostly spoken rite observed by the Lenape.[46] The Lenape, of the eastern Algonquin branch, had a twelve-day harvest festival that consisted for the most part of the local bands getting together for lengthy evenings of listening to recitations of the traditions, individuals sharing their own spiritual experiences, and prayers. The emphasis was entirely on Gitche Manitou.

---

[45] Spencer, Jennings, et al., *Native Americans*, 326–28.
[46] Schmidt, *High Gods*, 102. For a lengthier description of the Lenape ceremony, see ibid., 94–102.

In the dramatized Arapaho version, the first four of eight days are given over to setting up the ceremonial ground. A tall, straight cottonwood tree is chopped down (usually by women) and transported to the ritual area. A new large ritual lodge is built around it, and various representations connected to the creation myth are added. Certain people assume the role of the creator and the first pair of human beings. The main participants, the dancers, include the man who is sponsoring the event for that year and anywhere from ten to thirty others who have taken a vow. The regular part of the celebration starts on the fifth day when the participants enter the lodge bearing tufts of grass, reminiscent of those brought up from the sea by Turtle and Pipe-man in his guise as Red-headed Duck. Over the next three days the creation story and other parts of the mythology are acted out, while the participants spend their time in the lodge dancing themselves to exhaustion with a dance that consists for the most part of continuous swaying back and forth—perhaps representing the initial state of chaos. They always face the center pole that represents Pipe-man, who, in turn, stands for Gitche Manitou. The eighth day is a day of feasting, celebrating the renewed balance of relationships between humans, the manitous, and the Great Manitou.

The Inland Salish

Making firstfruit offerings is also a part of the inland Salish worship, but they do not include meat obtained by hunting. Again, it is not easy to cull out the premissionary religion from the records, but neither is it impossible. What emerges is a religious culture cultivating the practice of prayer to Amotken, both personal and public. There were standard prayers and personal prayers, as well as prayer gestures, whose nature and meaning can be found in other cultures far removed but definitely not taught by the Jesuit missionaries. They included such postures as the attitude of supplication and reaching for the power of god to come into their lives. Prayers among the Salish were times of whole-person involvement, not just a recitation of words. They would be accompanied by the aforementioned gestures or positions and deep expressions of emotion.

A widespread religious element among the Salish is the prayer dance, which takes one day. Schmidt describes it as it was practiced among the Thompson River people.[47] The day's main activities consisted of four dances in the morning, a banquet, four dances in the afternoon, another feast, and four more dances in the evening. The last dance ended the festival, except for men of a certain age or status, who convened for a pipe-smoking ceremony in honor of Amotken.

The dance included every member of the community, and any taboos that might otherwise have interfered with someone's participation were disregarded. The people arranged themselves in three concentric circles: the married men and women with their children on the outside, next the unmarried women, and the unmarried men on the inside. The main chief positioned himself at the western side; his role was to recite prayers to Amotken and intone songs as they came to him by inspiration. Another chief on the east side had the job to make sure order was maintained. There were no musical instruments, and the people danced by moving along a semicircle and then reversing their direction to their original place, where they would reverse again, and so forth. During the dance they would, as alluded to above, get highly emotional; and many people would engage in the various prayer gestures as well. Most everyone wore a head scarf with long ends hanging down or fluttering in the air, which came in handy for two practical reasons.

I am assuming that the first use of the head scarf was intended simply to keep the geometry of the dance together since three concentric circles may not be easy to maintain. At some points the dancers in the outside circle (married folks) and those of the inside circle (unmarried men) would hold on to the ends of the scarves of the unmarried women in the circle in between for a time.

---

[47] This account is, again, based on Teit, *A Mythology of the Thompson River Indians*, recounted in Schmidt, *High Gods*, 118–21.

But, more importantly, the bandannas of the bachelors would become extremely important a while later, still in the course of the four morning dances. There came a moment when the chief would stop all of his chanting and call out that the time was now for any young people who desired to do so to touch each other. Stated in this manner, this announcement sounds like an invitation to lewdness, but it was anything but that. It was directed at those young men and women who had their heart set on marrying each other. One presumes, though one cannot verify, that in most cases, if not all, there was a previous understanding. People of either sex were allowed to initiate the contact during this intermission. A woman could walk up to a man, grasp the ends of his headscarf and thereby signal that she wanted to marry him. A man could walk up to a woman and touch her lightly on the breast to declare his matrimonial intentions. These minimal gestures, performed publicly before the community and in the context of a worship ritual, were sufficient for the two young people to be considered married from that point on. No further elaborate ritual was required, presumably because anything additional could not really add anything significant to this commitment in the sight of the entire community and God. The morning dance would resume; and the noon banquet, which was also accompanied by prayers, served as a wedding feast as well as an expression of the community united in faith. I need to add here that as is typical of the *Primitive* culture circles, lifelong monogamy was the rule, and adultery was virtually unthinkable.

Summary

We have reviewed the three representative cultures Schmidt used in his lectures on the supreme being in America. I chose to use them because on the whole readers of this book will be more likely to have some basic background about these groups than about the people, such as the pygmies of Africa, who, in Schmidt's view are even closer to resembling what may have been humanity's primordial religion.

The point was to illustrate to what conclusions Schmidt's methods led him.

Still, we must not omit one other aspect of this original monotheism. Schmidt was convinced that the basic faith of the people in God the Creator also testifies to the fact that there was a revelation behind their conviction.

Revelation

I suspect that most people who adhere to a monotheistic religion also believe in a divine revelation. In fact, many of them may believe in the one and only God because that fact has been revealed in the Bible, the Qur'an, or other sources of revelation. Now we have seen that the *Primitive* people on their most basic level also believe in one god. Did they also receive divine revelation? Lang said no, but Schmidt said yes—a distinction well worth remembering in light of future criticisms.

Schmidt regarded all of Genesis to be historical and authoritative, though he was clearly not a "young-earth creationist." Roman Catholic theologians at the time were dealing with different problems from their Protestant counterparts concerning biblical interpretation. Schmidt also accepted his own adaptation of human evolution as presented by paleontology. He interpreted it in terms of a direct special creation by God of each new species of hominids at certain intervals, culminating in the divine creation of *Homo sapiens*.[48] On that basis he could not accept that Neanderthal man would have been the ancestor of *Homo sapiens*, but Schmidt did consider him to be human (which I do not).

This halfway acceptance of evolution (though not evolutionism) needlessly left Schmidt with a number of issues he could not solve satisfactorily. For one, there was the question of which of the antecedents of *Homo sapiens* would have been the first to have had the

---

[48] Wilhelm Schmidt, *Primitive Revelation*, trans. Joseph J. Baierl (St. Louis, MO: Herder Book, 1939), 86–95.

conceptual capacity to receive a divine revelation, a question paleontology was attempting to solve by analysis of the cranial structures
of prehistoric remains. Schmidt thought the bones discovered at
Piltdown in England provided a puzzling but potentially helpful,
solution.[49] It did not work out that way.

When it came right down to it, Genesis remained authoritative
for Schmidt and took precedence over paleontological discoveries.
Concerning biblical interpretation, he felt that the biggest question
that needed to be addressed was whether Genesis 1 was a historical
account or merely a personal confession of the writer to his faith in
God as Creator. He cut through that issue quickly:

> Presently it will appear that the second chapter of Genesis
> begins, and continues uninterruptedly thereafter, a historical
> presentation of the primitive period of mankind based on
> original sources. Would it not be strange, then, were the first
> chapter alone to lack historical and documentary authority?
> Furthermore, the necessary connection between the first and
> the second narrative is so evident as to make [the position that
> considers Gen. 1 to be unhistorical] less tenable.[50]

Of course, Schmidt did not appeal to revelation as a source of
data for his scholarly work because doing so would have constituted
circular reasoning since acceptance of the revelation of God presupposes the existence of God. The question was whether the first
humans relied on their reason alone to infer that there was a God
or there was a divine revelation as well. Schmidt concluded that the
people must have received divine revelation in addition to whatever
rational insights they would have been able to come up with concerning the need for a Creator.

Schmidt did not believe the exact mode of this early revelation
was known, but *speaking as a theologian*, he thought its contents would
include the following, based on the first three chapters of Genesis:

---

[49] Ibid., 66–70.
[50] Ibid., 10.

God is the almighty Lord and Creator of all things, and consequently of man's singular origin. He is above all change and decay. His is the knowledge of good and evil; changeless and unshakable His holiness. He makes, judges, and avenges the laws of the moral order.

A man shall leave father and mother, and take to himself a wife for companion, one essentially like to himself and destined to the same spiritual fellowship.

By this marital union God chose to insure the propagation of the race; and through the first couple the race received from its Maker the duty and right to fill and rule the earth with all thereon.[51]

Schmidt goes on to stress that God is the human being's supernatural end. In other words, being in fellowship with God is the highest good for a human being. However, Schmidt adds that after the fall "now man must attain that end through God Himself, the Redeemer."[52]

When speaking as an ethnologist, the qualities stated above (e.g., monotheism, morality, and monogamy) are precisely what Schmidt found within the *Primitive* cultures. Now he did not close the door on humans being able to derive some of these ideas by means of their own intelligence and awareness of the world around them. Schmidt believed they were informed by general revelation, as it is described in the book of Romans, "His invisible attributes, that is, His eternal power and divine nature, have been clearly seen since the creation of the world" (Rom 1:20 HCSB). However, Schmidt did not think one could do justice to the similarity and universality of the monotheism of the least developed people groups by positing nothing more than ancient people brooding over the mystery of *Dasein.* Please allow me to quote a somewhat lengthier passage than is customary. Schmidt does not lose his objectivity here, but he states his point with an almost poetic elegance. Like a good poem, the passage can only have its full impact when read in its entirety.

---

[51] Ibid., 38–39.
[52] Ibid., 39.

Something of such intense force must have come upon
these most ancient human beings in an encounter that became
an all-encompassing destabilizing experience, penetrating
their entire being to its innermost core, so that immediately,
due to its overpowering might, it gave rise to the unity and
comprehensiveness that we observe in these, the oldest of religions.

This "something" could not have been merely a subjective
process inside of the human being himself; for then it could not
have held either the power or the complete blueprint of these,
the oldest of religions. There would have been no way in which
the clarity and solidity of their outlook of faith, as well as the
cultural forms associated with it, could have been implemented.
Neither could it have been a purely material thing or event, no
matter how unusual it may have appeared. For then it would
have become increasingly inexplicable how mere material stuff
could act on the combined personhood of these ancient people
with the power, firmness, and clarity that we admire in these, the
oldest of religions.

No, it must have been a powerful, mighty person, who
stepped toward them, and who was able to chain their intellects
with illuminating truths, to bind their wills with high and noble
precepts, and to win their hearts with enticing beauty and
goodness. And again, this person could not have been an inner
chimera or phantasm of mere human origin because such an
entity could not even have come close to possessing sufficient
actual power to cause the effects that we observe in these, the
oldest of religions. Instead, it must have been a person who came
to them as a genuine reality from somewhere outside of them,
and it is precisely the power of this reality that convinced them
and conquered them.[53]

Descriptions consistent with the supposition of a revelation are
also unanimously supported by the people themselves. The most
common statement falls along the line that the great ancestor of the

---

[53] Wilhelm Schmidt, *Der Ursprung der Gottesidee*, vol. 6 (Münster: Aschendorff,
1935), 492.

clan learned the truths about God from God and that he taught them as a continuing legacy to his descendants. There is a complete absence of any information that would point to humans as the originators of these beliefs. To quote Schmidt once more:

> The bottom line is that the reports we have from the adherents of the oldest religions themselves are not only merely disinclined towards the supposition that the religions were created by seeking and searching human beings; rather, worse yet, they do not even mention it with a single word. All their affirmative responses are directed to the side of divine revelation: It is God Himself Who taught humans what to believe about Him, how to venerate Him, and how they should obey the expression of His will.[54]

Let me stress this point again because it is so easily distorted: Schmidt does not base his ethnological conclusions on divine revelation. Instead, his ethnological conclusions entailed that the monotheism of the *Primitive* tribes must have been due, at least in part, to the fact that God revealed himself to them.

---

[54] Ibid., 480.

CHAPTER 8

Wilhelm Schmidt: Reactions and Critiques

In the German version of the first volume of *Der Ursprung der Gottesidee*,[1] published two years after it had been in print in French,[2] Wilhelm Schmidt lamented the lack of thorough factual critiques from which he could learn. There were a number of congratulatory reviews (including one from Andrew Lang[3]), a few dismissive ones deriding Schmidt's work on the basis of his being a Catholic priest, but only a few substantive ones.

When one looks over how Schmidt's work is regarded in general, it becomes clear that many criticisms are essentially maneuvers to set him aside, a fact that is corroborated by the constant misrepresentations of crucial aspects of his positions. There could be a number of

---

[1] Wilhelm Schmidt, *Der Ursprung der Gottesidee*, vol. 1 (Münster: Aschendorff, 1912), v. Unless I specify otherwise, my references will be to this edition.

[2] P. Guillaume Schmidt, *L'Origine de l'Idée de Dieu: Étude Historico-Critique et Positive*, 1ére Partie (Paris: Librairie Alphonse Picard & Fils, 1910).

[3] Andrew Lang, "Review of *L'Origine de l'Idée de Dieu*" in *Folk-Lore* 21 (1910): 516–23. Lang was by no means entirely uncritical of Schmidt, pointing out for example that on a footnote on p. 131 of *L'Origine*, he attributed a false opinion to him. Schmidt deleted that note (and rightly so) from the German version.

reasons for this phenomenon. For example, Mircea Eliade at least partially blames the fact that in its final form *Der Ursprung der Gottesidee* ran to 11,000 pages in German. He adds:

> No wonder few historians of religions read all of this enormous treatise! Despite its polemical excesses (chiefly in the first volume) and apologetic tendencies, *Ursprung der Gottesidee* is a great work. Whatever one may think of Schmidt's theories on the origin and growth of religion, one must admire his stupendous learning and industry. Wilhelm Schmidt was certainly one of the greatest linguists and ethnologists of this century.[4]

On the whole these are kind words from Eliade in the light of some things he says later in the same book. However, Eliade may also be too indulgent with his colleagues here. The habit of writing reviews that dismiss Schmidt out of hand for some irrelevant reason goes back to a long time before there were twelve volumes of *Der Ursprung*. We need to recall that the first version of the first volume had run in French in the journal *Anthropos* as a series of articles from 1908 through 1910. Subsequently, it was issued as a stand-alone book (still in French) in 1910. This original edition ran to a mere 297 pages of text (316 counting the four helpful indices). When Schmidt lamented the absence of good reviews, let alone the fact that there were a number of ones that gratuitously panned his book, he was referring to this short edition in French, and this statement occurs in the preface to the still relatively short German edition of 1912. Numbers of pages had nothing to do with it.

These people who wrote without having read were the primary target of Schmidt's rhetoric, as they should have been. The greatest part of the early editions of *Der Ursprung*, in French and in German, was devoted to Andrew Lang, both for his own theories and as a springboard for Schmidt's elaborations. Schmidt also criticized the views of those who were making groundless assertions with

---

[4] Mircea Eliade, *The Quest: History and Meaning in Religion* (Chicago: Chicago University Press, 1969), 23–24.

regard to Lang, monotheism, and himself or distorting the facts. Whether one wishes to call doing so "rhetorical" or not, undertaking such critiques is what scholars (including Eliade) do. Considering the discussions we have been following, involving Lang, Müller, Hartmann, Tylor, Howitt, etc., there can be no question of rhetorical excesses in Schmidt's lament (just recall Howitt's unintelligible explosion, as mentioned in chap. 5). It would seem that only a lack of perspective—focusing on Schmidt's writings without looking at the entire discussion—would lead one to allege excesses in his writing style.

As we have seen, the world of ethnology had been filled with quite a bit of fact-twisting and a priori denunciation. Should one give E. B. Tylor a free pass on his dubious about-face concerning the high gods in America? Should one let Howitt get away with basing his conclusions not on his observations but on the unsupported imagination of L. H. Morgan?[5] Schmidt did not think so, and, as we mentioned at the outset, he was hoping other scholars would interact with his material rather than think up quick and clever ad hominem putdowns. Furthermore, I might just add the reminder that it is also a part of a scholar's work to read big books.

Thus, it appears to me that insofar as scholars have not studied Schmidt, such a possible deficit has little to do with the fact that his major tome ran to 11,000 pages. Even when the second German edition of the first volume of *Der Ursprung* came out in 1926, it "only" ran to 800 pages, which is certainly no longer a quick read but still less than the combined two volumes of Tylor's *Primitive Culture*, which people all over the world have read and admired.[6]

---

[5] Bernhard J. Stern, ed., "Selections from the Letters of Lorimer Fison and A. W. Howitt to Lewis Henry Morgan," *American Anthropologist* 32 (1930): 257–79. This article leaves no doubt that Fison and Howard were seeking to establish Morgan's theories, thus putting the conclusion ahead of the observation.

[6] I believe the overall dialogue on Schmidt, insofar as anyone wishes to engage in any, would be greatly improved if scholars who express opinions on him would first have read, say, at least a cumulative 500 pages or so of his writings, which is not

There is no question in my mind that one of the obvious reasons for the rejection of Schmidt is that what he found at the origin of human culture (as close as one can come to it) was marital faithfulness in monogamy, straightforward honesty, altruistic sharing while respecting another person's property, and a general aversion to shedding human blood unnecessarily.[7] And, of course, at root there was the idea of submission to the will of the one God. This is clearly an ad hominem observation, but, given the intent of many prominent anthropologists since the 1930s to promote cultural relativism, which many of them used to justify a moral relativism and demonstrate it in their own lives, it is difficult to imagine many of them giving a fair hearing to a work that leads to such conclusions.

Furthermore, one could conceivably even go out on a limb and argue that simply evading Schmidt's writings is to concede that he had won his case. At first glance, saying so seems to be merely an argument based on equal parts of arrogance and silence. However, in light of the fact that anthropological scholarship has pretty much delegitimized raising the question of origins altogether, that suspicion might not just be partisan rhetoric.

Pettazzoni and Monotheism

By the time we get into the 1920s, the attempts at large, worldwide syntheses of human culture begin to fade out. Curiously, J. G. Frazer's *Golden Bough*, despite its thoroughly fictional nature, continued to arouse fascination among readers a hundred years ago, and it still does so today. Nevertheless, with a few exceptions, ethnologists started to back off from the search for an origin of religion, or, for that matter, other theories that attempted to treat religions beyond certain

---

very much, but would definitely inject more understanding into the discussion. Some people have done so and more, of course.

[7] See Wilhelm Schmidt, *Primitive Revelation*, trans. Joseph J. Baierl (St. Louis, MO: Herder, 1939), 109–24.

temporal or geographical boundaries. We will look at some of the exceptions in the next chapter.

However, one person, who called himself a "historian of religion" rather than an "ethnologist," attempted to erect a general system for the sake of understanding religion. This was Raffaele Pettazzoni of the University of Rome.[8] Judging from his writings, he always saw himself in direct competition with Schmidt, and—in contrast to most of Schmidt's other critics—to the best of my knowledge never said a single positive word about Schmidt's scholarly achievements, not even in the customary manner of insincere flattery. Pettazzoni's argument is straightforward and easy to understand and thus lends itself to being used as a quick critique of Schmidt. It is also remarkably beside the point and contrived.

An Arbitrary Definition

If consistency is the hobgoblin of bureaucrats, then surely definitions are the hobgoblins of scholars caught in a pickle. To be sure, one needs to delineate the meanings of words to prevent misunderstanding, and sometimes doing so means providing a working definition. Also, there are times when the process of trying to establish the definition of a concept is a good teaching device. However, much of the time, occupying oneself with definitions turns into an easy way to focus on something other than the subject matter or to rework the meaning of a word so as to get out of a difficulty.

In an argument he repeated multiple times, Pettazzoni focused on the issue of original monotheism by raising questions on the definition of *monotheism*. In the previous chapter I did qualify our basic conception of monotheism, but I doubt any reader—at least those not previously acquainted with Pettazzoni's thought—would have had a problem with the basic idea that monotheism is a form of

---

[8] Raffaele Pettazzoni, "The Formation of Monotheism," in *Essays on the History of Religions*, trans. H. J. Rose (Leiden: Brill, 1954), 1–10.

religion that recognizes and worships only one God. But Pettazzoni stated there was an essential element to monotheism we could only find by focusing on the great historical monotheistic religions of the world: Judaism, Christianity, Islam, and early Zoroastrianism. Then we would also be able to come up with a more accurate, universal definition of *monotheism*. He explains, "The great monotheistic religions, those whose monotheism is past all doubt, which have declared themselves monotheistic from their very birth, and have always represented themselves as that and nothing else, are surely those to which we must have recourse first of all in any enquiry concerning monotheism and its formation."[9]

What Pettazzoni concluded from this analysis of these later, highly developed religions was that true monotheism must be defined as *a reaction against an established polytheism*. In all of these cases, which he believed provided the standard exemplification of the word *monotheism*, what he found was that a particular culture had been practicing a polytheistic religion. At some point a prophet arose (e.g., Moses, Jesus [or Paul; we are given an option], Muhammad, or Zoroaster), who challenged the establishment and taught that in contrast to the polytheism currently being practiced, there was only one God. This pattern, and this pattern alone, claimed Pettazzoni, captures the authentic meaning of *monotheism*. In order to have true monotheism, he declared unreservedly, there must first of all have been polytheism, not in the sense of monotheism evolving out of polytheism, as Tylor contended, but in the opposite sense of monotheism being a reaction *against* polytheism. "This, then, is the outcome of the study of the monotheistic religions. We arrive at an idea of what monotheism really is, an idea which is not theological nor speculative, but purely historical, following the principle according to which the true nature of a historical fact is brought out by its formation and its development (*verum ipsum factum*)."[10]

---

[9] Ibid., 5.
[10] Ibid., 9.

Even if Pettazzoni had been correct, the principle he invoked was clearly out of place. The issue here was not some factual truth, as he made it sound, but the application of terminology to historical events, which cannot be decided by singling out certain events as paradigmatic and saying that only they are the true referents for the term in question.

Pettazzoni's beginning point already showed that he was heading in the wrong direction. He made it sound as though the point of elaborating on the discovery of primitive original monotheism was intended to provide the best understanding of monotheism in general, and he asked:

> From an objective point of view, what justifies this preference for the religions of the uncivilized in the monotheistic controversy? Are they really the best qualified to impose themselves upon the study of such a religious phenomenon as monotheism, which for its part has so much greater importance in the history of religion generally? Why then should we not devote ourselves, with as good grounds, to the polytheistic religions of the various civilized nations of antiquity?[11]

Why not, indeed? It may certainly be true that we can learn more about the nature of monotheism by studying these four religions and their scriptures than by analyzing the beliefs of preliterate people. But that was not the point of either Schmidt's or Lang's work. They were not intending to contribute to the "monotheistic controversy," whatever Pettazzoni may have meant by that term. Their purpose was not to come up with the optimal understanding of monotheism but to account for the fact that among certain cultures people worshipped a single god.

Having created this novel definition of *monotheism*, Pettazzoni then applied it to the monotheism of preliterate cultures:

---

[11] Ibid., 10.

[F]rom the historical point of view I cannot attach myself to
the theory of "primitive monotheism." If we keep, as I do and
as one must do, the name of monotheism for the negation of
polytheism, as it appears in the great monotheistic religions of
history, the result is that monotheism presupposes polytheism
by the very fact of denying it. In so far as it is a negation of
polytheism, monotheism cannot be the first form of religion, as
the theory of "primitive monotheism" supposes.[12]

Pettazzoni was absolutely right given the rules he had just established. If the only acceptable definition of *monotheism* were "the negation of polytheism," one could certainly not apply that term to the
belief in a supreme being among indigenous cultures. But what an
amazing feat of word magic he was accomplishing here! Monotheism
logically implies the denial of polytheism, and historically there were
occasions when monotheism came up as a result of a reform against
an established polytheism. However, although it may be correct to
say that Moses was a "reformer," it is not clear against which established polytheism he was supposedly directing himself. The Egyptian
pantheon comes to mind, but he did not reform Egyptian religion.
The Hebrews were practicing various religions while in slavery in
Egypt, but to say that there was an established polytheism among
them is going too far. Nor does it really make sense to say that Christianity, whether one designates Jesus or Paul as the founder, was a
reform or rebellion against Greek polytheism. The early Christians
came out of monotheistic Judaism, and Christianity, though receiving
converts out of Greek religion, did not change it.

To derive a binding definition for the term from the historical
occasions selected by Pettazzoni is pure caprice. Schmidt, dealing
with this definition, which is, after all a matter of language, was sufficiently versed in Italian to read and quote Pettazzoni's works in that
language. He had stayed in Italy for a time while establishing the Vatican's ethnological museum. In a tongue-in-cheek remark expressing

---

[12] Ibid., 9.

his incredulity, he asked whether this definition was maybe a peculiarity of the Italian language with which he was not familiar. In any event, he was sure the word did not carry that baggage in English, French, or German. Further, even if Pettazzoni were correct in stating that his was a valid definition of *monotheism*, which is doubtful, the one currently used is at a minimum of equal validity.[13]

Paul Radin and Bogus Precision

In North America anthropology developed on more individualistic terms as an academic discipline than in Europe; consequently, it did not start out under the absolute dictates of E. B. Tylor and the *evolutionist* school. Following Schmidt, let us distinguish between the theory of evolution, which was supposed to be a scientific conclusion, and the philosophy of *evolutionism* with its a priori framework of an automatic series of developments only waiting for details to be plugged in from location to location. American ethnology did not start out on a basis of Tylorian evolutionism, and it has self-consciously and publicly avoided a direct tie-in with a theory of the evolution of religion. The corollary question comes up as to whether anthropologists, despite the outward denials of the theory, are nevertheless actually adopting an evolutionist view when they analyze specific cultures and religions. We will need to come back to that question in the last chapter.

There can be no doubt that American anthropology, under the leadership of Franz Boas (1858–1942), who is sometimes called the "Father of American Anthropology," has never been fond of global schemes. It has traditionally focused more on solid descriptions of particular cultures (ethnography) than on advancing connective schemes among them (ethnology). Let us sum up this point by saying that American anthropologists on the whole shied away from global pronouncements.

---

[13] Wilhelm Schmidt, *Der Urspung der Gottesidee*, vol. 6 (Münster: Aschendoff, 1935), xxi.

One American ethnologist who took this matter to the extreme was Paul Radin, who spent most of his professional life studying and writing about the Winnebago tribe.[14] In terms of theory and methodology, he placed great emphasis on the idea that an anthropologist should focus primarily on writing monographs based on years of observation of a particular culture. The first part of such a monograph should consist entirely of data collected by the field worker in direct collaboration with local individuals. Furthermore, the investigator must know the language of the people whom he is studying. Then the second part of the monograph should be a thorough analysis of the people and their culture, which does not leave out any important factors. The report should limit itself to the group being studied, and theories should not go any further than the interaction between the people and their culture. History plays a part only if it is derived from immediate knowledge and if we know that it has affected the tribe's culture in specific ways. Thus, anything like the culture-historical method, which of necessity has to be global in its approach and reach back into prehistory, was not legitimate for Radin. Most American anthropologists agreed that there never could be sufficient data to construct a worldwide pattern, but Radin did not even think that a limited pattern should be established.[15]

Radin criticized the culture-historical method by using Graebner as its representative, which is certainly appropriate since he was the one who first assembled in writing the methodology of the culture-historical school. He literally wrote the book on it.[16] However, Radin

---

[14] Among Paul Radin's works, the one to which we will refer the most here is *The Method and Theory of Ethnology* (New York: Basic Books, 1933). Other noteworthy writings of his include: *Monotheism Among Primitive Peoples* (London: G. Allen & Unwin, 1924), which became incorporated into *Primitive Man as Philosopher* (New York: Appleton, 1927); *The Road of Life and Death: A Ritual Drama of the American Indians* (Princeton, NJ: Princeton University Press, 1973); *The Trickster: A Study in American Indian Mythology* (New York: Greenwood Press, 1956).

[15] Radin, *Method and Theory*, 87–129.

[16] Fritz Graebner, *Methode der Ethnologie* (Heidelberg: Carl Winter's Universitätsbuchhandlung, 1911; repr., University of Michigan).

had obviously never read Graebner's book; he never referred to it directly, and he did not cite it anywhere either. Evidently the only source he used to find information on the culture-historical school was Schmidt's pages devoted to that topic in *The Origin and Growth of Religion*.[17] Even though *The Origin and Growth* is a good and helpful work, it was intended as a manual, and thus it is limited in its scope; the discussion of the culture-historical method is certainly abbreviated there.

Let us recall that the distinctiveness of the culture-historical method lies in the establishment of criteria as tools to uncover the chronological sequence of various cultures in a given area. The idea is, obviously, to make such inferences by setting up a method that allows us to do so objectively rather than speculating or guessing. As we saw in chapter 6, the method was based on identifying cultural forms and how they are related to each other within a particular culture, as well as what happens to them when different cultures come into contact with each other.

Radin had at least two problems with this approach. First, he objected to what he considered to be quantitative ethnology,[18] by which he meant establishing relationships between cultures entirely by counting various cultural artifacts. As though one were establishing the distribution of certain kinds of rocks in a given area, one would award the honor of being the originator of a form to the culture with the highest number of occurrences. Radin thought such argumentation was specious, particularly because, according to his view, the selection of items considered to be significant was based on the investigator's subjective preference. Furthermore, Radin argued, if similar forms appeared in two cultures, they might differ in their

---

[17] Wilhelm Schmidt, *The Origin and Growth of Religion: Facts and Theories*, trans. H. J. Rose (London: Methuen, 1931). The German original is Wilhem Schmidt, *Handbuch der Vergleichenden Religionsgeschichte: Ursprung und Werden der Religion* (Münster: Aschendorff, 1930).

[18] Radin, *Method and Theory*, 130–82.

meanings in each culture; thus, they should not be correlated with each other.

We must respond that if anyone was carrying out purely quantitative ethnology, it certainly was not the culture-historical school. Cultures are complex, and there is more to the culture-historical method than counting occurrences of particular items or, for that matter, complexes of items in different cultures.

On the other hand, one cannot totally do away with looking at cultural forms and even doing a quantitative analysis of their distribution at times. How else can one distinguish between different cultures than by looking at their cultural forms? Furthermore, with regard to the idea that they often carry different meanings in different cultures, that is a fact beyond dispute. But I do not need to know what deep meaning may be associated with the observation that a culture may have decorated pottery before I can assert that it has decorated pottery, whereas the tribe next door may not have any pottery at all. Furthermore, we need to keep in mind that for the culture-historical school nonmaterial forms, such as religion and mythology, as well as the meanings of particular forms in different cultures, are a part of the data; viz. they constitute forms as well. Thus, they are included in the investigation of a culture. Thus, Radin was really attacking a straw man in this respect. The idea that Graebner's work was nothing but subjectively counting selected forms from culture to culture certainly constitutes a misrepresentation.

The second problem Radin had with Graebner, as mediated by Schmidt's summary, is the establishment of a set of criteria by which we can attempt to assess the chronological priority of one culture over another. These rules, we should remember, pertain to the ethnologist's method; they are intended to be tools for the investigator to identify various strata of cultures. Nevertheless, Radin misinterpreted them as universal laws of cultural development, and he was offended by them. In his own words, "There is something compelling in the effrontery with which Graebner lays down the laws that govern cultural growth, and this is probably the reason for his very great influence in Germany and Austria."[19]

We see here, first of all, a total mix-up between a methodology, used for the purpose of investigation, and laws that supposedly direct a culture in its development. As we emphasized before, a highly significant aspect of the culture-historical method was that contrary to the views of Tylor and the evolutionists, there were no laws governing cultural growth.

And, of course, one wonders in what sense Radin finds it appropriate to label Graebner's method as "effrontery," particularly since it is pretty clear that the closest he had come to Graebner's writings was by reading Schmidt's summary. If Graebner's methodological principles really were laws that govern cultural growth, he might be accused of manifesting quite a bit of *hubris*, but even then he would have done nothing that Tylor, Morgan, or Frazer had not also done. So why should his work be considered an effrontery? I have no answer. And the statement that it is probably this alleged effrontery that lead to the popularity of this method among Austrians and Germans is, as Schmidt calls it, "impudent."[20] We will leave Radin's legacy in that respect in his own hands.

Radin did not actually go into the specifics of Graebner's method. He stated that "with Graebner the desire for chronology became an obsession and the obsession a dogma,"[21] which could not be a meaningful assessment since it had not been based on the study of Graebner's own writings or acquaintance with him as a person, even if it were true. It is not. Toward the conclusion of the two and one-half large-print pages he devoted to his vilification of Graebner and his German audience, Radin declared that "ethnologists have been far too kind to [Graebner]. . . . Instead of examining the foundations of

---

[19] Ibid., 79.

[20] Wilhelm Schmidt, *The Culture Historical Method of Ethnology: The Scientific Approach to the Racial Question*, trans. S. A. Sieber (New York: Fortuny's, 1939), 55.

[21] Radin, *Method and Theory*, 78.

his method, showing their complete inadequacy and the fallacious nature of his reasoning, and then paying no attention to it, scholars have permitted themselves to be beguiled into examining the extent to which his predicated culture strata hold true."[22]

Radin certainly followed the part of his recommendation not to pay attention to the culture-historical method, as made clear by his inability to present it correctly. As for the rest of his exhortation, he manifestly did not bother to examine the foundations of Graebner's method himself, thus making his assessment of its alleged inadequacy or fallacious reasoning worthless.

Radin not only threw stink bombs at Graebner, based on what he had culled out from Schmidt's *Origin and Growth*, but he also subjected Schmidt himself to the same treatment.[23] He correctly acknowledged that in the culture-historical method, the geographical areas where two cultures intersect are of particular importance because there we can see the results of contact and "crossings," which frequently provide us with the data to determine which culture superseded the other one.[24] This is correct, and one may wonder what Radin could conceivably find wrong with this principle, which is primarily a methodological directive on how to proceed in studying cultures, not a conclusion. Radin did not address the principle in any detail but once again brought out the broad brush argument that this procedure was too subjective and left it at that.[25]

---

[22] Ibid., 80.

[23] Schmidt, in his treatment of Radin in *Origin and Growth*, was positive toward him, even to the point of minimizing Radin's statement in an early article that the religion of American Indians was animism in the Tylorian sense, a statement Radin would certainly not have made in later years (either because of its content or because of its universality). Schmidt, *Origin and Growth*, 164–65. On the matter of primitive monotheism, Schmidt expressed disagreement with Radin in *Origin and Growth*, 201–4, but emphasized Radin's positive contributions. The fact that Radin's anti-German/Austrian venom also included Schmidt appears to rule out that it was based on the political direction in which Germany appeared to be heading at the time of his writing.

[24] Ibid., 163–67; Schmidt, *Origin and Growth*, 236.

[25] Radin, *Method and Theory*, 164.

Such assessments betray an artificial skepticism that one cannot possibly sustain. Were Radin's studies of the Winnebago not also based on observations and, therefore, subjective? What is here that is so subtle that it could be utterly distorted by the subjectivity of an ethnologist? Surely anyone studying cultures is familiar with areas where two cultures overlap and has observed the results of such intermingling: viz. the hybrids and the manner in which some forms of one culture have become dominant. True enough, it requires a subject to undertake observations, and in that sense all observations are "subjective." But it does not follow from this truism that any observation is as good as any other one or that subjectivity is always so overpowering that it compromises the trustworthiness of an observation beyond all help. Such a criticism based on subjectivity is almost always *ad hoc* and selective. One wants to know: Exactly what is being obscured by the involvement of the observer? The answer is most likely a pretty subjective one.

Radin continued his critique. He cited a passage from *Origin and Growth* in which Schmidt discussed how we can figure out whether a particular form has originated with a specific culture rather than having borrowed it from another. Once again the point concerns the ethnologist's methods, not the creation of rules that govern the behavior of cultures.

> No element belonging to one culture can have any inner connection with the analogous element in another culture, *so far as its development is concerned.* For the many-sided peculiarity of a culture is the result of its separate and independent existence throughout a considerable extent of time, apart from all other cultures. Consequently, the development of its several elements has been wholly independent likewise, and not in any way affected by the analogous elements of another culture, or in any way affecting them in their development.[26]

---

[26] Radin, *Method and Theory*, 165; Schmidt, *Origin and Growth*, 236.

This long statement comes close to being a tautology, which one can phrase far more simply as: *A culture differs from others because it has developed independently of other cultures.* Its point is directed against those critics who think Graebner and Schmidt were teaching that development in cultures was directed by various laws. To the contrary, the history of the human race is filled with people who created new objects and implemented new ideas. But if we want to credit a particular culture with having given birth to a new form, we must be able to identify it as distinct from others, which requires that we have some reason to believe that it has developed independently of other cultures.

But how can one identify the culture of the origin of a cultural element among various groups? Oftentimes, one cannot do so. As I stated previously, having a method to acquire knowledge does not mean having acquired omniscience, and Schmidt did not claim any. Still, insofar as one engages in attempts to identify the original cultures for various elements, it is reasonable to say that the probability of success is drastically lowered if similar elements are found in abundance in a number of adjacent cultures. We can say that a single culture developed a new item only if that culture has been isolated from others long enough to produce the item. Implicit in Schmidt's statement is a limit on what we can know, not a recipe for knowing the unknowable.

Radin, however, continued to misinterpret Schmidt so that Schmidt would look as though he was claiming more knowledge with greater certainty than he actually did. For the next excerpt I will give you Radin's paraphrase together with the actual statement made by Schmidt, as translated by Rose, as well my own translation which may serve as a control but needs no further explanation. I am highlighting important differences between Radin's and Rose's translations.[27]

---

[27] Radin, *Method and Theory*, 165–66; Schmidt, *Origin and Growth*, 237 (emphases added).

Radin's Paraphrase	Rose's Translation of Schmidt	My Translation of Schmidt
With regard to the origin of the individual forms, the theory lays down the two following rules: 1. Cultural elements are to be explained only from ideas and associations appertaining to the culture to which it belongs.	And now we can lay down an important and **general** rule, consisting of two parts: a. Every cultural element can be explained, as regards its origin, only from the ideas and associations belonging to that culture to which itself [sic] belongs, and **not from any general guesses as to what may have been; still less of** course from the ideas and associations of a foreign culture.	Thus we obtain an important general two-sided rule: a. The origin of each element of a culture can only be explained on the basis of the ideas and relationships within the culture circle to which it belongs, not on the basis of any general weighing of probabilities, let alone on the basis of the ideas and relationships of another culture circle.
2. With the specific culture **only** the older forms of a given element are **specifically** significant for explanations as to origin, for **they reflect most accurately** the various influences, physical and mental, to which the original appearance of that particular element is to be ascribed.	b. Within a given culture, it is the oldest forms of any element which are **especially** significant for the explanation of its origin, for **they come nearest to reflecting** the influences, physical and mental, to which the first appearance of that element was due.	b. In the course of explaining the origin of any element within a culture circle, the oldest forms of this culture element are of particular significance since they are most likely to reflect the physical and psychological factors, which allowed the element to appear for the first time.

Figure 8.1. Comparison of Radin's Paraphrase and Rose's Translation.

Schmidt's point was a corrective to hasty universalizing. He was directing himself particularly against hypotheses that attempt to explain the origin of an item within a culture on the basis of either purely a priori grounds or data that properly belong to another culture. In his summary of the first part, Radin broke off without Schmidt's clarifications and made the rule look like a stark and unbendable commandment rather than a caution to would-be identifiers of possible origins of a form (and we need to come back to this point shortly).

In the second part, he added "only," a word Schmidt would have inserted had he meant it to stand there. Schmidt said that the older forms were "especially" significant; Radin turned this word into "specifically," thereby creating an odd syntax and, again, raising the impression of greater exactitude than Schmidt intended. Finally, when Schmidt acknowledged a lack of precision by saying that the older forms "come nearest to reflecting" the situation surrounding their original invention, Radin is contriving the appearance of higher precision when he says that "they reflect most accurately" the original situation. Schmidt's phraseology distances itself from a direct representation; Radin's version lets the reader assume accuracy, with the *greatest* accuracy being reserved for the older forms. This difference is significant because, again, Radin's formulation attributes to Schmidt a greater degree of exactness than Schmidt is promising. We cannot accuse Radin of misquoting Schmidt since he is giving a paraphrase rather than a direct quote, but it is certainly obvious that he paraphrased Schmidt in a misleading way so as to enhance what he considered to be a problem with Schmidt. Perhaps Radin might have responded to this charge by saying that he was merely intensifying Schmidt's "real" intentions; if so, he got it wrong.

Having set up this second straw man, Radin moved on: "What such fictitious precision leads to is characteristically enough indicated by the three stages this school predicates."[28] He then gives a rather care-

---

[28] Radin, *Method and Theory*, 16.

less summary of Schmidt's *Primitive, Primary,* and *Secondary* cultures, including Schmidt's assertion that the three stages are blended in South America. All of that material is not "predicated" by the culture-historical school, as Radin put it, but inferred by Schmidt. Radin highlighted only a few out-of-context details that he found amusing—which they are without the context, as is true for any assertions in any book.

Radin did not clarify why Schmidt's conclusion of having arrived at different stages of cultures is intrinsically objectionable. As to the "fictitious precision," we just saw that Radin himself created this fiction in order to enhance what Schmidt actually said for the sake of satire. Schmidt did not make the promises that Radin accused him of making, but he set up strict rules to follow if one wants to have any success in establishing a sequence of cultures at all. Radin's purely emotive conclusion is to go back to his lame assessment of Graebner: "What can one possibly say to such schematization except to reiterate our previous characterization that with Graebner and his followers the search for chronology became an obsession and the obsession a dogma?"[29]

Since to all appearances Radin never seriously engaged with Schmidt's or Graebner's arguments except for reading a few pages out of *The Origin and Growth,* he certainly could not have said anything further. And since he also did not provide an accurate analysis of them in writing, his short diatribe does not seem to be of much use other than to illustrate the sad attitude of many scholars to Schmidt and the pseudo-criticisms that continue to abound. But those little baseless nuggets of criticism are what survive. Thus, Radin's objections have a significant value for us as we begin to think ahead to original monotheism in the context of Christian apologetics. We need to realize that just as Radin only picked out a few pages of Schmidt for his critique, contemporary people are likely only to pick a few lines out of someone's summary of Radin and believe Radin had gotten the best of Schmidt.

Radin and the Primitive Gods. Still, having brought up Radin, we cannot leave him without finding out what he had to offer in return.

---

[29] Ibid., 167.

Let us begin by asking how he dealt with the supreme beings of the *Primitive* cultures. Interestingly, he originally contributed to the accumulation of data that supported Lang's and Schmidt's theories with some early reports concerning Central Californian tribes. At one time he even applauded Lang, to whom he referred as "the most courageous of thinkers," endorsing the correctness of there being high gods at the beginning of many cultures.[30] Some writers, including the present author, admittedly not having read Radin's works sufficiently at that time, had inferred incorrectly that he was, therefore, a supporter of Schmidt.[31] However, the similarity with Lang or Schmidt stops at the point of all three of them accepting the reality of the belief in a supreme being among certain preliterate cultures. From there they parted ways.

Radin turned belief in monotheism into a triviality. He claimed that in all cultures, regardless of how simple or complex they may be, the same personality types are always present that we see among ourselves.[32] There are those who are pious and those who care little about religion; there are those who are given to deep thought and introspection, and there are those who simply do whatever is pragmatically best for them; there are those who attempt to puzzle out the mysteries of the universe, and there are those for whom it is sufficient to live in the universe without further questioning. It is those who are given over to reflecting, questioning, and speculating who may arrive at the conclusion that there must be a single God, while others, who are members of the same community, will not care and merely pursue whatever is traditional insofar as they may be concerned with religion at all.

Consequently, for Radin there really is no such thing as a monotheistic culture. There may be cases in which the reflective personality type is dominant, in which case we can talk about a religion in

---

[30] Radin, *Monotheism Among Primitive Peoples*, 18.

[31] Winfried Corduan, *A Tapestry of Faiths* (2002; repr., Eugene, OR: Wipf & Stock, 2009), 48.

[32] Radin, *Monotheism Among Primitive Peoples*, 55–60.

which monotheism is dominant as well. However, according to him, this possibility is really not all that significant since any such beliefs are merely due to the fact that people with the appropriate personality traits have asserted themselves more than people with different psychological dispositions.

Lang and Schmidt both agreed that the reason in so many cultures monotheism was faint and without a vital cultus for the supreme being was degeneration. People turned away from the Creator towards spirits and gods, whom they thought they could manipulate. The memory of the supreme being remained, but they started to focus their worship on inferior entities. In contrast, Radin did not accept any theory of degeneration. According to his view, when there is a rudimentary belief in monotheism without a great amount of animism, this fact is actually due to the presence of a second being, the trickster, whose traits begin to dominate and crowd out the all-good, divine Creator.[33] We encountered the idea of a trickster before in the context of the Maidu creation myth, where this role was being played by Coyote. Radin avowed with assurance that the trickster belonged to the earliest form of human thought. He described him thus:

> In what must be regarded as its earliest and most archaic form, as found among the North American Indians, Trickster is at one and the same time creator and destroyer, giver and negator, he who dupes others and who is always duped himself. He wills nothing consciously. At all times he is constrained to behave as he does from impulses over which he has no control. He knows neither good nor evil yet he is responsible for both. He possesses no values, moral or social, is at the mercy of his passions and appetites, yet through his actions all values come into being.[34]

Therefore, in such cultures where the supreme being is only vaguely recognized, according to Radin this is the case because the trickster has taken on greater importance than the supreme being.

---

[33] Ibid., 22.
[34] Radin, *The Trickster*, ix.

One is nonplussed at what one reads here. Suddenly there is both precision and certainty and a claim for specifically what belongs to the earliest thoughts of all humans. After having ridiculed the ethnologists who thought it could be possible to establish a chronological sequence of cultures, and after having insisted that any such attempt at cultural history was categorically impossible, Radin declared with great assurance that the idea of the trickster went back to the origin of human culture.

How can Radin be so sure of this claim? The "fictitious precision" he misleadingly attributed to Schmidt appears to be mere guesswork compared to the certainty Radin invokes here. Let me hasten to add that there is no ethnological confirmation of this claim since, for one thing, not all cultures to which Radin applies his explanation demonstrate the presence of a trickster. Radin's certitude derives from the fact that he already knows what the earliest people must have been thinking.

Let me explain. I stated earlier, when I began the discussion of ethnology in America, that regardless of how much one focuses on a precise, accurate, and complete collection of data, the writings (Radin's ideal monographs) still need to have some basic principles according to which the data are interpreted. In fact, Radin insisted that it is the obligation of an ethnographer to transcend to the depths of the culture under scrutiny, a task that includes exploring the meaning of various cultural elements for its members. The tool Radin used to carry out this exploration was depth psychology, also known as psychoanalysis or analytical psychology, the theories of Freud and Jung.[35]

We need not belabor the self-contradiction that runs throughout Radin's book on ethnological methodology as a consequence. But we can now discern even greater significance in how Radin truncated the first part of Schmidt's rule on how to discover the origin of a particular form among different cultures when he left out Schmidt's

---

[35] Thus, Radin's *The Trickster* concludes with an essay by Carl Jung, 195–211.

qualification, "not from any general guesses as to what may have been; still less of course from the ideas and associations of a foreign culture."[36] Surely, using the theories of European psychoanalysts, whether rightly or wrongly, is the importation of "ideas and associations of a foreign culture."

Carl Jung advocated the idea that humanity had a "collective consciousness" that manifested itself in the appearance of various recurring themes in cultures around the world. These are not just ideas but images that are as likely to come out in artwork and dreams as in the narratives of mythology. Thus, according to Jung, when we recognize the appearance of these themes, which he called "archetypes," we align them with other occurrences in different situations and possibly ascribe to them some kernel of meaning they appear to share in all cases. The trickster is such a Jungian archetype; we already mentioned that in numerous cultures there is a trickster figure, and we described what, in general, his role is. Whether one wants to invoke a "collective consciousness" or some other mechanism at root is an issue that does not need to detain us here; there can be little question that certain symbols appear to stretch across time and cultures.

However, it is a leap to go from the recognition of recurring symbols in many cultures to argue that since the trickster is a Jungian archetype, we can therefore assume with certainty that he must have been a part of the earliest form of human thinking. This is a capricious resort to a psychological frame of reference, which Radin posits not only without evidence, but even without the *possibility* of evidence, since he took such a strong stance against the possibility of identifying the oldest cultures. I do not see how one can reconcile this fundamental inconsistency in Radin's writings. What I can say is that it certainly represents a flight into the irrational, which is a point we will emphasize further in the next chapter.

---

[36] Schmidt, *Origin and Growth*, 237.

Emendations

We are clearly not making headway in finding solid criticisms of Schmidt's work. That does not mean there are not some items in Schmidt's writings that are in need of correction. The problem is that, to a large extent, few critics ever went sufficiently into analyzing his method or its application to come up with meaningful critiques. As a matter of fact, some things in Schmidt's system do not hold up any longer, and we do need to make the necessary adjustments. Then we can deal with some meaningful criticisms.

In an earlier book I stated that Schmidt's "particular take on original monotheism rises and falls by his anthropological conclusions. If they are accurate, then his theory is well defended, but to whatever degree they can be questioned, the theory also becomes more questionable."[37]

I am going to stand by that statement, even as I will now raise some questions concerning Schmidt's anthropological conclusions. In the process his conclusions concerning original monotheism certainly do become more questionable, at least for a moment. However, if answers to the new questions come up in the process, nothing is lost, and I believe such to be the case.

I mentioned in the last chapter, in the context of the Native American cultures, that Schmidt had the disadvantage of not knowing of the archaeological discoveries being made just as he was writing. Some of those finds have made an impact on Schmidt's reconstruction of cultural history, some positive and some negative. Furthermore, we need to take into account some other issues in ethnology. Our intended outcome is, after all, not to establish the truth of Schmidt's theories, but to establish the truth per se insofar as we are capable of doing so, an opinion with which Schmidt definitely concurred.[38] Thus, we will give ourselves the freedom to make some needed adjustments in light

---

[37] Corduan, *Tapestry*, 48.
[38] Schmidt, *Ursprung*, vol. 1, 258.

of current knowledge. Paradoxically, perhaps Schmidt's final conclusions may just be strengthened in the process.

Let us now consider the changes we need to make to our overall scheme in the light of reason and evidence. The bottom line is that on good grounds contemporary anthropology leads us to rethink Schmidt's alignment of the *Primary* and *Secondary* cultures.[39] A general unspoken prohibition also exists against attempting to establish chronological sequences of different cultures. However, in actuality it is impossible not to think in terms of successions in time, and, as long as we stay faithful to culture-historical criteria, we need not bind ourselves to that pro forma exhortation.

Let me start by saying that there is no issue with the idea of a genuine difference between the hunting-gathering stage (frequently referred to as a "foraging" economy) and the horticultural or "gardening" stage. As human cultures developed, many of them shifted from food gathering to food production. Thus, people started to nurture plants and even keep small gardens. At the same time, one can frequently notice a correlation between this mode of producing food and a general increase in the level of the material culture, but there is no necessary causal relationship in that direction. This acknowledged distinction between foraging and horticultural economies gives us a positive anchor point for the adjustments that follow.

Second, the existence of pure hunting cultures, as illustrated by the idea that the Paleo-Indians of the Clovis culture (see the previous chapter) survived entirely on mammoths and other extinct mega-fauna, is not reasonable. Everywhere people hunted, they also supplemented their diet with plant foods. So the most fundamental way of life continues to be that of hunting combined with gathering

---

[39] Susan Andretta and Gary Ferraro, *Cultural Anthropology: An Applied Perspective*, 8th ed. (Belmont, CA: Wadsworth), 147–76. I need to thank my son, Nicholas Corduan, especially for first clarifying to me the contemporary standpoint of various issues in anthropology. Subsequently, I found them documented in the extremely detailed textbook by Andretta and Ferraro. In the discussion below, my assertions on contemporary anthropology are documented in this book.

edible vegetation. Thus, contemporary views agree with Schmidt that the most basic human economy is hunting and gathering.

But that fact also means that Schmidt's view of a pure culture of hunters on the *Primary* level is not really supportable. Cultures that attained the level of more sophisticated hunting techniques also engaged in horticulture, and hunting never existed on its own, as we said. It may be safe to say that any general increase in material culture is also likely reflected in an increase in the effectiveness of hunting utensils, but we cannot use the occupation of hunting as a distinguishing mark for a separate culture circle. Thus, the cultures that Schmidt identifies as the patrilineal "hunting" cultures are patrilineal "hunting-horticultural" cultures. However, that fact does not rule out distinguishing between the strands on the *Primary* level that are matrilineal, patrilineal with totemism, and patrilineal with an open family concept.

There is also an issue with the pastoral, nomadic cultures being on the same chronological level as the "hunter-horticultural" cultures.[40] As a matter of fact, all of the last six volumes of *Der Ursprung* are dedicated to the various people groups who might come under this heading, and it becomes clear that Schmidt was well aware of the fact that many of them at a minimum can be as easily associated with *Secondary* cultures as *Primary* ones. There clearly has to have been some continuity. It would be silly to erect an absolute barrier here because we cannot dictate to the people of the past what they were supposed to have done, and so, if some people within the *Primary* context raised some goats, we can forgive them, as well as ourselves for thinking of herding as something without antecedents.

But there's another wrinkle. Schmidt made a serious miscalculation with regard to the pastoral nomads, the correction of which places his conclusions on even safer grounds. As we've mentioned, he believed the beginnings of humanity occurred in Asia and the

---

[40] Ernest Brandewie, *Wilhelm Schmidt and the Origin of the Idea of God* (Lanham, MD: University Press of America, 1983), 93.

pastoral cultures also originated there. He tied their emergence to the domestication of the horse. In his scheme, then, the African pastoralists came later in time, but they did not ride horses. Much of sub-Saharan Africa is open savannah, and horses would have been handy, so if African herders were supposed to be related in culture to Asian ones, what happened to the horses? When Schmidt wrote volume 7 of *Der Ursprung*, he apologized that, due to the easier availability of material on African cattle herders, he was starting his exploration of pastoralists out of chronological sequence because he believed he should have begun with Asia.

Two significant events in this context have occurred since Schmidt wrote those words. For one, insofar as archaeologists have been able to pinpoint a time when the domestication of the horse began, it was much later than could be reconciled with it being a full-fledged culture circle alongside the horticulturalists of the *Primary* cultures. This discovery caused a great amount of consternation for Wilhelm Koppers, a fellow member of the Vienna school, who had even written parts of Schmidt's *The Culture Historical Method of Ethnology*,[41] and, according to Brandewie, this issue was the catalyst that caused him eventually to renounce the whole idea of culture circles.[42]

But archaeology has many tentacles. It may have shown that the horse came later in history than suits the theory of human beginnings in Asia. But, then again, it has also contributed to the now-favored notion of humanity's origin in Africa.[43] And in that case the domestication of the horse is no longer a problem. The circle is intact! We simply have to lay out the geographical expansion for it differently, which is true for all circles assuming the African origin. Finally, the appearance of the nomadic cattle herders in Africa seems to be timed close to the origin of agriculture on that continent as well, so another

---

[41] Specifically, Schmidt mentions that Koppers wrote pp. 13–19 and 81–124 of the book (Schmidt, *Culture Historical Method*, xxi).

[42] Brandewie, *Wilhelm Schmidt*, 93–94.

[43] Fazale Rana and Hugh Ross, *Who Was Adam? A Creation Model to the Origin of Man* (Colorado Springs: NavPress, 2005), 27–39, 125.

potential discrepancy is avoided by moving the pastoralist circle into the vicinity of the *Secondary* cultures.

So we need to reorganize the *Primary* culture(s) somewhat. On the grand view, apparently only one basic economy succeeded the simple foragers of the *Primitive* cultures, namely a somewhat more advanced culture, most easily recognizable by horticultural practices, in which hunting was also practiced and in which extensive domestication of animals was not yet known. Then on the *Secondary* level the two forms of agricultural cultures are joined by the pastoral nomads. Since contemporary anthropology is leery of discussions of developmental lines, the identification of, say, the social trajectories are not an object of inquiry, but perhaps they should be. Despite Brandewie's hints in this direction,[44] the social structures of societies and their manners of counting descent, including totemism, do not occur happenstance and are not subject to frequent revisions. There is no reason not to acknowledge Schmidt's correlations here since the various cultures have not changed their ancient history over the past hundred years.

The question comes up as to whether we have lost anything in the process of allowing for these alterations. The answer is definitely not. We have not actually undercut anything that is integral to Schmidt's conclusions but have simply rearranged the patterns somewhat. We have altered the designation of the circles to a small extent, allowing for two horticultural circles, one of which is patrilineal and totemic, *possibly* with a greater emphasis on hunting, and the other one being matrilineal and *possibly* with less emphasis on hunting. We have also moved the true pastoralists tentatively down to the *Secondary* level. However, the records of the actual cultures are still the same, and the affinities of cultures within that circle need not be dismissed. Let us remind ourselves that the idea of culture circles was never an end in itself. Revising some of the specifics of culture circles exactly as described by Schmidt does not negate the criteria by which we can discern the sequences and layers of cultures or their interrelatedness.

---

[44] Brandewie, *Wilhelm Schmidt*, 73.

Two of Schmidt's most important conclusions stand untainted by this small shift in the geometry of cultures. It still remains true that the *Primitive* cultures represent the ones that most closely resemble what may have been the original human culture. Furthermore, regardless of where one places the pastoral nomads, they, in general, maintained the original monotheism most clearly. The intermediate stages may need to be rearranged, but the connections still remain, and Schmidt's conclusions really are not seriously disrupted by them.

Brandewie's Substantial Criticisms

With the *Primitive* circles still safely lodged in the position allocated to them by Schmidt, we can focus on the criticisms against his theory by people who were more knowledgeable than our first two major examples. We can use the book written by Ernest Brandewie, a retired professor of anthroplogy, as a good summary of such critiques.[45] His book consists of two parts: a 126-page introduction to Schmidt and his work, including a critical analysis, followed by translations of excerpts from the first six volumes of *Der Ursprung*. These excerpts are bound to be of great value to anyone interested in the content of Schmidt's work since the work as a whole has not been translated into English and probably never will be. Before saying anything critical, I need to applaud Dr. Brandewie for providing this service, as well as for making sure his translation of German turned into real English, which often meant turning one sentence into three or four. A translation must first present the message of the author correctly, and a slavish literalism can stand in the way of doing so.

However, I need to point out that there are also some problems with Brandewie's translations so that at times Schmidt's thoughts are no longer represented accurately. For example, Brandewie freely abridges passages, not merely curtailing verbosity but sometimes leaving out important qualifications. He also displays an unfamiliarity

---

[45] Ibid.

with a number of German idioms and even common expressions, which he sometimes translates by surmise rather than by consulting a dictionary. Thus, one must be aware that citing from his translations involves the risk of using material that is not always accurate. (See appendix B for a significant case in point.) Furthermore, I cannot help but wonder whether some of the incomplete understanding demonstrated by some of the problems in the translation may not have contributed to an all-too-ready disposition to accept certain criticisms as valid.

On the whole Brandewie is sympathetic to Schmidt in the sense that he is highly appreciative of his works but concludes that, in the final analysis, Schmidt's theories are no longer tenable. His criticisms are for the most part ones that have been made in the past, some of them stemming from Schmidt's original coworkers, and one must be careful to distinguish those that Brandewie appears to endorse and those that he reports only but apparently may not accept himself.

We have already addressed a number of these critiques in passing. Others are such that their nature makes lengthy commentary either unnecessary or impossible. I include among those:

1. *The Ontological Status of Culture Circles.* The whole question of whether the circles are real cannot be answered by anthropology. It is easy to say that, insofar as predicates and sets of things have reality, the ethnologist discovers real relations and real sets of cultural features distributed over real people groups. They are the product of the ethnologist's mind, to be sure, but the ethnologist is applying his categories to reality, while allowing reality to correct his categories. Then the issue first of all comes down to truth, not reality. However, since truth is what corresponds to reality, any further inquiry concerning the reality of the culture circles leads us into metaphysical issues that are best left alone in this context because they do not contribute to the more important ethnological matters.

Brandewie phrases this problem in terms of whether circles are real or merely tools, and he finds Schmidt to be inconsistent on this point. But this is a false disjunction because, given his Thomistic background, a "tool" would still have reality as an Aristotelian form for Schmidt. Thus, a simple reading of the text by anyone with a different philosophical orientation must reveal ambiguity. Understanding the problem as a metaphysical one, ethnology cannot provide a satisfactory answer, regardless of which direction it goes, and the ethnologist is best served by limiting his discourse to questions of truth or falsehood.[46]

2. *Concerns That Come Down to Schmidt as a Person or a Scholar.*[47] Brandewie stays far away from any abusive ad hominem argumentation. Still, such matters as whether Schmidt was sufficiently scientific in his thinking, remained systematic in his conclusions, accused everyone who disagreed with him of evolutionism (which I'm not sure is true), or overlooked alternative explanations may or may not be accurate assessments, but they are not conceptual criticisms to which one can respond substantively. They certainly do not vitiate his conclusions.

3. *The Red Herring of "Definitions."*[48] As I have argued earlier, this matter can become a no-win issue for any author because it lacks substance. The best defense for such banter is to ask the critic to define or clarify what he or she means by the word *definition*. Language always contains some ambiguity; even propositions expressed in symbolic logic are no exception, and there is no instrument, metaphysical or linguistic, to eliminate it entirely. But we can achieve clarity without artificial definitions, and we must leave ambiguity where the language itself will not liberate us from it.

---

[46] Ibid., 98.
[47] Ibid., 116–18.
[48] Ibid., 89–104.

4. *The Aura of Epistemological Uncertainty that Surrounds the Entire Critical Discussion.*[49] In various comments along the way, and particularly in the section on Schmidt and science,[50] it appears that Schmidt is being held to a standard that is reminiscent not just of Newtonian but of Euclidean science, viz. to begin with apodictic postulates and definitions and then proceed only with the level of mathematical certainty. We already stated in connection with Radin's critique that Schmidt's standard concerning his final conclusions is more moderate than that. Schmidt's language, conforming to the custom of the times, may have contributed to unrealistic expectations, but we should know better nowadays. An empirical science can neither work in such rigid fashion, nor can it promise the certainty of a purely logical deduction. On the other hand, the absence of any imaginary "absolute certainty" does not detract from the genuine truth of a statement.

Still, Brandewie raises some meatier problems. Let us isolate two criticisms, each of which embodies a number of corollary questions.

The Assumptions Underlying Culture Circles

Brandewie states that the attempt at culture circles was worth trying but ultimately needed to be discarded in the hope that better techniques will aid in coming up with better models. He partially blames their apparent lack of success on some tenuous assumptions underlying Schmidt's culture-historical methodology.

> . . . these assumptions being, first of all, the general stability or constancy of culture, especially of culture circles, and secondly the tight organic connection between diverse elements of any culture circle, which both strengthened the assumption of stability, and enabled reconstructions to be made freely, also in

---

[49] See, for example, ibid., 76.
[50] Ibid., 78–83.

prehistory. The two assumptions mutually reinforce each other. But two supportive assumptions do not make for certitude, nor does this situation exempt us from testing these assumptions.[51]

As an aside, I don't understand two phrases here. One is the phrase "also in prehistory." Why did this clarification need to be added? Are we not all agreed that reconstructing prehistory is what Schmidt's work is all about? My second question is why Brandewie feels the need to emphasize that "this situation" (and I'm not entirely clear on what he means by that) "does not exempt us from testing these assumptions." Isn't critical assessment of another scholar's work what we do? Thankfully, much of contemporary dialogue is not as abrasive as, say, Radin's criticism of Graebner and Schmidt, but surely we don't need to justify testing each other's truth claims.

The important item in that quotation is, of course, Brandewie's statement of Schmidt's two assumptions and his assessment thereof:

1. the stability and constancy of cultures and culture circles; and
2. the organic connection of elements within culture circles.

First, I'm wondering to what extent these concepts are still assumptions and should not be thought of as conclusions. It appears to me that they may have been more accurately labeled as assumptions a hundred years ago but that today they are at a minimum hypotheses with some support. I will continue to refer to them as "assumptions" so as not to confuse things, but I believe their status today is stronger than that. It would appear that the challenges Brandewie laid down as to how they could be tested, namely by archaeology and history, can be met.[52]

Concerning (1), cultures are constantly changing but in many cases only in minor respects. This is where the episodic archaeological record concerning North American Indians is of great help.[53] The

---

[51] Ibid., 104–5.

[52] Ibid., 79.

[53] This summary is based on Robert F. Spencer, Jesse D. Jennings, et al., *The Native Americans: Ethnology and Backgrounds of the North American Indians* (New York: Harper & Row, 1977), 1–36.

summary below is rough; its only point is to demonstrate that there is a lot of plausibility to the idea that cultures remain fundamentally unchanged over long periods of time. If we accept a common set of dates for Paleo-Indian history, the immigration into Alaska began about 25,000 BC. Archaeologists have discovered a bone that had been shaped by human beings into an instrument used to scrape meat from hides from that time, and a reasonable inference is that at that time they were hunter-gatherers. Then we have a gap in any further artifacts lasting for about 10,000 years. The few artifacts dated toward the close of that long silent period are heavily debated and would still leave a surprisingly long gap, and the indication is that at the end of this time, the people were still pursuing a hunting and gathering economy. Finally, we get to the arrowheads and spearheads of the so-called Clovis culture, dated to about 10,000–9,000 BC, and these people were, of course, hunter-gatherers; the limited archaeological evidence indicates a fondness for mammoth. The next culture for which we have enough finds to provide a separate identification is the Folsom culture of about 9,000–8,000 BC, in which the primary game had shifted to a now-extinct species of bison. Next came the "Archaic culture" (c. 8,000–1500 BC), followed by the "Woodlands culture," in which we have the first samples of pottery. From around 800 BC on, we see a number of mound-building cultures, referred to as the Adena, Hopewell, and Effigy cultures. For all of this time, even with a few cultural developments, such as the introduction of pottery in some areas, the economy remained that of hunter-gatherers. Eventually some horticulture showed up, and that's basically where it remained until European contact beginning around AD 1500. Some tribes were on the horticultural level, but for the most part, their economies appear to have been identical to that of their presumed ancestors of 27,000 years ago. Subsequent to European arrival, many changes were rippling over the continent—some of which affected tribes even when their actual contacts with Europeans would still be several hundred years away.

Let me add a historical example to my point, and again, I apologize for the broadness of my example, but the extent covered by it is its point. How much did the culture of Egypt really change in about 6,000 years? It was an agricultural economy long before the upper and lower kingdoms were united, even longer before the pyramids were built. Dynasties changed; writing evolved from pictographs through the alphabet of the hieroglyphics to a simplified style. Foreign invaders and foreign rulers adopted Egypt's culture rather than imposing theirs on Egypt. The priesthood perpetuated and multiplied all the while maintaining a firm grip on the country and regaining their prominence immediately after it had been set aside for one brief moment. Despite relatively minor changes, the economy continued to be based on what the fields along the Nile could produce, and the changes that were made for the most part had the purpose of preserving the overall status quo. Egyptian culture remained distinctively Egyptian culture. I am not unaware of the rich and event-filled history of Egypt and don't want to trivialize it, but with all of the cosmetic changes its culture underwent, its fundamental culture remained unmistakably enduring. History certainly records major changes in some cultures, most of them due to various crises; however, internal fundamental changes within a culture, not triggered by some event from the outside, can be slow.

In a move that is not at all clear to me, Brandewie ties the questionability of assumption (1) to the further criticism that the conception of the culture-historical method is focusing too much on cultural traits as though they were individual objects, such as artifacts accumulated in a museum.[54] The method seems too formal, putting too much emphasis on the elements of cultures as things rather than allowing for the creativity of people, as well as the intellectual, spiritual side of cultures.

One must admit, particularly after reading through Graebner's or Schmidt's books on methodology, that a description of the culture-historical method per se is likely to create the impression of counting and sorting blocks of different shapes and colors. Brandewie cites

---

[54] Brandewie, *Wilhelm Schmidt*, 75.

Wilhelm Mühlmann to the effect that "the school of culture-history forgot that culture is carried by living people."[55] Brandewie disagreed with Mühlmann's assessment to a degree but nonetheless made a concession that "the entire culture-historical school often treated the social and religious dimensions of cultural life as if they were a canoe form, or a house type, independently of the people who were religious, who lived in certain kinds of systems and the like."[56]

It's never easy to respond to critiques based on impressions because one can't argue with the subjective perception a person may have. And I certainly would like to pin a medal on anyone who has read the aforementioned two books on methodology. Still, an ethnologist who has studied the other books by Schmidt should know that, appearances aside, this is not how Schmidt approached cultures. In terms of establishing relationships by way of the correct methodology, there is no other way of treating the humanistic side of cultures than as artifacts. An important tool in tracing the development of the Protestant Reformation in England, for example, is by cataloging the changes in the *Common Book of Prayer* during that time. But to do so does not mean to forget the personalities, the struggles, and the emotions behind the print. We can put names to those individuals, which is not open to us for the people of prehistory. We can remind ourselves of the fact that their personalities, struggles, and emotions were just as real as those of the three Thomases: Cranmer, Cromwell, and Moore. But in the meantime, we must tend to our artifacts.

However one wants to read this issue, there seems be a non sequitur in tying this questionable understanding of the method to Schmidt's conception of the nature of human cultures. There comes a point when one needs to take an author's word for what he is doing or intending to do, particularly in light of what he has done. Schmidt's

---

[55] Wilhelm Mühlmann, *Geschichte der Anthropologie* (Bonn: Universitätsverlag, 1948), 144, cited in Brandewie, *Wilhelm Schmidt*, 75.
[56] Brandewie, *Wilhelm Schmidt*, 75.

short book on *High Gods in America* is a good example of what the outcome of the method is. It does not focus much on the material and purely external aspects of the cultures at all, except insofar as they contribute to establishing the necessary time lines. But from then on, the content is devoted to the myths and rituals of the representative tribes. In fact, at various points Schmidt praises the creativity and original thought that comes out in his analysis. Given the similarities that allow us to allocate them into their culture circles and relationships, they have also created settings for those common elements that are unique and attractive in each of them. As I said above, how this matter ties into the assumption that, left alone, cultures tend to be stable, I cannot discern. In short, assumption (1) seems to be, at a minimum, a good assumption.

With regard to assumption (2), the organic connection of elements within a culture or culture circle, it seems odd even to raise a serious question about this assumption once one has agreed that there are cultures and culture circles that deserve the name. The "assumption" seems to be an analytic statement, one that is true simply by virtue of what the words mean. Can one speak of a culture without intending to mean a single essentially coherent collection of traits? If there is a serious split in the manners and customs of a people, wouldn't we say that two cultures are vying for dominance?

But let us treat the assumption as a factual statement so the objection has merit. The potential problematic nature of this assumption presumably lies in the idea that once the presence of a certain culture circle has been determined, the ethnologist may feel free to fill out certain lacunae in one culture by taking recourse to "types" that he derived from a different culture. If so, that's risky business, and Schmidt acknowledges as much. To the extent that he may have gone too far in doing so, he needs to be criticized.

But illegitimate extrapolation is not necessarily entailed by the proposition that cultures and culture circles are organically connected wholes. Furthermore, there really is no reasonable alternative to positing a fundamental unity on any level of cultures one might be investigating. We can see certain incoherent cultures at times as a direct consequence of a migration or an invasion, but they are going to settle back into some form of equilibrium. Thus, cultures may have changed from their original "independent" culture circles due to influence from other cultures and thus created new "dependent" culture circles, to use the proper jargon, which means the newly formed culture circle is dependent on a synthesis of elements from several culture circles. The result is still going to be a setting in which the people connect up the various elements to fit together as an organic whole. In short, we can be sure that Schmidt's two "assumptions" are safe.

The Criterion of Quantity

Let me begin with a quotation.

> Schmidt also said that the more distant cultures are, the
> more similar items we need to prove genetic, i.e., historical,
> connection. But as two cultures are further removed from each
> other, in time or in space, the fewer clear similarities we can
> expect to find. The principle deteriorates precisely where it
> is supposed to apply strongly. The Central California groups
> share much more with the Algonkians [sic] than these do with
> the Fuegians, or these Amerinds (in turn) do with African and
> Asiatic pygmies. Yet, the method requires just the opposite![57]

Brandewie makes this assessment in the context of discussing Schmidt's criterion of quantity, and it appears that he is treating it in isolation from the other criteria. However, the criterion of quantity can never stand on its own; it always presupposes the criterion of quality or form. It appears as though this criticism is based on the fact that Schmidt is not doing something that would be even more objectionable, namely assigning relationships between cultures simply on the basis of counting forms. Brandewie's examples, rather than

---

[57] Ibid., 73.

constituting a *reductio ad absurdum* of Schmidt's method, demonstrate the need for a thorough grounding of a quantitative approach in a prior use of the criterion of quality. Radin rightly objected to quantitative ethnology, insofar as an ethnologist would actually count and correlate cultural elements arithmetically, but Schmidt is not guilty of it and should not be found guilty for being innocent.

It should be obvious that an ethnologist has to make a distinction in the nature of forms for his purposes. Like it or not, there is a certain amount of subjectivity in doing so; thus, one must take care not to let the subjectivity overpower the objectivity, which is supposed to be provided by specifying criteria. This is why Schmidt's book on the method consists of more than 300 pages rather than just two. Furthermore, this objection demonstrates exactly the reason nonmaterial forms including linearity, totemic groupings, and mythology, are so crucial.

Regardless of their "pedigree," ethnic groups of different origin, once settled into a particular environment, are going to resemble each other closely in many external material matters, which are essential for the sake of survival in that particular environment. Borrowing of cultural artifacts, particularly again on the more superficial material level, is also to be expected. However, certain aspects that are integral to a particular group, many of which are the immaterial forms, are not as likely to be similar.

Consider the two cases Brandewie brought up in the quote above. What does it signify, that the Central Californians have more in common with the Algonquins than with the Fuegians? First, although Schmidt places all three of these groups onto the level of *Primitive*, he assigns them to different culture circles. The Tierra Del Fuegians belong to Schmidt's Southern culture circle, whereas he places the Californians and Algonquins together into the Arctic culture circle. Clearly the North American tribes have a lot in common because they reside in North America, whereas the Fuegians manifest significant differences from them because they live in Tierra Del Fuego. So, why should the Fuegians be closer in culture to the Central Californians than the Californians are to the Algonquins? Is it because they are, according to Schmidt, closer in age to each other than to the Algonquins? If so, then assumption (1) of the previous objection would have to be raised to the level of a law together with the directive to all cultures that if they must change, they may only change along preset patterns.

One cannot have it both ways. Either the human beings who are the bearers of culture are creative human beings or they are not. It is illegitimate to criticize Schmidt for allegedly ignoring the human side of cultural development and then expect uniformity in the superficialities of two cultures remotely separated. To choose another example along the same line, surely one does not expect Eskimo culture to be similar to Central Californian culture and expect the Eskimos to survive the arctic winters. What binds them together is not what they eat, specifically what clothes they wear, or exactly what kind of houses they live in: clearly they are on a cultural level of minimality. They are foragers living in a nontotemic society practicing monogamy with few cultural innovations that go beyond the need for survival. These fundamental traits must outweigh those traits that are only a function of adaptation to the environment.

Let us review the basics of Schmidt's theory. Two points are given, not just as assumptions or axioms but also as fundamental observations on the history of humanity: one (which Schmidt could not have stated with as much assurance as we can now) is the single and unique origin of humanity, *Homo sapiens*, at one point in space and time. The other one is the fact of migration, not because of some wanderlust that is intrinsic to human nature but because lesser developed cultures were always under pressure from more developed cultures (or environmental factors) to yield ground, to be absorbed, or to cease to exist altogether. A corollary is that we are most likely to find cultures that are the least developed and have the greatest chance of resembling the culture of the original migrations of people on the geographic fringes. Some of these cultures clearly adapted and went on to greater complexity. But it surely is not by either accident or choice that these cultures are found in Southeast Australia,

Greenland, Tierra del Fuego, the African jungle, or on the Andaman Islands. I must repeat what I said earlier: if one does not understand that the least developed cultures *must* have wound up continents apart, one does not really understand the culture-historical method or the nature of migration.

It would be wrong to expect the cultures that fall into this category not to have made some adjustments (drastic ones in some cases) in order to survive in the areas into which they were pushed. Perhaps some didn't, but we would not know about them now because they would have gone extinct. Consequently, it strikes me as a serious misunderstanding of the entire method to expect the Central Californians to have greater similarity, measured purely quantitatively, with the Fuegians than with the Algonquins, or, again, purely quantitatively between the North Americans or the pygmies of Africa or Asia. To think otherwise is to put the criterion of quantity way ahead of the criterion of quality, the reality of human creativity, and common sense. The quotation by Brandewie assumes a one-sided caricature, and I cannot help but think that, on reflection, he knew better.

Conclusion

As I have hopefully shown, it is not necessary to accept all of Schmidt's ideas in every detail. In fact, insofar as we can adapt Schmidt's theories to contemporary discoveries without losing the central point of his arguments, the more his major conclusion, namely the presence of an original monotheism in the least developed cultures, is going to be strengthened. Schmidt was not infallible, but the representative criticisms of his work that I have shown here do not undercut his basic point.

Brandewie brought up some meaningful criticisms, but they were rather tendentious in nature and certainly were far from fatal for Schmidt's theory. Unfortunately, critiques in the style of those by Pettazzoni and by Radin are the ones we are most likely to encounter—that is to say, critiques based on distortion and polemic. At the same time, while such inadequate critiques were leveled against Schmidt, his critics had nothing substantial to offer in return and still do not. Instead, scholarship turned to irrationality and called for a lifelong moratorium on the question of the origin of religion. We shall describe these events in the next chapter.

CHAPTER 9

Eliade, Otto, and Durkheim: Escape into the Irrational

In the first chapter I called special attention to the time about fifty years ago when many scholars decided to forego the search for an origin of religion. They had come to the general conclusion that the origin of religions was not to be found in space/time history. We have now returned to that time. Our main representative for the earlier preview was Mircea Eliade, and it is only appropriate that we start with him once more.

Mircea Eliade

Mircea Eliade (1907–86) was a man of many interests and occupations. Born in Romania, he began his studies there but eventually finished his doctorate in Calcutta under the well-known Indian philosopher, the Cambridge-educated, Surendranath Dasgupta.[1] His dissertation was a study of yoga, which was published in French shortly

---

[1] Surendranath Dasgupta, *A History of Indian Philosophy*, 5 vols. (Calcutta: Motilal Banarsidass, 1922–52).

after its conclusion but later was thoroughly revised and amplified for reissue in 1954; it has been considered to be an authoritative discussion of the topic ever since.[2] Eliade also wrote novels, short stories, and plays. His association with the nationalistic governments in Romania prior to World War II resulted in several diplomatic positions but prevented his return to his home country after the Soviet Communist takeover. He finished his career with a lengthy stay at the University of Chicago from where he wrote numerous influential works.

In his book *The Quest*,[3] which can be construed as a eulogy for the search for the historical origin of religion, Eliade includes several short references to Wilhelm Schmidt, some of which I have already mentioned earlier in this book. We cannot lose track of original monotheism as our main concern, but at this point our focus is shifting to a certain extent. As we refer to some representative writers, we will mention their reactions to Schmidt and Lang, but the objective of this chapter is to show that their alternative was a flight into an irrational world where history was no longer history, *origin* no longer meant "origin," and inconsistent speculative theories were acclaimed as truth to substitute for historical data. Eliade is a good representative of this phenomenon because he had the courage to affirm that this was precisely what was happening. If some of the points in this chapter seem repetitive, I shall take it as a compliment indicating that my previous discussions have been clear enough to be remembered. So let us begin with Eliade's critiques of Schmidt, as we must, but then also ask what he has to offer in return.

I shall present some fairly lengthy quotations, but I need to interrupt them from time to time so as not to build up too great a pile of corrections since the reader might not remember all of the details by the end. I would like to state for the record that insofar as I highlight

---

[2] Mircea Eliade, *Yoga: Immortality and Freedom*, trans. Willard R. Trask (1935; repr., Princeton, NJ: Princeton University Press, 1970).

[3] Mircea Eliade, *The Quest: History and Meaning in Religion* (Chicago: Chicago University Press, 1969), 45–46.

points where Eliade shows a lack of knowledge of Schmidt's views, these deficiencies should not necessarily be thought of as ipso facto vitiating the contributions Eliade has made to the phenomenology of religion. The point is that phenomenology (a subjective description) and history (an objective narrative) are two different things, and the problem with all three of the representatives in this chapter is that they let phenomenology take the place of history, which can only create incoherence.

In the first passage I wish to bring up, Eliade complains about Schmidt's supposed excessive rationality in attributing the discovery of God by preliterate people to a purely logical inference. He alleges: "[Schmidt] neglects the obvious fact that religion is a very complex phenomenon—that it is, first of all, an experience *sui generis*, incited by man's encounter with the sacred."[4]

What a strange thing to say in light of Schmidt's own assertions! Apparently Eliade included himself when he said that there were too many pages in *Der Ursprung der Gottesidee* for a scholar to be expected to read them all, as we mentioned in the last chapter. He clearly did not read or remember volume 6,[5] nor, surprisingly, the section in the second edition of volume 1, in which Schmidt interacts with Pettazzoni,[6] nor Schmidt's separate book *Primitive Revelation.*[7] Schmidt could not have made his point any clearer that the belief in God, as found in original monotheism, did not have a purely rational basis but ultimately stemmed from an encounter by human beings in all of their dimensions with a personal God who revealed himself. To continue:

> Schmidt was inclined to think that all the irrational elements represent a "degeneration" of the genuine, primordial religion.
> The truth is that we do not have any means to investigate this

---

[4] Ibid., 25.

[5] Wilhelm Schmidt, *Der Urspung der Gottesidee*, vol. 6 (Münster: Aschendoff, 1935).

[6] Wilhelm Schmidt, *Der Ursprung der Gottesidee*, 2nd ed., vol. 1 (Münster: Aschendorff, 1926), 676–77.

[7] Wilhelm Schmidt, *Primitive Revelation*, trans. Joseph J. Baierl (St. Louis, MO: Herder, 1939), 109–24.

"primordial religion." Our oldest documents are relatively recent. They take us no further than the Paleolithic age; we ignore everything of what prelithic man thought during many hundreds of thousands of years.[8]

In a move that needs to wait for further clarification below, Eliade consigns all elements not consistent with theism to the category of the "irrational." Since on the previous page he had made brief reference to the culture-historical method, apparently the statement that "we do not have any means to investigate this 'primordial religion'" means we cannot observe it directly, which is undeniably true. But similar considerations are true in any science; the scientist must draw inferences to get beyond mere observation.

I must assume that Eliade's word "documents" here is supposed to refer to "evidence" or "documentation" in a broad sense beyond written materials because, surely, Eliade knew that written records give out a long time before one gets as far back as the Paleolithic era. Whatever he meant by this word, Eliade claims that there are no "documents" earlier than this era, and thus, he triumphs, we see that ipso facto Schmidt could not possibly account for the earliest religion of humanity.

Eliade creates more confusion than critique here. It would appear that "prelithic" humans, viz. people who do not even make stone tools, are represented by some of the tribes of Southeast Australia, who figure in both Graebner's and Schmidt's application of the culture-historical method. But then again, they are members of our species *Homo sapiens*. And if Eliade means to include prehuman hominids (nowadays technically "Hominians"), as his reference to hundreds of thousands of years indicates, he is making a highly debatable judgment. Should, for example, Neanderthal man be included in an analysis of human culture? One of the weak points of Schmidt's own writings is that he tried to accommodate the results of the human paleontology of his day in his theory, which caused him a lot of

---

[8] Eliade, *The Quest*, 25.

confusion.[9] I am inclined to think that if we discuss human culture, it is best to stick with those who are human, i.e., *Homo sapiens*, and not to include those creatures (including Neanderthal "man") who are not considered to be our true ancestors, not even by many scholars committed to human evolution.[10] To continue with Eliade: "It is true that the belief in High Gods seems to characterize the oldest cultures, but we also find there other religious elements. As far as we can reconstruct the most remote past, it is safer to assume that religious life was from the beginning rather complex, and that 'elevated' ideas coexisted with 'lower' forms of worship and belief."[11]

There is no need to repeat that clearly the culture-historical method had not found itself into Eliade's toolshed. Still, why is it safer to begin with "lower" forms? He says that the religions were complex right from the beginning, and I am thankful that he does not stipulate an *Urdummheit* ("primordial stupidity") as some German scholars did.[12] But when Eliade refers to monotheism as "elevated" and other forms, say animism, as "lower," the choice of words already betrays an evolutionist commitment. If the evidence points in the direction of original monotheism, why is it "safer" to ignore it and to stipulate other forms as concomitantly present? Eliade does not say.

In another section Eliade began with a somewhat patronizing summary of Lang's theory and then commented on Schmidt's influence on it in a rather startling way. Again, I need to interrupt the

---

[9] Schmidt, *Primitive Revelation*, 44–70.

[10] William Howells, *Mankind in the Making: The Story of Human Evolution* (Garden City, NY: Doubleday, 1959), 231–42.

[11] Eliade, *The Quest*, 25.

[12] This term stems specifically from the pen of K. Th. Preuss (1869–1938), who in his earlier articles attributed an *Urdummheit* to early human beings. According to his theory, once human beings had barely evolved past their bestial nature, they started fumbling about unsuccessfully with attempts at magic in order to control their environment. Finding themselves entirely ignorant or "stupid" (*dumm*) with regard to the workings of nature, they then turned to religion and art. K. Th. Preuss, "Der Ursprung der Religion und Kunst.Vorläufige Mitteilungen," *Globus* 86 (1904): 321–92; and 87 (1905): 333–419. He eventually became a supporter of primitive monotheism, though not on the basis of the culture-historical method.

lengthy quotation several times so as not to have to store up too many corrections.

> [A theory of preanimism] is that of Andrew Lang, postulating a belief in a High God at the beginnings of religion. Though almost ignored in England, this hypothesis, corrected and completed, was later accepted by Graebner and some Continental scholars. Unfortunately, one of the most learned ethnologists of our time, Wilhelm Schmidt, elaborated the hypothesis of the primitive belief in High Gods into a rigid theory of a primordial monotheism (*Urmonotheismus*). I say unfortunately because Schmidt, though a very able scholar, was also a Catholic priest and the scientific world suspected him of apologetic intentions.[13]

So, why didn't the "scientific world" read Schmidt in order to confirm or falsify the suspicions? In fact, it would not have taken much effort to see that he openly connected his ethnological theory to an apologetic for Christianity, just as other scholars were advocating their points of view in order to promote atheism and agnosticism. As stated above, anybody suspecting his intent needed only to look at volume 6 of *Der Ursprung der Gottesidee* or the separate book *Primitive Revelation* to find their "suspicions" confirmed. Still, what difference does that make, as long as the author is not insidious about his stance? Regardless of whether the purpose of a scholarly work is to promote a point of view, and such is usually the case, the important consideration is still whether what an author writes is correct. Or perhaps the "scientific world" was afraid of not being able to refute Schmidt's conclusions?

And what is one to make of the phrase, *Schmidt, though a very able scholar, was also a Catholic priest*? People who repeat this refrain should recognize that what they are doing in the process is just plain confessing to bigotry, either against scholars who practice a religion in general or against Catholic scholars in particular; both are possible. In reading various works of scholarship, to whatever extent this issue does make a difference, I would certainly place more confidence in

---

[13] Eliade, *The Quest*, 45–46.

the scholarship of the person who is committed to a divinely ordained standard of morality than that of someone who thumbs his nose at such values. And I'm afraid the story as we have encountered it in this book bears out this point, as we have seen so many writers break away from the evident data in order to maintain their naturalistic theories.

If I may add three points of correction concerning Andrew Lang. To repeat, he never went so far as to say that one could claim with assurance that religion began with belief in a high god. He had an intuition that it might be so, but he said that, as far as he could assess the evidence scientifically, in some places religion may have begun with animism and in others with belief in a supreme being.[14] Second, I have no clue to whom or what Eliade could be referring when he said that Lang's theory was "corrected" and "completed." By whom? He couldn't have meant Schmidt because Eliade brought him in subsequently. There was no "correcting" or "completing" except insofar as Lang defended his view in the intellectual arena and made some unnecessary verbal concessions. And third, whatever the status of Lang's theory of primitive monotheism may have been, Fritz Graebner never accepted it.[15] Graebner's significance was that he formalized the culture-historical method of ethnology,[16] which Wilhelm Schmidt adopted and adapted for his purposes; but Graebner never went along with original monotheism. Like Frazer and others, he believed that in human cultural development there was a preanimistic stage of belief in an impersonal magical force, which preceded the religious stage of animism.

Eliade continues:

---

[14] Andrew Lang, *The Making of Religion*, 2nd ed. (Charleston, SC: Bibliobazaar, 1900; 1st ed., 1898), 279–80.

[15] Fritz Graebner, *Das Weltbild der Primitiven: Eine Untersuchung der Urformen weltanschauendlichen Denkens by Naturvölkern* (Munich: Verlag Ernst Reihhardt, 1924), 4, 144n4.

[16] Fritz Graebner, *Methode der Ethnologie* (repr., University of Michigan; orig., Heidelberg: Carl Winter's Universitätsbuchhandlung, 1911).

Furthermore, . . . Schmidt was a thorough rationalist, and tried
to prove that the idea of God had been grasped by primitive
man strictly through causalistic thinking. As Schmidt was
publishing the monumental volumes of his *Ursprung der
Gottesidee*, however, the Western world witnessed the irruption
of quite a number of irrationalistic philosophies and ideologies.
Bergson's *élan vitale*, Freud's discovery of the unconscious, Lévy-
Bruhl's investigations of what he called the prelogical, mystical
mentality, R. Otto's *Das Heilige*, as well as the artistic revolutions
of dadaism and surrealism, mark some of the important events in
the history of modern irrationalism. Thus, very few ethnologists
and historians of religions **could** accept Schmidt's rationalistic
explanation of the discovery of the idea of God.[17]

Eliade is telling us here that the majority of the ethnologists and
historians of religion were unable to accept Schmidt's conclusions.
Why not? Because these conclusions were rational, and rationality was
supposedly no longer acceptable in certain circles. I am intrigued, or
maybe even amused, by the phrase "few could," which implies a general inability. Apparently the people in question would not have been
able to accept rational conclusions, even had they wanted to, because
irrationality reigned, which, I'm sorry to say, unavoidably sounds a
bit like academic *Urdummheit*, viz. making an axiom out of irrational
thinking. More accurately, I would say, some people did not *wish* to
accept Schmidt's rational (not rational*istic*) conclusions and opted for
some irrational escape. Surely they could have been more rationally
oriented had they decided to follow their capacity for reasoning.

This paragraph is also mixed up in other ways. We need to clarify to whom rationality and irrationality are attributed. At times the
investigator (e.g., Lévy-Bruhl) was clearly rational, but he thought his
subjects were not actually irrational but prerational. Other writers
or artists (e.g., Freud),[18] were, indeed, irrational and were expressing

---

[17] Eliade, *Quest*, 46 (emphasis added).
[18] Mircea Eliade, "Cultural Fashions and the History of Religions" in *The History of Religions: Understanding Human Experience*, ed. Joseph M. Kitagawa (Atlanta:

their irrationality by means of their work. On the whole one might even say that it is not entirely rational to bundle all of these figures, ranging from Otto to Dali, together into one single phenomenon called "irrationalism."

Partially Eliade was reporting on an era prior to him, but in doing so, he was not just commenting on what occurred in his recent past, but he was taking us back to the roots of his own thought. Eliade saw himself clearly in the role of continuing the work of Rudolf Otto, and the distinction he saw between himself and Otto was one of vantage point and detail.[19]

Eliade and a number of other scholars who shared similar views wound up teaching at the University of Chicago, where they became known as the "Chicago School." They also worked under their highly confusing preferred self-designation, the "History of Religions School."[20]

The crucial question now comes up in what sense Eliade and his colleagues used the term "history." As we have seen already, it could not have meant the establishment of a number of events into some chronological sequence or to provide greater detail and coherence to narratives of the past. Let us recall Eliade's pronouncement, as quoted in the first chapter: "So, after more than a century of untiring labor, scholars were forced to renounce the old dream of grasping the origin of religion *with the aid of historical tools*, and they devoted themselves to the study of different phases and aspects of religious life."[21]

So, as we remarked earlier, the study of "history" in this usage is apparently not the same as the study of history as normally carried out by historians. But then what does "history" mean for the "History

---

Scholars Press, 1987), 23–25.

[19] Mircea Eliade, *The Sacred and the Profane: The Nature of Religion*, trans. Willard R. Trask (New York: Harcourt, Brace & World, 1959), 8–16.

[20] In German they were simply designated as scholars in the *Religionswissen-schaft*, "the science of religion," a rather generic term but at least not as potentially misleading as the English designation.

[21] Eliade, *The Quest*, 50 (emphasis added).

of Religions School"? Eliade explains, beginning with a rhetorical question.

> Is religion an exclusively historical phenomenon, in the same way as, for instance, the fall of Jerusalem or of Constantinople? [No, but f]or the student of religion "history" means primarily that all religious phenomena are conditioned. A *pure* religious phenomenon does not exist.[22]

Thus, in the parlance of the History of Religions School, being "historical" is not so much a matter of being located somewhere on a particular spot among events on a time line but refers to a quality of the event or object observed. It means that the people observed by the anthropologist and the elements of their cultures are conditioned by their context as well as by the fact that they occupy a place in human culture and history. The same thing applies to the anthropologist. In fact, it is the human being's nature to be conditioned by all of human history.

At this point, given the last statement, it becomes difficult to sort through precisely what Eliade is expressing here. On the one hand, he says about his use of data without regard to ordering them in time or geography,

> From the historical-cultural point of view, such a juxtaposition of religious data pertaining to peoples so far removed in time and space is not without some danger. For there is always the risk of falling back into the errors of the 19th century and, particularly, of believing with Tylor or Frazer that the reaction of the human mind to natural phenomena is uniform. But the progress accomplished in cultural ethnology and in the history of religions has shown that this is not always true, that man's reactions to nature are often conditioned by his culture and hence, finally, by history.[23]

---

[22] Ibid., 52. [Words in brackets were supplied by me for the sake of clarity.]
[23] Eliade, *Sacred and Profane*, 16.

The problem is that when we look at Eliade's actual work concerning preliterate societies, whatever he may have intended by asserting "history" seems to get lost quickly. He constantly repeats his principle that primitive human cultures do not have a history except insofar as they direct themselves to the time of *the beginning*, the time of the mythical ancestors. This approach is perhaps epitomized in *The Myth of the Eternal Return*,[24] where he makes the point over and over again that human beings of an archaic mind-set do not have a history in our sense, only a cycle of myths that draws them back to their conception of the primordial origin of their world. A good example for Eliade's paradigm is the "Dreamtime" of the Australian indigenous people, which, at least for some tribes, appears to be the beginning and end of all time and the mystical location in which all ritual actions become real. To quote from the introductory section of *Eternal Return*, "If we observe the general behavior of archaic man, we are struck by the following facts: neither the objects of the external world nor human acts, properly speaking, have any autonomous intrinsic value. Objects or acts acquire a value, and in so doing become real, because they participate, after one fashion or another, in a reality that transcends them."[25]

A little further he says with reference to gestures or rituals:

> This conscious repetition of given paradigmatic gestures reveals the original ontology. The crude products of nature, the objects fashioned by the industry of man, acquire their reality, their identity, only to the extent of their participation in a transcendent reality. The gesture acquires meaning, reality, *solely* to the extent to which it repeats a primordial act.[26]

Thus, if the cultus of archaic people invariably acquires its meaning through emulation of a mythological time, as Eliade puts it, *in*

---

[24] Mircea Eliade, *The Myth of the Eternal Return*, trans. Willard R. Trask (Princeton, NJ: Princeton University Press, 1954), 3–4. This book was published in 1959 as a Harper Torchbook under the title *Cosmos and History*.

[25] Ibid.

[26] Ibid., 5 (emphasis added).

illo tempore, literally "in that time," pointing back to the time of the ancestors, then it certainly leads one to wonder in what sense the analysis is "historical."

On the other hand, it begins to become clear why Eliade and his colleagues were saying that the origin of religion is not "historical" but "metaphysical." What Eliade has done is (1) insisted on the historicity of human beings and their culture, (2) reinterpreted this historicity into a specific metaphysical quest for an ideal age, and (3) equated the archaic person's "history" with a metaphysics of an ideal origin. This is a speculative belief and not what we would commonly understand by "history," viz. a series of events in time.

Consequently, it appears to be unavoidable to accept that there is definitely a paradox, likely an inconsistency, and probably a streak of irrationality running through Eliade's works. Let us continue to pursue this line of investigation and look more closely at the work of Rudolf Otto, whom Eliade included in his list.

Rudolf Otto

Rudolf Otto's (1869–1937) writings cross over the fields of theology, philosophy, and religious studies. He enriched his research by taking several trips abroad, which included lengthy stays in India and Africa. Some of his later well-known writings, *Mysticism East and West*[27] and *India's Religion of Grace and Christianity Compared and Contrasted*,[28] incorporate careful studies in comparative religion with Christian theology. He is best known for his book *The Idea of the Holy*, which appeared in German in 1917.[29] Otto began the foreword of this celebrated book by stating:

---

[27] Rudolf Otto, *Mysticism East and West: A Comparative Analysis of the Nature of Mysticism*, trans. Bertha L. Bracey and Richenda C. Payne (New York: Collier, 1932).

[28] Rudolf Otto, *India's Religion of Grace and Christianity Compared and Contrasted*, trans. Frank Hugh Foster (New York: Macmillan, 1930).

[29] Rudolf Otto, *The Idea of the Holy: An Inquiry into the Non-Rational Factor in the Idea of the Divine and Its Relation to the Rational*, trans. John W. Harvey (New York: Oxford University Press, 1923).

> In this book I have ventured to write of that which may be called "non-rational" or "supra-rational" in the depths of the divine nature. I do not thereby want to promote in any way the tendency of our time towards an extravagant and fantastic "irrationalism," but rather to join issue with it in its morbid form. The "irrational" is to-day a favourite [*sic*] theme of all who are too lazy to think or too ready to evade the arduous duty of clarifying their ideas and grounding their convictions on the basis of coherent thought.[30]

As it stands, this declaration certainly appears to be a straightforward repudiation of Eliade's inclusion of him in a set, with, say Dadaism, a movement in the world of art that repudiated conventional forms in society, as expressed in art. But a repudiation of nomenclature does not necessarily imply a repudiation in substance. Even though he rejected outright irrationality, the consequence of Otto's thought is ultimately not all that different from the use Eliade made of it because, at least in this book, it led to an unsubstantiated preference for subjective intuitions over rational methods in delineating the nature of religion.[31] In other words, what Otto claimed here, and what he actually wound up doing, were not the same things.

Otto's stated intentions are based on the notion that prior to the time of his writing this book with its new thesis, the study of religions was almost entirely devoted to its rational side. By that he meant scholars looked at the beliefs, concepts, and mythology exclusively from the vantage point of its intellectual content. Even rituals, art, and worship practices were being explained in conceptual terms, as beginning with the rational doctrines of the beliefs or mythologies, and then acting out the narratives or precepts derived from them.

---

[30] Ibid., vii.

[31] It should be pointed out here that there are significant differences between Otto and Friedrich Schleiermacher, who wrote about a century earlier. Schleiermacher inferred from a universal "feeling of absolute dependence" to the reality of the Absolute that constitutes the object of our dependence, whereas Otto began with the experience, a direct experiential encounter with the Sacred. See Friedrich Schleiermacher, *The Christian Faith*, 2nd ed., trans. H. R. MacIntosh and J. S. Stewart (Philadelphia: Fortress, 1976), 12–16.

We need not pursue the question of to what extent Otto's assessment was true; he certainly could not have meant it as a universal description of all work before him. Still, it was Otto's conviction that such forms of analysis at best addressed only half of what religion was all about, namely precisely only the beliefs and practices that can be described in objective words and sentences.

According to Otto, it is a big mistake to ignore the fact that there is a deep, nonrational side to a person's religious experience. You can see by that statement that we have switched subjects from "religion" to "religious experience." Otto's implied point is that you cannot talk about "religion" without taking into serious account the experience of the person who practices the religion. And it is here that the nonrational becomes of utmost importance. If one practices a religion fully in accord with its rational precepts, this participation must have been preceded by a direct personal experience based on an encounter with "the Holy." Such an experience presumably applies to all authentically religious people but is particularly manifest in those who are really outstanding members of a religion: the founders, visionaries, and mystics.

One cannot present a clear verbal explanation of "the Holy." As we just saw, it is supposed to be nonrational and beyond concepts; therefore, it excludes being captured directly by words. Still, people are often fast to discuss the ineffable. As Samuel Johnson pointed out with regard to Jacob Boehme, "If Jacob saw the unutterable, Jacob should not have tried to utter it."[32]

And so Otto's expression "the Holy" nowadays has a fairly clear referent. It entails an experience that goes beyond words but can be circumscribed sufficiently by its empirical effects so that there is no question that one is referring to Otto's brainchild and nothing else.

The centerpiece of this idea is that the person has an encounter with "the numinous," a term derived from the Latin word for

---

[32] Quoted by Alasdair MacIntyre, "Is Religious Language So Idiosyncratic That We Can Hope for No Account of It?" in *Religious Language and the Problem of Religious Knowledge*, ed. Ronald E. Santoni (Bloomington, IN: Indiana University Press, 1968), 50.

the divine realm. It refers to the usually sudden awareness of having encountered the sacred, which transcends any conceptual understanding and is so powerful that it will utterly change one's life and way of seeing things. Because it lies deeper than our words and concepts, the experience occurs without being limited to particular cultures, geographical areas, or times.

There are two crucial aspects to this realization of the Holy. It is a mystery that evokes fear, hence one part of the experience is designated as the *mysterium tremendum*. In light of the Holy, individuals recognize their sinfulness and unworthiness to be in its presence, and they fear this sacred purity will justifiably destroy them. However, the other side of the experience is the *mysterium fascinosum*, which is to say that the Holy is attractive; it draws people to itself. At the same time as people become aware of their sin and unworthiness, they also become aware of love, grace, and acceptance. Thus, to make contact with the Holy is, as Otto insists, not just a feeling, but it is a direct experience on all spiritual levels that leads persons to see themselves and the entire world in a whole new light.

One can immediately raise the question of whether each religious person has had the experience Otto describes, but I'm not sure it would make much of a conceptual difference because Otto's thesis is clearly not empirical but a priori. He gives examples, which may illustrate that there have been people who have had this experience in the past but they do not prove that necessarily all religious people fall into this category. Nevertheless, he states unequivocally that this encounter with the Holy is the basis of religious experience and, therefore, of religion as a whole.

Otto insists that this nonrational experience is only one-half of what religion is all about, and in his later works he once again focuses on the conceptual side of religion and does not read subliminal, nonrational elements into what various authors are saying. However, even though in *The Idea of the Holy* Otto contends that the nonrational and rational aspects are the warp and woof of religion, in this book his protestations notwithstanding, the nonrational definitely receives priority not only in the focus of his discussion but in the fundamental place which he accords to it for religion. He even states that if it were not so, viz. if the historical and conceptual side came first, there could be no religion (see below). This view seems to be overstated and puzzling since his starting point was that one should ultimately not separate the two; as it stands, it appears to be arbitrary and not sustainable.

Now let us be clear on what Otto is doing. He is saying that a fundamental experience of the Holy is what ultimately characterizes the nature of religion. To look at the negative side of this contention, the nature of religion is not ultimately characterized by conceptual beliefs accrued over history. Thus—and this is the really crucial point—to find the origin of religion we should not look at historically developed beliefs but at the role religion plays in the human psyche. And so we begin to see how the word *origin* became dehistoricized and was reinterpreted into something psychological and metaphysical rather than an act or event in space-time history.

This view of the nature of religion is brought out by Otto's own reaction to the thesis of original monotheism. The year of publication for *The Idea of the Holy*, 1917, places these remarks subsequent to Andrew Lang's death and the publication of both the French and German versions of *Der Ursprung*, though Otto manifested no familiarity with the latter. Let us once again look at a fairly lengthy quotation in stages.

> Finally, it is only upon our assumption of an *a priori* basis of ideas and feelings that an explanation is forthcoming for the interesting phenomena to which Andrew Lang rightly drew attention. These do not, of course, support the hypothesis of a "primitive monotheism," that offspring of missionary apologetic, which, eager to save the second chapter of Genesis, yet feels the shame of a modern at the walking of Yahweh "in the garden in the cool of the day."[33]

---

[33] Otto, *The Holy*, 133.

Otto declared that his understanding of religion, as set forth in the previous pages of *The Idea of the Holy*, was going to provide the only viable explanation for the "phenomena" exposed by Lang. It would have helped if he had been more specific in stating exactly what precisely needed explanation, but that matter becomes clearer as he proceeds: The problem is the appearance of apparent monotheism among some people whose culture supposedly is not yet ready for it. Thus, his starting point with an evolutionist-hierarchical scheme is obvious. The gratuitous unkind second half of the quotation would perhaps be more effective if it was clear what Otto was getting at. If he meant to say that the view of the supreme being in original monotheism was less anthropomorphic than the depiction of Yahweh in parts of the Bible, he had obviously not read the books he cited, which included, for example, the anthropomorphism of the Southeastern Australian deities.

Otto took the position that no naturalistic basis (which he clarified by enumerating "animism," "pantheism," and unspecified "others"[34]) could account for Lang's data and that only his subjective approach would be able to do so. Even though the word "others" leaves room for a lot of possibilities, we can agree with that part of the statement since he specified "naturalistic," though how his approach can do so to the exclusion of other positions that are not entirely naturalistic remains to be seen. One may also question how it came about that Otto would be able to speak with such finality on this matter, and all I can offer by way of explanation is that apparently doing so is a perquisite of taking a purely a priori approach apart from studying the evidence.

Otto carried right on to reveal what he called the "essence" of Lang's (actually Howitt's) discoveries: There are tribes in which their belief in a high god vastly exceeds the rest of their religions and mythologies. For many such cultures, this belief is due to the

---

[34] Ibid.

lengthy influence in the past by a higher theistic religion, long forgotten by now (except apparently by Rudolf Otto). This heritage would explain why many of these tribal people responded so positively to missionaries and had been stimulated to recognize the god of their own heritage in the god preached by the missionaries.[35]

However, Otto concedes that not all cases of monotheism in preliterate cultures could be explained in that way. He asserts: "But though the theory of a surviving tradition is often applicable, there are many of these cases in which it is impossible to apply it without doing violence to the facts. In these we have clearly to do with anticipations and presentiments rather than survivals."[36]

Otto illustrates this point with an analogy to Gypsy musicians who, though backward in other aspects of their culture, have an advanced sense for music. Similarly, he claims, the cultures with a supreme being manifest an innate disposition toward religion that outstrips by far the rest of their cultural capability. It is an anticipation of the future direction of religious development. Otto contends that this explanation could only be derived from a subjective understanding of people and religions.[37]

We must agree entirely with Otto in the last sentence of this summary. It is clearly only on the basis of a subjective approach that the notion of original monotheism as a harbinger of future developments can be entertained because, as we know, the historical sequence almost always goes in the other direction. In the histories of cultures where we find a supreme being, in most cases we also see that the cultural trajectories move into the direction away from monotheism and into the various possibilities of degeneration. Let us recall that Eliade, for example, exaggeratedly said that such a movement toward the *deus absconditus* was *always* present, which is also not accurate.[38]

---

[35] Ibid., 134.
[36] Ibid.
[37] Ibid., 135.
[38] Eliade, *Sacred and Profane*, 125.

However, Otto contends that inquiry based on historical principles or the notion of a primitive revelation would be unable to account
for this anomalous monotheism. To follow what Otto wrote in this
paragraph, we must grant him an implied premise that the preliterate people arrived at the awareness of a rudimentary monotheism by
a process of powerful introspective reflection. Otto asks his readers
to think back to some moment in time when they felt utterly sure in
their commitment to their religion. He called this phenomenon "the
self-attestation of religious belief in one's own mind."[39] Naturalistic
psychologists, he asserted, should take this idea more seriously, but so
should scholars who approach religion from a historical perspective.
Since the origin of religion lies in the subjective experience of the
individual, a historical approach would prevent the recognition of
this subjective factor, and, in effect, make religion impossible. Having
tried to explain what Otto was saying, here is the direct assertion:

> The upholders of the theory of "Primitive Monotheism" . . . show
> no less serious disregard of this central fact than the naturalistic
> psychologists. For if the phenomena we have been considering
> were based simply and solely on historical traditions and the dim
> memories of a "primeval revelation," as on such a theory they
> must be, this self-attestation from within would be just as much
> excluded as before.[40]

But "why?" as the previous owner of my copy penciled in the
margin. Why does a historical inquiry or the memory of an objective
revelation in the past exclude that the subjects of the inquiry had
strong subjective experiences? Otto had by now gone much further
at this point in the book than he had indicated originally. He had said
that the rational and the nonrational went hand in hand, but at this
point he seems to be showing heavy favoritism for the nonrational;
He does so without a convincing reason.

---

[39] Otto, *The Holy*, 135.
[40] Ibid.

Schmidt's criticism of Otto's ideas concerning the origin of religion comes down to the judgment that Otto "makes not the faintest attempt at proving any of his propositions whatsoever,"[41] an assessment with which it is impossible to disagree. One can certainly take exception with Eliade's grouping Otto together with Dadaism and Freud, but, for the sake of our subject, the word *irrational* applies just as well as *nonrational*. The bottom line is that he placed the "origin" of religion outside of the historical and objective and into a contrived psychological and subjective scheme. Worse than that, he was dismissive of an inquiry into the historical facts as interference, preferring his own speculative interpretations regardless of whether they could be proven. That last step is certainly irrational.

Émile Durkheim

To fill out this picture, let us turn to one other, different attempt at explaining the origin of religion. What makes the following thesis different is that it attempts to explain the origin of religion on the basis of seemingly historical events in time, complete with claims as to the chronological development of all religions. Still, when all is said, the origin supposedly described in historical terms is not really supposed to be a historical origin. The theory in question is the idea propagated by Émile Durkheim that the root of religion lies in totemism and that its essential nature is to fulfill a social function.

Émile Durkheim (1858–1917) was a French sociologist. In fact, he was among the first scholars in France to adopt that label for himself, and he was largely responsible for including sociology as an accepted discipline in the world of French academics. His last book was his treatment on the origin of religion.[42] It became particularly popular because of his conception of religion as a social phenomenon

---

[41] Wilhelm Schmidt, *The Origin and Growth of Religion: Facts and Theories*, trans. H. J. Rose (London: Methuen, 1931), 142.

[42] Émile Durkheim, *The Elementary Forms of Religious Life*, trans. Carol Cosman (1912; repr., New York: Oxford, 2001).

based on the method called functionalism. Functionalism explains various aspects of society from the perspective of their contributions to the welfare of the group.[43] At least a major part of his thesis is expressed by the dictum, "The god of the clan, the totemic principle, must be the clan itself, but transfigured and imagined in the physical form of the plant or animal species that serve as totem."[44]

Please allow me at this point to give you a rough synopsis of Durkheim's proposal. The nature of the proposal, more than its content, is of interest to us. Since most of his factual assertions are wrong, a lengthier discussion would have to involve pursuing numerous tangents. A short summary that I hope presents his position accurately, along with my brief disclaimers, should suffice. For the points that become important for us, we will, of course, provide documented references and quotations. Durkheim's theories on totemism are based on the data derived from the tribes and clans of Southeastern Australia.

Durkheim contended that

1. All cultures at one time passed through a stage of totemism (an unverified, false assumption based on the priority that Durkheim gave to the priority of social organization).
2. Most of the year the clans had little or no contact with one another (which is also not true; if they did not, how could there be marriages or, for that matter, warfare?).
3. There was an annual gathering of all clans, bringing together all members of the larger group (the phratry, or, as I prefer to call it, the moiety, usually identified with the whole "tribe"). During this time, special ceremonies were performed. (This statement is also not accurate. If Durkheim is referring to the initiation rites, they were called by the clans, and members of other clans and tribes showed up for the ceremony. Thus,

---

[43] Functionalism also became a dominant theory in England as well, initiated by Bronislaw Malinowsky. See his collection of essays in *Magic, Science and Religion* (Garden City, NY: Doubleday Anchor, 1948).

[44] Durkheim, *Elementary Forms*, 154.

these were not occasions of cohesion of a single social group. Other than that, there were no annual moiety-wide rallies.)

4. The excitement produced at these occasions induced a state of euphoria or ecstasy ("effervescence") in the minds of the people, leading them to recognize a spiritual force (*mana*) permeating this gathering. (This construction is based entirely on Durkheim's imagination.)

5. This tribe-wide experience of individuals linked together by the same totem served as a vehicle of cohesion for the entire community. (This idea cannot be true in light of the fact that there were no single-larger-social-unit gatherings of the type Durkheim posits.)

6. The practices originally derived from these totemic celebrations survived and grew even as societies changed and religions became more sophisticated. By its nature, religion serves as the "glue" of society. Let us look at Durkheim's own statement summing up the central part of his theory:

> All this leads us back to the same idea: that rites are, above all, the means by which the social group periodically reaffirms itself. And in this way perhaps we can manage to reconstruct hypothetically the way the totemic cult must have first arisen. Some men, who felt united in part by blood ties but even more by a community of interests and traditions, gathered and took stock of their moral unity. For the reasons we have proposed, they were led to imagine this unity in the form of a special kind of consubstantiality: they thought of themselves as participating in the nature of a specific animal. For them, under these conditions, there was only one way to affirm their collective existence, and that was to affirm themselves as animals of this same species, not only in the silence of consciousness but through physical acts. These acts constituted the cult, and clearly they must have consisted of

> movements imitating the animal with whom man
> identified. So understood, imitative rites seem to be
> the first form of the cult.[45]

Durkheim's careful delineation of exactly what the earliest human beings must have thought is intriguing, particularly since, according to his theory, similar deliberations must have occurred around the globe many times. Just as Tylor had argued in his day that even the most sophisticated monotheism is nothing more than animism with a really big spirit, Durkheim proceeds to derive all further religions from this early totemic cultus. The totemic animals turned into spirits, the spirits into gods, and the gods eventually gave way to God. Inspired by the notion of the totem feast as conjured up by Robertson Smith[46] (who also supplied the foundation for Freud's conjectures), Durkheim took the development of the associated actions all the way from people imitating their clan animals to Christian communion as an advanced totemic rite.[47]

Given all of the previous discussion in this book, I trust that the reader will recognize that Durkheim's scheme, even though loosely based on the anthropological reports from Australia, consists of generalizations and inferences that cannot be supported. To his credit Durkheim showed awareness of Strehlow's descriptions, which were generally ignored. Since he did use Australia as his particular database, it is, of course, of particular interest to us how he dealt with the phenomenon of supreme beings among Australian indigenous people. Concerning this discussion, Durkheim's sources apparently did not go any further than Lang's *Making of Religion* and Tylor's "Limits of Savage Religion." Regardless, there can be little doubt that to whatever extent Lang's theory provided an obstacle to his pan-totemism, he could not let it survive.

---

[45] Ibid., 287.

[46] Ibid., 249. W. Robertson Smith, *Lectures on the Religion of the Semites*, 2nd ed. (London: Adam and Charles Black, 1894).

[47] Durkheim, *Elementary Forms*, 250.

Of all of the descriptions of the Australian supreme beings by various critics of Lang and Schmidt, Durkheim's is one of the most accurate and fair.[48] His critique is also among the least substantial,[49] a fact that should probably be considered as a good thing since he did not go out on a limb on this topic with absurd counter-assertions to obvious truths. Still, it did not hold up. After providing a digest of Lang's summary of Howitt's descriptions, he mentioned Tylor's borrowing-from-missionaries hypothesis, followed by Lang's theory of indigenous origin. Durkheim underplayed Lang's conclusion that the local people arrived at the knowledge of a supreme being by seeing him as the maker of everything[50] and attributed a theory of revelation to him, which he did not hold. He then stated, "But the facts do not support either Tylor's sceptical [sic] hypothesis or Lang's theological interpretation."[51]

Unfortunately, what Durkheim called "facts" were not facts but interpretations, and he went on to shoehorn the material on Australian supreme beings into his theory of totemic origin. He agreed that the supreme beings were indigenous but asserted that they also were derived from the earliest totemic systems. In many cases, he claimed, the totemic being for a group was an exalted ancestor or a culture hero. Becoming increasingly endowed with conceptions of superior power, he was eventually transformed into a deity. As we have seen in earlier instances, Durkheim took notice neither of the fact that the strongest belief in a supreme being occurred in the tribes where there was no indication of an earlier totemic system, nor, as we showed in chapters 4 and 5, that a correlation between an exalted ancestor or a culture hero could not be sustained.

All of the above information on Durkheim's views is in a sense preliminary. The point is now to examine what exactly he meant

---

[48] Ibid., 210–13.

[49] Ibid., 213–16.

[50] Andrew Lang, *Myth, Ritual and Religion*, 2nd ed., vol. 1 (London: Longmans, Green, 1913; first ed., 1887), 330.

[51] Durkheim, *Elementary Forms*, 213.

in his descriptions. It certainly appears that he is referring to real events in real time, and there are plenty of passages to sustain that impression. For example, he states in the context of including some examples from North American Indians in his analysis, even though he considers them to be on a culturally higher plane than the Australians: "So, though American totemism is further from its origins than Australian totemism, it has more effectively preserved the remnants of certain important features. . . . At the same time, it will put us in a better position to understand how totemism is connected to subsequent religious forms and to place it in the context of historical development."[52]

Or, in another place, we read: "Furthermore, we are convinced that totemism is the most primitive religion that can be observed at present, perhaps the most primitive that has ever existed. Indeed, totemism is inseparable from clan-based social organization."[53]

Then, having made a quick argument to the effect that there is no society without division into clans, Durkheim continues: "A religion so closely allied with a social system of such surpassing simplicity can be considered the most elementary we know. If we manage to find the sources of the beliefs just analyzed [in the previous chapters], we may discover at the same time the causes and sparks of humanity's religious feeling."[54]

Can there possibly be any doubt that Durkheim is relating his theories on totemism to states of affairs that have obtained in the past and that he is writing an objective history that spans from the origin of religion within a totemistic society to its later forms? Even right before he pulls the rug out from under our feet, so to speak, it still looks as though constructing history is what he is doing.

As [religion] progresses historically, the causes that called it into existence, though still exerting their influence, are now viewed

---

[52] Ibid., 82–83.
[53] Ibid., 126.
[54] Ibid.

through a vast system of distorting interpretations. . . . We shall
see how in primitive religions, the religious phenomenon still
bears the visible imprint of its origins; it would be more difficult
for us to infer those origins by considering only more developed
religions.[55]

Of course, he is right in saying that reconstructing any history
can be difficult because of distorting factors, including the historian's
own subjectivity, and so it seems to be a good idea to go back as far
in time as possible to uncover causes. Thus, chronology seems to be a
central element of Durkheim's inquiry.

But wait! Despite all of these references to the history of humanity, Durkheim denies that he is actually interested in any event in the
time/space matrix.

> Our study, then, is a way of taking up the old problem of the
> origin of religions *under new conditions*. Certainly if what we
> mean by origin is an absolute first beginning, the question is not
> in the least scientific and must be firmly dismissed. There is no
> crucial moment when religion began to exist, and the point is
> not to find a way to transport ourselves there by thought. Like
> any human institution, religion begins nowhere.[56]

At the risk of understatement, these assertions are seriously at
odds with the language Durkheim uses throughout the rest of the
book, where his constant model is an evolutionary sequence of developments. But let us see what we can make of these assertions.

"Origin" certainly means a beginning in time; it is almost always
difficult to figure out what the qualification of "absolute" adds to a
word. In this case, it really adds nothing. The "origin" of something
is the first time it has become actual. If the adjective "absolute" is
supposed to intensify the fact that this was the first time, that would
be redundant. But if the intent of calling it the "absolute origin" is to

---

[55] Ibid., 9.
[56] Ibid. (emphasis in original)

mystify the event (and I suspect that is the case), that's a purely rhetorical move, and we might as well drop the adjective.

To move on, it would be one thing for Durkheim to say that science has so far not produced any reliable information on the chronological origin of religion, or even, as others have said, that science is so far incapable of providing information concerning religion's beginning. But Durkheim condemns the question as unscientific, which is an entirely gratuitous verdict. Why should we accept it as such other than out of deference to *monsieur le professeur?* Even if a scientific question does not have an answer at present, even if no scientific answer seems to be possible (such as ascertaining both the location and the momentum of an elementary particle at the same time—the Heisenberg principle), that does not make the question unscientific.[57] Certainly no person of academic standing was searching for an actual way of mental teleportation backwards in time to "the crucial moment when religion began to exist"; even more modest historiography has never had time travel at its disposal. But if the matter truly were beyond scientific inquiry and there were no scientific answer, then no factual answer would be possible, either positive or negative. Then Durkheim's assertion that there was no such point would be just as unscientific and meaningless as anyone's statement defending its existence. If the question is ruled out of bounds, a negative answer does not have special privileges. Finally, one is certainly thrown for a loop by the enigmatic assertion that "religion begins nowhere."

I believe Durkheim's reasoning behind this astonishing declaration is as follows. Human beings are by their nature social animals; that means that wherever human beings are present, the social institutions that come with being human must also be present. Since his point in the book is to show that religion is a social institution, religion must also always have been a part of being human.

---

[57] See the discussion by Milton K. Munitz, *The Mystery of Existence: An Essay in Philosophical Cosmology* (New York: Appleton, Century, Crofts, 1965), particularly 33–47.

Still, if this is the reasoning Durkheim uses, he has not yet reha-
bilitated himself from the above criticism that would apply to himself
as well as to others. Furthermore, assuming that we have reinstituted
the validity of the question after all, it would appear that Durkheim
is committing a non sequitur. Unless he also accepts the eternal existence of humans, which I seriously doubt, there had to have been a
beginning to the human species. Moreover, if he contends that there
can be no humans without social institutions including religion, the
"absolute beginning point of humanity" must also be the "absolute
beginning point" of religion among the other inevitable institutions.
To say that there is no such point, or that "religion begins nowhere,"
would entail that there was no beginning point for human beings
and that "humanity begins nowhere." I doubt Durkheim would have
accepted these statements as true, and there certainly would be no
good reason to accept them as anything but meaningless rhetoric.
The same problem besets his assertions concerning a beginning in
time for religion.

Durkheim now takes up a similar position to that of Rudolf
Otto. The search for the "origin of religion" is really the question of
what consistently makes people be religious. "The problem we pose
is entirely different. We would like to find a way of discovering the
ever-present causes that generate the most essential forms of religious
thought and practice."[58]

Durkheim is correct. This problem is "entirely different." It is a
new one, substituted for the previous one of a historical origin, and
in itself there is nothing incoherent in the problem he poses now. It
is intriguing that human beings seem to have a capacity for transcendence and a need for it to be fulfilled, and this phenomenon is a good
object of study for a phenomenology of religion.[59] But raising that

---

[58] Durkheim, *Elementary Forms*, 9–10.

[59] I have addressed this matter off and on in various writings. Winfried Corduan,
Handmaid to Theology (Eugene, OR: Wipf & Stock, 2009; orig. Baker, 1981), 61–80;
Mysticism: An Evangelical Option? (Eugene, OR: Wipf & Stock, 2009; orig., Grand
Rapids: Zondervan, 1991), 63–80; with Norman L. Geisler, *Philosophy of Religion*,

problem does not invalidate the previous one of a historical origin, let alone make it unscientific. To use one answer to respond to the other question creates only incoherence.

Unfortunately, Durkheim is guilty of precisely such an incoherence. He insists that he is searching for the "ever-present causes that generate the essential forms of religion." Very well, what are the results of this quest? First, he states that by "origin" he does not mean "a beginning in time." Then he ignores that assertion and refers us to primordial events in prehistoric cultures. He insists on the necessity of chronological sequencing because only the most primitive form of religion can answer his question, even though he has no method to distinguish between "earlier" and "later." He isolates totemism as the original form of all religion because it was presumably the earliest human social institution and tells us that, therefore, all religions are derived from totemism. Consequently, the "ever-present causes" are . . . ?

Before getting to Durkheim's conundrum, let me clarify his problem with a clear contrast. It would be easy, of course, to complete the above sentence with pointing to a single sufficient condition, namely "a consistent awareness of a Creator." Obviously Durkheim had no intention of taking that option. However, I do wish to point out the advantages this answer would have as a scientific hypothesis (keeping in mind that it would not by itself prove the existence of a creator). It would be a sound explanation, viz. one would not have to go through a complicated set of speculative hypotheses to show how the awareness of a creator can lead to religion; the transition, insofar as it makes sense even to think of one, is self-evident. It would fit what we know about the past thanks to the reconstructions that are made possible by means of the culture-historical methodology. It would also account

---

2nd ed. (Eugene, OR: Wipf & Stock, 2005; orig., Grand Rapids: Baker, 1988), 62–76; Winfried Corduan, *A Tapestry of Faiths: The Common Threads Between Christianity and World Religions* (Eugene, OR: Wipf & Stock, 2009; orig., Downers Grove, IL: IVP, 2002), 195–220. In the last-named book I make positive use of the insights of Jung, Otto, and Eliade but only with respect to their help for a phenomenology of religion.

for the continued practice of religion in the present. Finally, it ranks high in plausibility. Let me just put this last assertion in understated terms without tying myself to statistics: I'm sure a lot of people claim they are aware that there is a creator.

But how would or should Durkheim fill in that blank? Despite the clear statement of the problem, it is not clear what his answer could be. The ever-present causes that generate the most essential forms of religious thought and practice are . . . ? Should we put "totemism" in that slot? This would be a logical (albeit false) answer if he was thinking simply of historical origins, but he had clearly stated that this was not his aim. Furthermore, even if it were true that all cultures had passed through a totemistic phase (which it is not), we still could not plausibly explain the fact of religious consciousness in the present on the basis of a remote, inaccessible totemic stage in the past without inventing a history of religions that is out of harmony with the facts.

So maybe Durkheim should say that the "ever-present causes" are "the demands of a society for an institution that holds it together." Now this idea is logically possible, regardless of whether it is true; but, unfortunately for his case, it is also circular because Durkheim had already used that idea as an assumption in establishing that totemism was integral to the nature of any primitive society. It was already questionable in that context, but to make this unfounded assumption become the outcome of the entire study as well would, indeed, be irrational.

One might suggest that Durkheim should have written a different book, one in which he examined a sufficient sample of different religions and then showed that each of them had its primary purpose as a social institution for the sake of providing unity in society. However, such a study could only be a tour de force. Consequently, given the manifest implausibility of bringing off such a study, Durkheim took the back road of trying to show that since (a) totemism is the most basic form of religion, and (b) all religions are variations or extensions of totemism, and (c) totemism's function is to provide unity for a society; therefore, (d) all religions exist in order to provide unity for a society. In addition to the questionable truth of the premises, this is not a valid deductive argument either. It leaves the door open to the possibility that one of the changes a religion may undergo in its variation and extension of totemism could be the loss of its purpose as providing unity for society. Whether that has happened would have to be decided on the basis of an empirical investigation, and Durkheim would be right back with having to pull off the tour de force we mentioned.

There is no need to belabor this point any further. Durkheim's theory is based on erroneous interpretations of the facts, combined with a fundamental incoherence with regard to what constitutes an "origin" of religion. Discussions of Durkheim frequently close with the final observation that even though he was wrong in almost everything he said, his great legacy consists of the fact that he has demonstrated the essentially social nature of religion. I do not believe he has done any such thing. He assumed it, but he did not demonstrate it.

The Death of the Origin

And so we come to the demise of the search for an origin of religion. Anthropology continued on the inquiry for ways of describing the nature of religion, combining pragmatic methods (e.g., functionalism) with psychological ones (e.g., structuralism). Any theories that have become so broad as to include multiple cultures have been greeted with a great amount of suspicion. Clearly one cannot totally ignore the effects of history on a present-day culture, but to establish a sequence of cultures in history is regarded as questionable, and the search for an origin of religion is just plain not allowed. Thus, we arrive at the assessment by Tomoko Masuzawa:

> It has been some time since the question of the origin of religion
> was seriously entertained. Today, there is little sign of the matter
> being resuscitated and once again becoming the focus of the
> lively debate of old. Looking back upon the bold speculations
> of their forefathers, contemporary scholars of religion seem to

consider themselves to be in a new phase of scholarship, having
learned, above all, not to ask impossible questions. . . . Such is
the present-day assessment of these "theories," and if we still
study these ideas today, it is supposed to be only in order to
assist their more decorous—and more secure—second burial.[60]

In the meantime, there is the work of Wilhelm Schmidt, largely
unread, almost invariably distorted beyond recognition, dismissed
most often on the basis of misrepresentations, though sometimes
with critiques that legitimately question parts of his work but do not
negate his conclusions. Scholars will not ask the questions Schmidt
answered. However, that undeniable fact does not alter three truths
that emerge: (1) The conclusion of an original monotheism based on
a historical sequencing of cultures (i.e., an application of a culture-
historical method) stands, not unscathed, but unrefuted. (2) The
proposed alternatives to Schmidt's theory play fast and loose with
ethnological data, do not stand up to sound reasoning, and become
irrational. (3) There appear to have been four alternatives for anthropologists to consider for adoption with regard to the origin of religions:

    a.   the failed theories on religion, e.g., the animistic theory, based
        on naturalistic assumptions;

    b.   Schmidt's theory that led to a fundamental recognition of
        theism in the most basic human cultures;

    c.   escaping into an incoherent, irrational theory that cleverly
        passes off a psychological speculation as a historical descrip-
        tion, and vice versa;

    d.   putting a permanent moratorium on the question of the ori-
        gin of religion.

Most anthropological scholars today have chosen *d.* Now we
need to recognize that *d* is a reasonable choice if one recognizes the

---

[60] Tomoko Masuzawa, *In Search of Dreamtime: The Quest for the Origin of
Religion* (Chicago: University of Chicago Press, 1993), 1. In case anyone should be
wondering, Masuzawa does not reopen the issue either.

objective unacceptability of *a* and *c*, while also maintaining a *dogmatic antisupernatural outlook* that supposedly prohibits the possibility of *b*.

However, not everyone shares such an antisupernatural outlook. We should recognize that the dismissal of original monotheism does not imply it has actually been defeated on scholarly grounds. In the next chapter we will bring up further examples of how original monotheism has been preserved around the world.

CHAPTER 10

Monotheism Around the Globe

The subject matter of this chapter deserves more treatment than I am able to allocate to it in the constraints of this book. Other books address the topic from a different perspective.[1] Up to this point

---

[1] Don Richardson, *Eternity in Their Hearts: Startling Evidence of Belief in the One True God in Hundreds of Cultures Throughout the World*, 3rd ed. (Ventura, CA: Gospel Light Publications, 2005) popularizes not only a globally pervasive monotheism but further, with unbridled optimism, recounts parallels and anticipations of biblical beliefs in other cultures. In contrast to this book, it takes an anecdotal approach and focuses heavily on Richardson's theological interpretations, which lead to various exhortations concerning Christian missions. Richardson does not get involved in critical issues, and among varying documentary (not just explanatory) alternatives known to us, he merely presents the ones that fit in best with his thesis. The book is well worth reading as long as we keep in mind that it is a somewhat polemical introduction to the subject for a popular audience.

The essays in Aída Besançon Spencer and William Spencer, eds., *The Global God: Multicultural Evangelical Views of God* (Grand Rapids, MI: Baker, 2001), contribute to the insight that "God" and "The Western Conception of God" are not necessarily identical, and in the process some of the writers give explicit recognition of a knowledge of the one true God in indigenous religions. This is another worthwhile book, though it also does not deal with the fundamental scholarly issues that stand in the background of the monotheism it defends.

The books by Arthur C. Custance, collected by Evelyn White and published by the Arthur Custance Foundation under the heading of "The Doorway Papers,"

we have been concerned with the phenomenon of original monotheism as represented among the materially least developed people on the earth. We have stressed that in the materially most rudimentary of these people groups there is active worship of a supreme being. Further, we witnessed the decline of this belief in the single god and a degeneration into animism and magic, and the worship of various subordinate deities. Still, the belief in a high god has persisted to varying degrees. To return to the traditional terminology, God became *deus absconditus* (the disappearing god) and *deus otiosus* (the hidden god) but not always and everywhere. In the process of stressing the use of the culture-historical method so as to isolate the cultures that potentially represent the earliest human cultures, we have forced ourselves to ignore the widespread presence of belief in the high god where the cultures are not monotheistic any longer. Let us now lift that restriction.

In chapter 7, I mentioned the Kikuyu of Kenya, who believe there is one God, Ngai.[2] Ngai resides on Mount Kenya; he is the all-powerful and all-knowing Creator of the world and enforcer of morality. However, the people worship him only during extreme emergencies and then as an entire community. Once the situation has resolved itself, they ignore him once more. For the rest of the time, traditional Kikuyu people keep in mind the presence of the ancestor spirits and pay their respects to them. Thus, it only makes sense to classify the religion as a whole as animistic, but we should not forget that there is a god there as well.

The situation of the Kikuyu is in some ways typical for many African traditional religions. For some, such as the San people ("Bushmen") or the Maasai, worship of God is far more regular. For others, it is more suppressed. For the Zulu we have no definite evidence whether there was a high god prior to European contact, and, if so,

provide a lot of useful insights as well, as Custance incorporates a belief in "primitive monotheism" into a Christian philosophy of science; http://www.custance.org.

[2] Jomo Kenyatta, *Facing Mt. Kenya* (New York: Vintage, 1965; orig., 1938), 222–31.

we don't know what he might have been called, though there are a number of hypotheses. The Yoruba have a high god, Olorun, who has withdrawn himself, leaving a multitude of divinities (*orisa*) who now receive worship. John S. Mbiti attempted to cut through all of this diversity by arguing that ultimately all African religions focus on the one God. He stated that "sacrifices and offerings are directed to one or more of the following: God, spirits and living-dead ['ancestor spirits']. Recipients in the second and third categories are regarded as intermediaries between God and men, so that God is the ultimate Recipient whether or not the worshippers are aware of that."[3]

Richard Gehman responded to Mbiti's contention that this observation had taken him "beyond reasonableness,"[4] and one would be inclined to concur. Some tribes do not believe nature spirits and ancestors are intermediaries, and so Mbiti, with the best of intentions, crossed the boundary of what may be legitimately ascribed to a culture. Nevertheless, if recognition of a high god were not as frequent as it is, Mbiti presumably never would have made such a comment.

By contrast, even though we saw active worship of the one god among the Yuki, Maidu, Algonquins, and Salish, most Native Americans have no more than a minimal idea of a creator, and he is frequently so obscured as to be irrelevant or identified with an animal or a natural object. As mentioned in chapter 7, many of the North Central Californian tribes considered either Coyote or Eagle to be the creator. Here is another example: An Oglala man by the name of "Sword" gave the following explanation, translated by Burt Means:

> Every object in the world has a spirit and that spirit is *wakan*. Thus the spirits of the tree or things of that kind, while not like the spirit of man, are also *wakan*. *Wakan* comes from the *wakan* beings. . . . *Wakan Tanka Kin* signifies the chief or leading *Wakan* being, which is the Sun. However, the most powerful of the

---

[3] John S. Mbiti, *African Religions and Philosophy* (Nairobi: East African Educational Publishers, 1969), 58.

[4] Richard Gehman, *African Traditional Religion in Biblical Perspective* (Kijabe, Kenya: Kesho Publications, 1989), 142.

Wakan beings is *Nagi Tanka*, the Great Spirit who is also *Taku
Skanskan. Taku Skanskan* signifies the Blue, in other words,
the Sky.[5]

This account is somewhat confusing, and Sword laments that
even his own tribespeople constantly need clarification.[6] We must
recognize that *wakan* is not an impersonal force that pervades nature,
as some scholars have claimed,[7] but that it is always associated with
personal beings. Who is at the top of the spirit world for the Oglala
Lakota? Is it the "Great Spirit" of the sky, the sky itself, or is it the
sun? The wider context of Sword's account makes it clear.[8] The
"Great Spirit," whatever his relationship may have been to the sky
in the past, does not play a central role for the Oglala, though it is
still significant that he receives mention as the most powerful *wakan*
being. The sun tops the hierarchy of *wakan* beings. However, when
people pray, unless they have a specific concern that is associated
with a specific spirit, they should pray to *Wakan Tanka*, the totality
of the *wakan* beings conceived as a singular unity.

Wherever we look around the world, there appears to be at least
a memory of a supreme being. Now it may be tempting to construct
an argument for original monotheism based on the sheer prolif-
eration of the concept. However, let us remember that the gist of
Schmidt's work was actually to minimize the number of cultures
studied, namely those he could identify as the most *Primitive*, which
also turned out to be the most clearly monotheistic ones. Sociologist
Rodney Stark, who in two books is not afraid to venture the opinion
that anthropologists rejected the conclusions of Lang and Schmidt
simply because they did not want to face up to the theological

---

[5] J. R. Walker, "The Sun Dance and Other Ceremonies of the Oglala Division of
the Teton Dakota," *Anthropological Papers of the American Museum of Natural History*
16, no. 2 (1917): 152–53.

[6] Ibid.

[7] E.g., Ruth M. Underhill, *Red Man's Religion: Beliefs and Practices of the Indians
North of Mexico* (Chicago: University of Chicago Press, 1965), 21.

[8] Walker, "Sun Dance," 152–53.

implications, still appears to interpret Schmidt's argument as a case based on the accumulation of evidence rather than on the outcome of applying the culture-historical method, which he doesn't mention in these works.[9]

Global Testimony

Having said all of that, it does not mean the appearances of supreme beings in contexts other than *Primitive* cultures are irrelevant. After all, Schmidt's thesis includes the idea that the high god did not disappear spontaneously but was replaced in various ways by inferior spirit beings, while some cultures retained a more active memory and cultus of him. As we said in chapter 8, there are some serious doubts whether the fully developed nomadic pastoral cultures belonged to the *Primary* culture, but it remains to be the case that they, in contrast to other kinds of cultures, maintained a far clearer memory and even cultus of the high god than others. On the negative side, on the whole, for them the intertwining between the god in the sky and the sky (or heaven) itself became most likely.[10] We rejected the idea that the supreme being invariably developed out of the concept of a sky god, but the amalgamation of the god in the sky and the sky became a frequent phenomenon among the nomadic cultures.

Schmidt devoted the entire second half of the twelve volumes of *Ursprung der Gottesidee* to the pastoral nomads. A well-known African nomadic cattle-herding culture is the Maasai, whose land crosses Kenya and Tanzania. Their ethnic origin has been a matter of dispute, frequently distorted by various racial ideologies. Schmidt classified them as "Hamitoids," by which he meant that they were the descendants of

---

[9] Rodney Stark, *One True God: Historical Consequences of Monotheism* (Princeton, NJ: Princeton University Press, 2001), 38–40; idem, *Discovering God: The Origin of the Great Religions and the Evolution of Belief* (New York: HarperCollins, 2007), 55–62. Unfortunately, in these brief discussions Stark's enthusiasm for Lang and Schmidt did not preclude him from making a number of other factual errors.

[10] Wilhelm Schmidt, *The Origin and Growth of Religion: Facts and Theories*, 2nd ed., trans. H. J. Rose (New York: Humanities, 1936), 288.

"Hamite" people from Southwest Asia, who had migrated into Africa and intermarried with the local population.[11] This classification no longer stands up to contemporary concepts. The Maasais's language, called *Maa*, is distinct from that of their Bantu-affiliated neighbors (e.g., the Kikuyu) and from the huge Afro-Asiatic group (which is sometimes still called "Hamito-Semitic"). Contemporary linguistics assigns *Maa* to the *Nilo-Saharan* language family. This group is represented as far north as Chad and by the tribes of the upper Nile region to the east. The Maasai constitute its southernmost extension. The members of this language family are overwhelmingly pastoral nomads. The point is that the Maasai, as other pastoral people, stand out from the surrounding agricultural people in language, descent, and economy. The antagonism celebrated in the famous musical exhortation that "the farmer and the cowman should be friends,"[12] reflects a millennia-old global tension, as seen by the fact that agricultural and cattle-raising cultures went into different directions in their religions.

The Maasai are well known for their colorful form of dress, their focus on cattle, and their age-grade system of social organization, which includes a lengthy time for an individual to spend as warrior prior to becoming a junior elder.[13] Their religious practices include consistent ancestor veneration but also the worship of god, known to them as Engai, multiple times a day by all members of the community. Thus, they are a good example of a group of pastoral nomads that have retained the idea of one god who has not become hidden.

To return to Schmidt's examples, among the pastoral nomads of Asia, Schmidt included the Mongols, beginning with the notorious Genghis Khan prior to the time when their religion became

---

[11] Schmidt, *Der Ursprung der Gottesidee*, vol. 7 (Münster: Aschendorff, 1940), 4. (None of the expressions Schmidt uses here are intended to be in any way pejorative, though tragically, in some circles the baseless slander that the so-called curse of Ham vouchsafes the inferiority of African peoples has still not been erased.)

[12] "The Farmer and the Cowman Should Be Friends," music by Richard Rodgers, lyrics by Oscar Hammerstein II.; act 2 of *Oklahoma!* first performed in 1943.

[13] For a further description, see my *Neighboring Faiths*, 2nd ed. (Downers Grove, IL: InterVarsity Press, 2012), 219.

syncretized and then replaced by Buddhism. This is a summary of the picture that emerges from Chinese annals, which supply Genghis's self-reports as communicated to us by Schmidt.[14]

Genghis Khan was a man who directed all of his devotion to heaven, whom he thought of as the single true moral deity. Even though he acknowledged the reality of inferior spiritual beings, they bore little significance for him, and it would not be unfair to think of him as a monotheist in a rudimentary sense. He agreed with Islam right up to the point of thinking of Mecca as a holy city but did not think that God's presence could be particularly concentrated in any one location. Once, having conquered a particular Muslim city, he mounted the pulpit in the mosque and preached to the people that his coming was a direct punishment from God for their sinful lives. He directed his prayers to heaven and was convinced that heaven had called him to bring justice and goodness to all of the people currently under the rule of corrupt kings and princes. For the most part he manifested an almost supernatural calm and assurance, knowing that heaven was on his side. He saw himself as the bringer of purity, whether people wanted to accept it or not. Genghis Khan claimed not to enjoy shedding blood, but he was willing to do so without conscience pangs if he needed to. Here is an example of a message he sent to a city in Persia: "Know that heaven has given to me the rule of the earth, encompassing it from east to west. Those who submit will be spared. Woe to those who resist! They will be slaughtered, along with their children, wives, and servants."[15]

And so he did. Current books like to see in Genghis Khan the popular values of our day. They tend to extol his supposed tolerance, his institution of laws protecting those whom he considered to be oppressed, and his alleged policy of freedom of religion.[16] Concerning this tolerance and so-called freedom of religion, he could not help but make allowances on pragmatic grounds since there were not enough

---

[14] Schmidt, *Ursprung*, vol. 10, 12–23.

[15] Ibid., 14.

[16] Jack Weatherford, *Genghis Khan and the Making of the Modern World* (New York: Three Rivers Press, 2005).

Mongols around to administer his empire. He made use of the religious terminology of the people he was about to conquer when he politely requested their surrender, which he typically followed up with the complete obliteration of those who did not immediately comply, an idea foreshadowed a long time ago by the Assyrians (2 Chr 32:9–19).

Regardless of his claims to piety and his messianic claims, he was a man without a conscience who went where he was not invited and killed whoever objected to his presence.[17] For our purposes the point is simply this: claims to monotheism and even self-professed righteousness come with no guarantee that those who claim it live according to it. Further, as we have said before, receiving the label of "monotheism" does not mean the religion in question has any power to change lives, let alone provide salvation. Please keep in mind that we are now far removed from *Primitive* cultures.

The Supreme God in World Religions

It is not a logical corollary, but definitely a reasonable expectation, that the highly developed, enscripturated religions should have maintained some relationship with the god of original monotheism, and we have enough data to make this case in a number of situations.

Some Ground Rules

1. In order to qualify under this heading, the monotheism in question must be traceable to ancient, if not prehistorical, times. For example, insofar as the worship of Krishna in Hinduism may be considered to be theistic, it would not qualify because there is (on objective, academic grounds) no basis for linking him to the god of original monotheism.

---

[17] For a more traditional appraisal of both the greatness of Genghis Khan and his pathology, see Jeremiah Curtin, *The Mongols: A History* (Boston: Little, Brown, 1908), 141.

2. Our fundamental pattern is that a belief in one supreme creator god goes back to the earliest prehistory of various people
   groups. In certain cases more details may be attached to this
   belief. However, just as we saw on the preliterate level, there
   was constant pressure in the monotheistic cultures to supplant
   the primordial monotheism with other forms of religion. In
   many of the long-standing religions, monotheism has been
   out of the picture for many millennia while further deities,
   doctrines, and mythologies have accumulated. It would be a
   serious mistake to reincorporate the new indigenous myths,
   let alone its pantheon, into our reconstruction of the original
   monotheism so as to attempt to create a synthetic mythology
   more in line with biblical history but with little or no scholarly credibility. Such attempts, by burdening the discovery of
   the ancient monotheism with unnecessary, often speculative,
   embellishments, may even weaken the case for monotheism. It is a fundamental principle of science that a hypothesis
   with a more limited scope can be shown to be more probably
   true than one that includes more detail than the hypothesis
   requires. After the hypothesis has been proven, one can move
   on to the details, if one wants to, but one step at a time is the
   best policy here as in many other places.

First, we must address a popular misconception, namely the idea
of historical monotheism originating in Egypt. Then we can address
monotheism among the Semites, Indo-Europeans, and Chinese.

A Pharaoh's Attempted Monopoly on Religion

Before going into the story of Amenhotep IV, who turned himself
into Akhenaten, we need to realize that his innovation cannot come
under the heading of the persistence of original monotheism because
there is no linkage known to us of his worship of Aten to the ancient
prehistoric tradition of the supreme being.

Pharaoh Amenhotep IV, though originally not in the official line of succession, came to the throne as a gesture of love to his mother by his father Amenhotep III.[18] He was singularly unsuited to the office of king, and all but two years of his seventeen-year reign were spent in co-regency with some other person. During the two years when he was left without supervision, he was able to take drastic measures to impose on the rest of Egypt the fantasy world he had created for himself.

For the last hundred years or so, fueled by the romanticizing writing of James H. Breasted,[19] Amenhotep's story has been depicted as that of an idealistic young king who became convinced of monotheism and tried, albeit ineptly, to convert the Egyptian people to this new religion. Obviously, this innovation alienated the priesthoods of the traditional gods, who later ruthlessly exterminated his vision in favor of regaining their professional standing and reinstituting the same old polytheism and rituals. Scholars embraced this picture because they could use it to undercut the role of Moses, as well as the Hebrew people, in bringing monotheism to the world. So an obvious corollary was that (assuming a dubious thirteenth-century date for the exodus) even though his monotheism was not well received in Egypt, it did have an influence on Moses, who then made it the official worldview of the Hebrews. Amenhotep's famous hymn to Aten, the disc of the sun, certainly fits in well with a monotheistic understanding. Here are just a few significant lines:

> How manifold it is, what thou hast made!
> They are hidden from the face (of man).
> O sole god, like whom there is no other!
> Thou didst create the world according to thy desire,
> Whilst thou wert alone.[20]

---

[18] This introductory summary of Akhenaten is based on F. J. Giles, *Ikhnaton: Legend and History* (London: Hutchinson, 1970).

[19] See James H. Breasted, *The Dawn of Conscience* (New York: Scribner's, 1933).

[20] John A. Wilson, trans., "The Hymn to the Aton," in James B. Pritchard, *The Ancient Near East: An Anthology of Texts and Pictures* (Princeton, NJ: Princeton University, 1958), 227.

Aten is here portrayed as the only god and the one who created everything. The rest of the hymn reinforces this point of view. Multiple writers like to show obvious resemblances to one or more of the psalms, though they are not necessarily in agreement as to which ones. Psalm 104 is recognized by many; followed closely by Psalm 110. Others parcel out the hymn as composed of various parts of Psalms. It is hard not to see the resemblances, but they do not prove anything inasmuch as there are only so many things one can say in general in adoration of a creator god, and, if we looked at the entire hymn, we would also find some glaring differences.

On the surface it seems pretty obvious that Amenhotep IV attempted to convert Egypt to monotheism. This much is clear: This Pharaoh was committed to Aten and sincere in his belief that Aten was the only true God. He changed his name to Akhenaten, indicating his devotion to his god; built a whole new city, Amarna; intended to serve as both temple and royal residence; and, given the chance, decreed that the names and temples of all other gods should be eliminated forever.

We tend to assume that if someone comes up with a new idea in religion, he or she will set out to convert the rest of the world to their point of view. So a crucial question is: Did Akhenaten intend for all Egyptian people to start worshipping Aten? Far from it. Egyptian religion did not work that way.

Ever since the expulsion of the Hyksos from Egypt, there were two intermingling strands of religion in Egypt. The later one focused on Amun, the god of Thebes, while the earlier one was based on the cultus of Re, a sun god. Re was widely worshipped, but he was supposed to have had a particularly close relationship to the pharaohs, who were thought to be descended from him. Thus, the worship of Re always implied the recognition of the pharaoh as god. Some people prior to Akhenaten may have already specifically revered the solar disk as the essence of Re. Akhenaten picked up on this idea. Now, here is the ensuing reasoning. If the essence of Re was intrinsic to the pharaohs, and if Aten was, in fact, this essence, then the pharaoh was its unique and exclusive proprietor. Consequently, as far as Akhenaten was concerned, Aten was *his* god and not that of anyone else. The people were exhorted to acknowledge Aten, but there was only one way in which they could worship him, namely, in the way in which commoners in Egypt had always been instructed to worship the gods, by worshipping the pharaoh and his wife. Akhenaten's hymn closes:

> [*Everything is*] made to flourish for the King, . . .
> Since thou didst found the earth
> And raise them up for thy son,
> Who came forth from thy body:
> the King of Upper and Lower Egypt, . . . Akh-en-Aton, . . . And
> the Chief Wife of the King, . . . Nefert-iti, living and youthful
> forever and ever.[21]

Thus, if Aten were the one and only God, and he could only be worshipped by worshipping the Pharaoh, this was hardly a "monotheistic reform." Instead, it was the ultimate in egotism and delusions of grandeur. Akhenaten intended that he and only he (accompanied by the beautiful Nefertiti) should be the central deity of all of Egyptian cultus because he and only he, as pharaoh, had true knowledge of the unique and only authentic deity, Aten.

Rodney Stark evaluates Akhenaten's supposed reform in this way: "This first attempt to establish monotheism was doomed from the start because the Pharaoh failed to grasp that he needed to enlist support, rather than to simply order it done. His failure was to not have tried to build a social movement of committed believers."[22]

Stark's evaluation misses the point of what Akhenaten was trying to do. As Stark himself acknowledges, common people had always been excluded from temple privileges and had always been exhorted to worship deities vicariously through the Pharaoh, though it had not usually been laid out in as rigid a fashion as Akhenaten attempted. Akhenaten was not setting out to create a populist religion but to

---

[21] Ibid., 230.
[22] Stark, *Discovering God*, 161.

draw the ultimate logical consequence from the established pattern. "Support" for his egolatry could not have been enlisted; it could only be ordered. A corollary of his plan was that he demoted the priests of the various gods and temples to the same level as water carriers and field workers, requiring them all to worship Aten by worshipping him. The professional officiants were unhappy. Under other circumstances, if a new deity became mandatory, they might have been able to switch which god to serve. But by the nature of the "new religion," doing so was impossible; their entire lives as priests were over.

*A word needs to be said about the word *first* that is frequently associated with Akhenaten and his supposed monotheism. Aside from the fact that based on our ethnological conclusions, he was preceded by preliterate tribes all over the world, and looking at the matter from a historical point of view, he would not have been the first to promote monotheism. To write history, it is always best to begin with the data supplied by one's sources and to build the theories around them, rather than beginning with certain theories and questioning the reliability of the written sources because they do not fit the theory. (Unfortunately, liberal biblical criticism has forgotten that principle, but we need neither emulate them nor seek their approval.) If the written sources are explicit and clear, they should bear the brunt of the evidence. In this particular case I'm referring to the date of the exodus of the Hebrews from Egypt, for which the written sources are relatively limited, but could not be any clearer. They consist of two unequivocal statements in the Bible.[23]

First Kings 6:1 fixes the time of the completion of Solomon's temple at 480 years since the exodus of Israel from Egypt. The

---

[23] A similar situation exists with regard to the life of Zoroaster, the founder of Zoroastrianism. The literature states a date, namely 273 years prior to Alexander the Great. There is some latitude here, depending on which events from the time of Alexander and Zoroaster are matched up, but a time in the sixth century is pretty certain based on that number. However, scholars frequently ignore the written testimony of the ancient texts and come up with different numbers based on various other matters. See Winfried Corduan, "The Date of Zoroaster: Some Apologetic Considerations," *Presbyterion* 23, no. 1 (1997): 25–42.

completion of the temple is established with a good amount of reliability as having occurred in 966 BC. Counting back from there we get to a date for the exodus of 1446 BC. A verse coinciding with this long time span occurs in Judges 11:26, when Jepthah informed the King of Moab that Israelites had lived in their towns for 300 years. Given that time frame for Moses, Akhenaten's sun-and-self worship is unlikely to have influenced Moses' worship of Yahweh in time or in substance. We cannot devote any further space to discussing alternative dates for the exodus; for an overwhelming case that this date for Moses in the middle of the fifteenth century BC is not only correct but that other, later, dates are historically impossible, please see the discussion by Gleason Archer in his *Survey of Old Testament Introduction*.[24] To summarize, one is best off not to credit Akhenaten with a true monotheism, let alone with attempting to reform Egypt into a universal practice of true monotheism.

The Indo-European Supreme God

We now come to the payoff for the hard work of finding our way through some of the features associated with the study of Indo-European languages. Let us recall that officially the category "Indo-European" ("IE") refers to a language family, based on similarities in grammar and vocabulary. Physical genetic affinities among the different ethnic groups who were speaking IE languages cannot be completely ruled out but are not of interest in this study. Somewhere, thousands of years ago, a group of people spoke the IE ancestor language (proto-IE). We can now add a point for which we may not have been ready in chapter 2: the language family may also have spread by diffusion and cross-cultural interchange. Early on, this large tribe divided, and the languages of the resulting two groups took distinctive turns. All later IE languages have followed one of the two

---

[24] Gleason L. Archer, *A Survey of Old Testament Introduction*, 3rd. ed. (Chicago: Moody Press, 1998), 228–52.

options of this ancient division, which I shall call "trunks" in order to distinguish between this main division from the many later branches arising out of each of them. Scholars have picked an easily recognizable difference to refer to these two trunks, using their respective words for "hundred" and labeling them arbitrarily with the Latin *centum* (pronounced "kentum"), a word beginning with a hard guttural consonant, and the Avestan, *satem*, which starts with a sibilant.

Any features that are clearly common to both the *centum* and *satem* trunks are likely to reflect a feature close to proto-IE. Thus, for example, if there were to be some clear similarities between, say, Sanskrit on the one hand, and maybe Greek or Old Norse, on the other, we could fairly confidently surmise that this must have been an original expression in or close to proto-IE, which was continued on both trunks.

Finally, to finish this quick reminder, we are on safe grounds to invoke the philological principle that the language used by people would also reflect elements of their cultures on both their material and immaterial sides. The languages would not have expressions for, say, trees or angels if the people speaking them did not have an awareness of trees or a belief in angels. And if later IE languages on both the *centum* and *satem* trunks were to have similar words for trees and angels, then the people speaking an early language, close to proto-IE, must have shared those beliefs.

Such is the case for the name of a god who appears only occasionally in the earliest Hindu scriptures, the Rig Veda. He is called *Dyaus Pitā*. *Pitā* means "father," and the word transfers easily through most IE languages, appearing as *pater* in Latin, *patér* in Greek, and *Vater* in German. For Dyaus, its Sanskrit root is *div*, which is probably derived from a proto-IE radical **diw*.[25] Its original meaning was "to shine," so that *Dyaus Pitā* is the "Shining Father," which, without question, refers to the supreme god. In fact, **diw* and its variations also gave

---

[25] The asterisk in front of the word signals that it is a reconstruction of a basic phoneme inferred to have been present in a proto-language but never directly appearing in any actual languages.

rise to the more generic term for "god," which recurs in many IE languages, e.g., *deva* in Sanskrit, *daeva* in ancient Iranian, *divine* in English, *deus* in Latin, or *theos* in Greek. Since these expressions straddle both original branches, it is a reasonable inference that their origin goes back to the time prior to their split, which puts them close to proto-IE but allows for an unknown amount of time for development before the split.

But let us not forget about *Dyaus Pitā*, which is clearly a proper name, not just a noun. We picked him off the Indic branch on the *satem* trunk. By the time of the Rig Veda, the first scriptures of the Aryan immigrants into India, he plays a rather minor role; but where he is mentioned, it is always with the utmost respect to him as the father of all, who has been replaced in his administrative functions by other gods such as Indra and Agni. He resides in heaven, does not have an active cultus, and lets his presence be known from time to time by means of a thunderbolt. In other words, *Dyaus Pitā* is playing precisely the role of *deus otiosus* that one should expect in the polytheistic culture of the Rig Veda.

Many of the hymns of the Rig Veda are compositions of flattery to the gods in order to entice them to provide this-worldly wealth. Some, however, consist of deep reflections. Book 10, hymn 129, ponders the creation of the universe and leaves matters hanging. An earlier hymn, Book 1, hymn 164, comes to a more positive conclusion. The first thirty-two verses are given over to admiring the intricacy and complexity of the universe and its internal contemplation. There follows a contemplation of the wonders of the cow, together with a reference to an imperfect shepherd. Lost in this world of wonder, unable to explain it, the hymn seems to come to a climax when the writer declares: "Dyaus is my father, my begetter; my kinship is here."[26]

---

[26] Translation by Ralph Griffith, 1896. Found at http://www.sacred-texts.com /hin/rigveda/rv01164.htm.

Sanskrit: http://www.sacred-texts.com/hin/rvsan/rv01164.htm. We should clarify that the Sanskrit renditions of the text are most likely accurate in terms of language and content. However, the process that was used to generate these files

This statement becomes the anchor point as the author continues to marvel at the mysteries of existence. Much continues to be beyond his grasp, but he has reassured himself that behind it all is the one god. Now we need to keep in mind that what we have here is no longer monotheism but a nostalgic longing to return to the monotheism of the past. God created a world of order, and all the other deities are different ways of seeing him. This is the location of the famous statement, which has metamorphosed into "Truth is one, the wise call it by various names" and various other paraphrases that refer to an impersonal object. The crucial statement occurs in the midst of a list of various Vedic gods: "They call him Indra, Mitra, Varuṇa, Agni, and he is heavenly nobly-winged Garutmān. / To what is One, sages give many a title they call it Agni, Yama, Mātariśvan."[27]

This is admittedly a difficult verse to translate and exegete, but eisegesis in light of a worldview that is not found anywhere else in the Vedas does not help. The translator of this verse has capitalized the word "One," thereby making it easier to fit this statement into an impersonal, pantheistic worldview. But in this case, even if it fit into the context of the hymn or the Sanskrit demanded such a translation, it would be a serious anachronism, anticipating Shankara's Vedantic philosophy 2,000 years before Shankara. Sanskrit has no capital letters, and there is no good reason to translate *ekam* ("one") as anything but "one," the numeral expressing singularity. There is only one direct referent for the phrase, "what is one" in the entire hymn, namely, the one personal creator of everything, *Dyaus Pitā*.

In the Rig Veda, *Dyaus Pitā* serves as role model for the "younger generation of gods." In Book 4, 21:1, dedicated to Indra, rain god and king of the gods, we read: "May Indra come to us for our protection; here be the Hero, praised, our feast-companion. / May he

---

did not take cognizance of some of the combination forms of consonants in the Devanagari script. Consequently, consonant combinations are at times spelled out as two consonants in a row. This does not affect the actual content.

[27] Ibid.

whose powers are many, waxen mighty, cherish, like Dyaus, his own supreme dominion."[28]

In Book 10, 37:1 we learn that the sun god *Surya* is a son of *Dyaus Pitā*.[29] We also learn concerning Agni, the god of fire, in 45:8 of that same book: "Agni by vital powers became immortal when his prolific Father Dyaus begat him."[30] Thus, in this case, the mythology itself demonstrates a strong memory of Dyaus as the originator and lord of all. The Vedas are not consistent about the relationships among the gods, but a place of honor goes to the now-retired former supreme god, *Dyaus Pitā*.

The question is, can we find an analogue to *Dyaus Pitā* on other branches of the IE tree? Indeed, we can. Again we are profiting from our quick look at the IE family, which allows us to recognize analogues without getting confused by changes in some consonants. So we find on the *centum* trunk, among others:

1. on the Hellenic branch, the Greek *Zeus Patèr*
2. on the Italic branch, the Latin *Jupiter* (*Ju-piter*)
3. on the North German branch, the Old Norse *Týr*

The proto-IE name may have been **Dyeus*. Of the three mentioned, *Týr* is probably least familiar to most people, so I shall briefly focus on him. His early Old Germanic name, prior to further development may have been *Tiwaz*. There are a number of permutations of his name (e.g., *Tio* or *Tius*). In ancient Germanic writing the rune for "sword" (†) was his special symbol. Among our names for the days of the week, most of which are based on Norse deities, he presides over Tuesday. By the time he appears in the mythology known to us, his status has gone through a number of transformations. The

---

[28] Griffith translation, http://www.sacred-texts.com/hin/rigveda/rv04021.htm. Sanskrit: http://www.sacred-texts.com/hin/rvsan/rv04021.htm.

[29] Griffith translation, http://www.sacred-texts.com/hin/rigveda/rv10037.htm. Sanskrit: http://www.sacred-texts.com/hin/rvsan/rv10037.htm.

[30] Griffith translation, http://www.sacred-texts.com/hin/rigveda/rv10045.htm. Sanskrit : http://www.sacred-texts.com/hin/rvsan/rv10045.htm.

parallels to Dyaus, Zeus, and the other apparent cognates are strong enough to conclude that he is their counterpart and, thus, identical with the single supreme deity of the earliest Indo-Europeans. But, similarly to Dyaus in India, as polytheism replaced monotheism, Týr was supplanted from his supreme position and replaced by Wodan (Odin). Various myths make him out to be the son of either Wodan or Hymir, a giant. This inconsistency suggests the synthetic character of these myths. There is every reason to believe that in actual time he was worshipped as the high god in the sky before there was a cultus for Wodan or a mythology of Hymir.

In late verbal descriptions and even later pictures, Týr was pictured clad as a warrior, one hand missing and the other one holding a sword. According to the mythology, there was an evil wolf named Fenrir, who was causing great harm. The gods attempted to fetter him, but they could not come up with shackles strong enough. The dwarves were able to construct a chain that was unbreakable due to its magic power, but no one was able to bind Fenrir with it because he would bite anyone who came close to him. Týr volunteered to place his hand in Fenrir's maw so that the other gods could finish their work of restraining the wolf. They finished their task, but Fenrir had bitten off Týr's hand. So, even after he was no longer recognized as the supreme god, Týr continued to represent justice, self-sacrifice, and courage.

When the Roman historian Tacitus[31] wrote a lengthy report concerning Germanic culture and religion, he heavy-handedly equated Germanic gods with Roman ones, specifically Thor with Hercules, Wodan with Mercury, and Týr with Mars, the Roman god of war. These supposed equivalences apparently were commonly accepted by the Romans, and they were even adopted in northern Europe by the Germanic people who had raised Wodan over Týr. They were happy to designate him as a subordinate god of war. That this new designation came about due to Roman influence is

---

[31] Thomas Gordon, trans., *Tacitus on Germany* (New York: Collier, 1910).

supported by the fact that subsequent inscriptions frequently called Týr by the Roman name Mars, as R. M. Meyer describes.[32] However, Meyer goes on to use this idiosyncrasy to argue that Týr had been considered to be a god of war prior to what Tacitus said, which seems to be a backward argument. One needs to understand that Meyer was an evolutionist to the core, and he admittedly felt free to ignore the philological implications of the Dyaus-Zeus-Tîwaz identity and (by his own admission) invent a prehistory to the apparent original supreme beings in the proto-IE speaking culture. Furthermore, he also invented a subsequent history in which the tribes who remained true to Týr, the Saxons and Swabians, fought against those who accepted Wodan's supremacy, all the while supposedly relating to Týr as their god of war. Despite these corruptions of a deity by this triple-axis of Roman piety, alleged Germanic monolatry, and evolutionist historiography, they cannot erase the fact that here was a god who, at the time of his flourishing, had stood for righteousness. His weapon had not been the blade of the conqueror but the sword of justice.

We need to mention one other point to understand the IE high god. The decay from monotheism to polytheism had preceded the breakup between the *centum* and *satem* branches, and the pantheons on both trunks manifested a similar, fascinating twist. In general, the gods were known collectively by a term rooted in the same radical *diw* ("to shine"), which in Sanskrit came out as *div* and provided the same foundation for the name *Dyaus*, and the *devas* for the gods.

The example of India became the model applied to other IE groups, creating unnecessary confusion in the process. We'll follow it for the moment. The standard Sanskrit word for god is *deva*. But there appears to be a second, separate group of gods, sometimes translated as "lords," who are known as the *asuras* in Sanskrit, the ahuras in Persian, and the *aesir* in Norse mythology. The root of this

---

[32] R. M. Meyer, *Altgermanische Religionsgeschichte* (Stuttgart: Magnus-Verlag, 1909), 67–68.

word may go back to a proto-IE term meaning "life give," but this is not as clearly demonstrated as the root *diw* for the devas. This "*as*-group" still shows up in English in names with the syllable *os*, such as *Osgood, Oswald,* and *Osborne.* This is the common perception: the Indo-Europeans, once they had entered the polytheistic stage, found themselves with two opposing groups of gods, the *divs* and the *asrs*. Over the course of history, various cultures treated these two groups differently. In India the devas became viewed as the good gods while the asuras were consigned to the status of evil beings and demons. In Iran, under Zoroaster's revolution, the daevas were condemned as demons,[33] and one ahura, Ahura Mazda, was exalted as the single supreme god. In Norse religion the *aesir* are the main group, and they fought against a group known as *vanir,* a name of utterly unknown origin. So the puzzle is this: In some of the earliest IE days, though after proto-IE had been spoken, the culture seems to be relatively cohesive, but apparently there were not just one but two pantheons. There is no probability whatsoever to the idea of external influence from some other, similarly early culture. When the culture split, it was not on the basis of each side preferring one of those two groups of gods. But in the process of splitting, the tribes on both sides of the division appear to have taken both pantheons along with them, and then, only subsequently, took up one or the other as supreme. How can this be? This question is important for us because the identity of the high god, e.g., *Dyaus Pitā,* could, to some extent, depend on whether he belonged to the devas or the asuras.

It appears that we can take the greatest amount of inconsistency out of the situation by rethinking the idea that the devas and asuras were originally two competing groups. It is easy to see how such an understanding could develop, based on the observation of how these two sets of beings have functioned in Hinduism for the last 2,000

---

[33] In English the root *div* has also given rise to the word *devil.* It would be convenient to attribute that oddity to some cryptic post-Zoroastrian Persian influence, but I doubt that any can be demonstrated. So we'll have to leave this phenomenon in the box labeled "Unexplained—Speculations Invited!"

years or more, where they have been seen invariably as two groups in conflict, the relatively good devas in opposition to the relatively evil asuras.[34] With that scheme in mind, it is easy to go back to the Vedas and read the same split into them as far back as the earliest one, the Rig Veda. So we come to the Vedas, already prepared to see the devas as the group that will eventually be regarded as good and supreme and the asuras already as bearing the seed of their eventual transformation into the evil demons in the religion of the people.

Such an interpretation could never have arisen if scholars had started to read the Vedas first, without having been influenced by the later mythology, something that is admittedly difficult to do. If they had done so, they would have quickly discovered that a number of the most important gods are identified both as devas and as asuras. This applies, for example, to Varuna, a god of heaven, who, at times is credited with having been the first deity to have supplanted *Dyaus Pitā*, only to be defeated by Indra subsequently. In the Rig Veda, Book 1, 89:2, 3 Varuna is counted among the devas.

> May the auspicious favour [sic] of the **Gods** be ours, on us
> descend the bounty of the righteous Gods. The friendship of
> the Gods have we devoutly sought: so may the Gods extend our
> life that we may live. We call them hither with a hymn of olden
> time, Bhaga, the friendly Daksa, Mitra, Aditi, Aryaman, **Varuna**,
> Soma, the Asvins. May Sarasvati, auspicious, grant felicity.[35]

The word "god" in each case is *deva*. However, in other places, such as in Book 1, 24:14, he is definitely designated as an asura. "With bending down, oblations, sacrifices, O Varuna, we deprecate thine

---

[34] One has to add the qualifier "relatively" because in the epics (the Mahabharata and the Ramajana) and the puranas the behavior of the devas is from time to time not exactly above board, whereas there are some asuras who actually are fairly righteous in their actions, such as Bali, who permitted Vishnu to take back the universe for the devas by allowing him three steps.

[35] Griffith translation: http://www.sacred-texts.com/hin/rigveda/rv01089.htm (emphasis added).

Sanskrit at: http://www.sacred-texts.com/hin/rvsan/rv01089.htm.

anger: / Wise **Asura**, thou King of wide dominion, loosen the bonds of sins by us committed."[36]

In the latter case the eventual supremacy of Indra over Arjuna is oftentimes interpreted as a decisive aspect of the victory of the devas over the asuras, which could be read into 1,108:6 ("in battle we must contend with Asuras"[37]); however, "asuras" here could also simply refer to other members of that division.[38]

However, there is a serious problem with this whole view. It is not just Varuna's status as either deva or asura that is in question. The same ambiguity surrounds Indra, as exemplified in Book 1, 174:1: "Thou art the King of all the Gods, O Indra: protect the men, O Asura, preserve us."[39] More confusing yet, even *Dyaus Pitā*, the original head of the devas, is at time called "asura." For example, in Book 10, 67:2, he is called "Dyaus the Asura."[40] I can think of only three reasonable interpretations of this phenomenon. Either the composers of the Rig Veda were utterly confused, or it was patched together without anyone taking the time to bring it into coherence (which would be a similar approach that many critics have applied to the Old Testament), or we give the early Aryans greater credit for rational thinking and recognize that there was only one group of gods, usually called devas but at times also asuras. Eventually, by the end of the Vedic period, the asuras had become a subclass of the devas, with the membership still not entirely defined. By the time of

---

[36] Griffith translation. http://www.sacred-texts.com/hin/rigveda/rv01024.htm (emphasis added).

Sanskrit: http://www.sacred-texts.com/hin/rvsan/rv01024.htm.

[37] Griffith translation: http://www.sacred-texts.com/hin/rigveda/rv01108.htm.

Sanskrit: http://www.sacred-texts.com/hin/rvsan/rv01108.htm.

[38] Thus, for example, Arthur Anthony Macdonell, *A Vedic Reader for Students*, 1917, reproduced at http://www.sacred-texts.com/hin/vedaread.htm.

[39] Griffith translation, http://www.sacred-texts.com/hin/rigveda/rv01174.htm.

Sanskrit at http://www.sacred-texts.com/hin/rvsan/rv01174.htm. The Sanskrit word "asura" is clearly in the vocative case, apposite to "King Indra" (*rajendra*), and can only refer to him.

[40] Griffith translation, http://www.sacred-texts.com/hin/rigveda/rv10067.htm.

Sanskrit: http://www.sacred-texts.com/hin/rvsan/rv10067.htm.

the epics, the classical alignment of the devas as good gods and the asuras as evil demons emerged, but this was clearly a purely Indic development, long past the time when the Aryans split into their Indian and Iranian branches. If that is the correct view of the matter, then there is no paradox in Zoroaster's alleged condemnation of the daevas and exaltation of one of the ahuras, namely Ahura Mazda. Zoroaster called for the worship of one god and the rejection of all other supernatural beings as competitors to god. He used the term Ahura for God and referred to all of the other spirit beings as daevas, but this was not the victory of one pantheon over another. Similarly, there is nothing anomalous about the fact that the Norse people referred to their main gods as aesir; they just chose that particular designation within the IE language. The *vanir*, the enemies of the aesir, just happen to be their opponents; a group of battle-ready gods needs someone against whom to fight. The vanir show no resemblance to the *diw* group. They may have been indigenous gods of the land prior to Germanic and Norse invasions.

Thus there is no problem with the idea that Týr, the supreme god of the Norse pantheon, should be found among the *as* group of IE gods, whereas his counterparts, Dyaus, Zeus, etc., are on the *diw* side. The point is that these were not really sides, just two different appellations, which in some cases, especially Hinduism, turned into sides later on. Did *Dyeus*, which was perhaps the name of the original IE supreme god, belong to the *diw* or the *as* classification? The answer is both.[41]

God Among Semitic People

I trust that I may be forgiven if I do not interact with all of the thousands of books that have been written with regard to the Hebrew

---

[41] I must state that the need for a different construction than the traditional one of two competing pantheons only came to me recently and that the solution I have just described is not found in any of my previous writings. It removes the confusion from the Vedas and takes the mystery out of what happened outside of India.

people and their religion. I shall confine myself to a few observations in an area that has been explored extensively.

David Noss illustrates well my contention that frequently the rejection of an evolution of religion is merely verbal. When it comes to specific religions, writers frequently lapse into the old Tylorian scheme on a purely a priori basis. He describes the Hebrews before Moses (and before Abraham) by drawing a colorful picture of Bedouin life in the Syrian desert.[42] From there he goes on to ascribe to them an imaginary animism in which stones and pillars were the objects of worship because it was often believed that they housed "gods" or "godlings." According to Noss, the general name for any spirits, good or evil, was *el* (or *eloah*) in the singular and *elohim* (or *elim*) in the plural, only referring to a specific spirit if qualified by an adjective or place-name. As though following a manual written by Tylor, Noss concludes that the word *el* became the name for a single god as various groups, such as the Hebrews or Arameans, elevated the god of their choice to supremacy.[43]

None of these items, presented as facts to thousands of students each year, have any basis in evidence concerning the Hebrew people. In fact, there were no Hebrew people prior to Abraham, and, as Noss himself narrates, things drastically changed with Abraham, so there is no way in which any of the above could apply to any "pre-Mosaic" Hebrews. There were none before Abraham; they were exclusive worshippers of El-Shaddai, "God, the Strong" after Abraham.[44] There is no place to put these animistic nomads.

The fact of the matter is that where El appears, he is a supreme god, perhaps in the process of losing his stature (*deus absconditus* once more). If a backward extrapolation is possible, then El is a good

---

[42] David S. Noss and Blake R. Grangaard, *A History of the World's Religions*, 13th ed. (Upper Saddle River, NJ: Prentice Hall, 2008), 380–81. This description actually goes back to the earlier editions of the book under the authorship of Frank Noss, but David Noss has had many opportunities to change it if he cared to do so.

[43] Ibid., 382.

[44] It is not really necessary to add "El Shaddai" to "El" here on a consistent basis, but I am going to do so more than required to maintain clarity if possible.

candidate as representative of the original God in the Semitic circle, and with the way in which he appears in biblical circumstances, that possibility is increased.

For one thing, we can strengthen that observation by referring to the name *El Elyon*—"the most high God." This is a generic term, which people from the time of ancient Sumer on, applied to the highest deity. In the Bible, it occurs in Gen 14:18–19, in Abraham's encounter with Melchizedek, king of Salem and priest of "God Most High." The possibility that Melchizedek worshipped a pagan deity named El Elyon and that Abraham, in political correctness, accommodated himself to this false god, is eliminated by the fact that the same expression is used specifically to refer to Yahweh[45] three verses later (14:22) as well as in other parts of the Old Testament (e.g., Ps 78:35; Dan 4:2). To the contrary, Abraham recognized his own God, El-Shaddai, in the God whom Melchizedek served. Since Abraham served El-Shaddai exclusively, Melchizedek provides us a good instance for the ongoing monotheism among the Semitic people.[46]

There is an interesting side note, though, to the place of the Hebrews in the preservation of monotheism, which I can introduce with the following distinction: Melchizedek was a part of a people who were residential and agricultural. Abraham, at the time of their encounter, was a pastoral nomad. In fact, the true (as opposed to Noss's fictional) early Hebrews fit precisely the attributes Schmidt applies to people on this level. The transition of Abraham's clan from dwelling in a city devoted to the worship of the moon to recognizing the one God in heaven could be remarkable, depending on precisely what the relationship was between Abraham's family and the city of

---

[45] As one expects of a somewhat later historian, the narrator, traditionally Moses, uses the name for God that is uppermost in his mind, namely God's covenant name "Yahweh." There is nothing problematic here. Just consider the fact that we talk about "God" as the supreme deity of the Bible. Yet this word is of Germanic origin, and none of the biblical writers would have recognized it.

[46] So Richardson aptly describes the persistence of monotheism among non-Hebrew people as "the Melchizedek factor." Richardson, *Eternity*, 25–29.

Ur. The fact that his clan pursued a pastoral nomadic lifestyle seems to indicate that at least a sizable number of his people resided outside of the city with their livestock.

The Bible does not give us an account of how idolatry and polytheism arose historically. We know that Abraham came from a line of people who worshipped a moon god, but we don't know where that chain was broken. With all that we have learned in the course of this study, there is good reason to believe there were other monotheists around besides Melchizedek. Further, there were multiple opportunities to learn about the one God, not to mention the probability of there having been a live memory carried all along in Moses' own family.

In accord with Schmidt's analysis of the pastoral cultures, Abraham's social group was not totemic or even exogamous. Robertson Smith[47] inferred that the Israelites must have had a totemic society, primarily based on their practice of sacrifices, which he linked up with the imaginary totem feast. Since totemism is primarily a social arrangement, he should have first examined the way in which the society functioned. A quick genealogical reflection (based on Gen 11:27–31; 22:20–24; 28:2) should clear up this matter.

There was a man named Terah, who hailed from the city of Ur. As a city, Ur's culture would have been classified as *Tertiary* on Schmidt's scheme, but Terah's clan somehow continued the pastoral pattern of existence (which we are allowing to hover around the *Secondary* level): "patrilineal and an open family." Terah had at least three sons and a daughter (not all by the same wife): Abraham, Haran, Nahor, and Sarah. Abraham married his half-sister Sarah. Haran had died by the time the report officially begins, and we don't know who his wife was, but he had at least three children: a son named Lot and two daughters, Milkah and Iscah. Terah's third son, Nahor, married Haran's daughter Milkah, who was his and Abraham's niece, Lot's sister, and

---

[47] W. Robertson Smith, *Lectures on the Religion of the Semites*, 2nd ed. (London: Adam and Charles Black, 1894).

Terah's granddaughter. By today's Western standards, as well as the subsequent Mosaic Law, these marriages would have been forbidden. The subsequent unions would not have been illegal, but they definitely remained in the larger family: Abraham and Sarah's son was Isaac, who married Rebekah, the daughter of his cousin Bethuel, one of Nahor and Milkah's sons. Rebekah became the mother of Jacob, who married both daughters (Leah and Rachel) of her brother Laban, and, thus, were Jacob's cousins. We see that in typical nomadic fashion, they were patrilineal with no divisions within the family. These marriages were definitely endogamous if the concept even applies. And, if it is legitimate to apply Schmidt's conclusions back to a different specific situation now, it is to be expected that they as pastoral nomads were carriers of monotheistic concepts. But of course, as an argument for a more general pattern, it would be circular.

To continue how well the Hebrews exemplified the pattern, when these nomads took up residence in Egypt around the nineteenth century BC, they were thoroughly disliked by the agricultural Egyptians, whose prejudice was enhanced during the Hebrews' stay by the coming and leaving of the Semitic *Hyksos*, the "Shepherd Kings." By the time of the *Hyksos*'s departure, the dislike had turned into animosity, and the Israelites finally made their escape, the exodus. The Israelites had waffled around while they were in Egypt (Josh 24:14–21), some of them adopting Egyptian religions and others worshipping Mesopotamian gods; but after the exodus, Moses called them all back to their monotheistic origins, which immediately put them at odds religiously with the inhabitants of Canaan, the Promised Land to which they were heading. Baal, in all of his various forms, was primarily associated with fertility, a typical belief for an agricultural society, such as the Canaanites. As the Hebrews settled in Canaan, they moved into an agricultural existence themselves so that the Canaanite gods became enticing to them. And so the historic conflict concerning allegiance to Yahweh or Baal began. However, even as the Hebrews gave up their pastoral existence, and despite many struggles, they managed to retain and further the cause of monotheism.

El Elyon continued to be used by different people in different contexts. As stated above, the best way to make sense of the term is to see it as a generic expression used by different groups for their own conception of the highest god. Thus in some areas, El Elyon might refer to *Sin*, the moon god; in others to El himself, and in yet others to an unknown god above El. Specifically, in the Arabian peninsula, where religion on the whole had turned into a smorgasbord of animism, polytheism, and idolatry, there was a small group, called the *Hanif*, or "righteous ones," who confined their worship to El Elyon, or *al-ilah*, as it was transformed. Now, in the town of Mecca, "Allah," which is the generic term for "god" in Arabic, had received all sorts of interpretations, including the idea that he had fathered three daughters. Some people may have used the term al-ilah to refer to a moon god, though there is little direct evidence thereof. These excrescences notwithstanding, when Muhammad began his reform and called on the people to worship one God alone, it was the pure al-ilah of the Hanif that he clearly had in mind. He eschewed the idea of Allah producing offspring, and he clearly forbade associating Allah with the moon numerous times (e.g., Qur'an 6:67 and 2:289; also 6:54; 10:2, 33). Thus, El Elyon had once again manifested itself as the god whose origin lay with the beginnings of humanity.[48]

China's Clear Heritage: Shangdi

David Noss writes concerning Shangdi, the ancient Chinese god in heaven, "This Ruler on High . . . was a sort of ancestral figure, a vaguely conceived being located in the upper regions of the sky; he was far from being the Almighty God of Western religions, it seems, for he had no clearly defined character and sent down no messages preserved in scriptures."[49]

---

[48] For a further discussion of the impossibility of the Islamic Allah being a moon god, see my discussion in *Neighboring Faiths*, 2nd ed., 112–14.

[49] Noss and Grangaard, *History*, 259.

Rodney Stark's description of Shangdi consists of a number of quotations. Let me separate out. Two are attributed to John S. Major's article "Shang-Ti" in the *Encyclopedia of Religions*, the other one was penned by Stark himself.

> When a ruler died, he became an ancestral spirit, and the eldest ancestor spirit became known as Shang-ti, the "High God, or God Above." (ref. to Major)
> [Shang-ti was] thought of as a cosmic god, dwelling in or above the sky at the apex of the rotating heavens. Indeed, [he] might have been a deified embodiment of the pole star itself. (Major) Shang-ti also is known as the Jade Emperor. (Stark)[50]

This god must, indeed, be a wondrous being, who is both a "sort of ancestral figure" perhaps specifically "the eldest ancestor spirit"; and a "cosmic god," located in the "upper regions of the sky" and "in or above the sky," while maybe being an "embodiment of the pole star"; as well as being both "vaguely conceived" and identified with the Jade Emperor, concerning whom there is a rich mythology.

Stark's observation is correct to an extent. Initially Daoism (*dao-jia*) was a philosophy with little direct personal application. A numbers of factors contributed to its development as a religion (*daojiao*),[51] including the arrival of Mahayana Buddhism with its many Buddhas and Bodhisattvas, divine beings in human appearance. In competition, Daoism developed its own pantheon. The Jade Emperor, Yü Huang, first appeared during the second Han dynasty (AD 25–220) but did not attain general acceptance as supreme deity among Daoists until the Tang dynasty (AD 618–907), whose early segment was marked by a significant influence of Buddhism.[52] Because the memory of

---

[50] Stark, *Discovering*, 252. Note the various ways of Romanization of Chinese. I am essentially following the newer Pinyin method, whereas a number of sources, particularly older ones, use the older Wade-Giles style.

[51] For a lengthier treatment of this development, see *Neighboring Faiths*, 2nd ed., 401–5.

[52] See "The God Most Adored: the Jade Emperor" at the official website for Chinese culture, China.org; http://www.chinaculture.org/gb/en_aboutchina/2003-09/24/content_25159.htm.

Shangdi as the god of heaven was still alive, and it is awkward to have two supreme beings, it was only natural that there would be an informal intermixing of the names. On the whole, though, it would be a serious mistake to equate Shangdi with Yü Huang. Shangdi was the one god in heaven going back to prehistorical times; the Jade Emperor was a much later conception. The worship of Shangdi was always under the emperor's supervision; the Jade Emperor is a god designed for the people. In contemporary Chinese Bibles, the word "Lord" is translated with *Shangdi*; and it is inconceivable to substitute *Yü Huang* for it.

We can quickly dismiss the two descriptions of Shangdi mentioned above, the ones that tie him to being a "sort of ancestral figure," and the one connecting him to the pole star. If he had been an ancestor, one would certainly be right in adding the expression of uncertainty "sort of." One is left to wonder, "what sort?" E. T. C. Werner[53] hypothesizes that Shangdi was a previous emperor, setting standards for the present emperor on earth. There is certainly nothing unusual about the thesis that gods developed out of the fear or veneration of the departed, going all the way back to Herbert Spencer. There is also no question that ancestor veneration has been a significant practice in China for a long time. However, there is nothing to connect Shangdi directly to any specific ancestor (even a previous emperor) or ancestor worship in general.

Nor is there any good reason to believe he was an embodiment of the pole star. Before dismissing this notion as utterly absurd, we need to be aware that Daoism in its earliest religious phrase, included the idea of "star deities," viz. the belief that the stars were gods. Thus, it is possible that under this system, Shangdi was assigned to the pole star. But if so, again, Shangdi had a long history prior to the Daoist innovation of star deities.[54]

---

[53] E. T. C. Werner, *Myths and Legends of China* (London: George G. Harrap, 1922), 94.

[54] Daniel L. Overmyer, *Religions of China: The World as a Living System* (San Francisco: HarperSanFrancisco, 1986), 38–39.

In a tour de force to prove that neither Shangdi nor his later appellation, Tian (also spelled T'ien), were actually gods, Werner writes, "That Chinese religion neither was or is a monotheistic worship of God is further disproved by the fact that Shang Ti and T'ien do not appear in the list of the popular pantheon at all, though all the other gods are there represented."[55]

This strange argument recoils on Werner because it so clearly establishes the difference between the popular pantheon and Shangdi and Tian. *Of course* one does not see either of them among the contemporary gods, and it would be absurd to expect to see them there. As I said above, in all of the cultures at which we are looking in this chapter, we need to be sure to distinguish between the original monotheism with whatever cultus we can clearly identify as belonging to it and the later polytheistic religions that pushed the original God into the background. Clearly, the popular pantheon belongs in the second category, and it would be a mixed-up situation if one found Shangdi listed along with, say, Yü Huang, Mazu, Guanyin, Nüwa, or the threesome of Fu, Lu, and Shu. Werner has inadvertently just helped us see that there is something special about Shangdi.

Knowledge of the history of ancient China has, until recently, relied on documents that went back as far as the time of Confucius. That hasn't meant that we could just assume it was unreliable (just as one can't assume the unreliability of the Old Testament just because it is old), but it left a number of holes. The earliest dynasty of which we had certain knowledge that it existed was the Shang dynasty (BC 1766–1077), but much of its details had remained shrouded in mystery. Allegedly, preceding the Shang, was the Xia dynasty, but there were no plausible records to verify its existence. Over the last twenty years there have been concerted efforts by scholars with strong credentials to look more closely at China's ancient history. A result has been that, at a minimum, the Xia dynasty has been confirmed to have existed for several hundred years prior to the Shang, and a lot more

---

[55] Werner, *Myths and Legends*, 97.

details have been uncovered concerning both the Shang and the Zhou dynasties.[56] In Chinese mythology the period before the Xia dynasty constitutes a golden age of perfection, and the accounts of it are incompatible with one another, suffused with Daoist and Confucian mythology. Inconsistent descriptions cannot possibly be verified logically, though future discoveries may unveil a different, historically acceptable, and logically coherent description of an ancient civilization. The more recent discoveries have also underscored the importance of Shangdi.

Shangdi stands apart from the mythologies of China, and I cannot emphasize sufficiently how much any attempt to connect him to the later gods of Daoism undercuts his special standing. Even with the existence of the Xia dynasty now established, our more accurate records still begin with the Shang dynasty, and there we see Shangdi as the high god in the sky.[57] He has become somewhat remote; as an all-good being he does not require an extensive cultus; his regular public worship services are performed by the king on behalf of the kingdom; he is the author of a code of morality and will definitely punish both the people and the rulers if they do not abide by it. In short, he is the god of original monotheism.

In his book *Finding God in Ancient China*,[58] Chan Kei Thong pulls together from numerous Chinese sources the various properties of Shangdi so as to leave no doubt about his sharing the attributes of the God of the Bible. According to Thong, Shangdi is sovereign, eternal, immutable, all-powerful, all-knowing, ever-present, infinite, love,

---

[56] Chan Kei Thong and Charlene L. Fu, *Finding God in Ancient China: How the Ancient Chinese Worshiped the God of the Bible* (Grand Rapids, MI: Zondervan, 2009).

[57] *Di* means ruler and is used of human beings as well as God; *Shangdi* means the "most exalted ruler" and applies to God alone. The word *Shang* in *Shangdi* is not identical with the word *Shang* referring to the dynasty.

[58] I need to be clear that I am not endorsing all of Thong's interpretations of certain data, for which there is no need to expand on at this point. However, his collection of data is excellent.

holy, full of grace, good, faithful, merciful, compassionate, just, righteous, and wise.[59]

In the history of China, the Zhou dynasty replaced the Shang dynasty, and the reason the new set of kings gave for why this had been possible was because the kings of the Shang had departed from the moral expectations and become corrupt. So Shangdi set the Shang kings aside and gave the kingdom to the rulers of the Zhou dynasty. Their ultimate fall has also been attributed to their lack of obedience to Shangdi. During the time of the Zhou, a shift in nomenclature took place. Rather than referring to Shangdi, the god living in heaven, people started to talk about heaven (*Tian*) when referring to the same personal god. There is no reason to believe that by *Tian* they meant the actual physical sky, but, insofar as we have met several times throughout this book advocates of the unsubstantiated idea that ancient people turned from worship of the sky or heaven to worship of the god in the sky, we have here a substantiated case where the movement went in the other direction. In any event, the references to "heaven" here do not impersonalize the deity; in contrast to long-standing interpretations, it is now becoming increasingly clear that even Confucius, when he spoke about the "mandate of heaven," was referring to a personal god.[60]

A cultus of Shangdi was maintained right up to the end of the Chinese Empire in 1911.[61] Over the years it had become corrupted by including other gods in the ceremony, but it was purged again under the Qing dynasty so as to focus on Shangdi alone. The emperor served as priest, ideally three times a year, performing a burnt animal offering on behalf of the people, in which the meaning of a reconciliation with God was dominant. As had been the case all along, the emperor was representing all of the people, and common people would not be anywhere near that ceremony. But does that mean common people

---

[59] Thong and Fu, *Finding God*, 88–106.

[60] See Kelly Clark, Zhan Qingxiong, and Xu Yi Yie, eds., *Ethics, Religion and Society* (Shanghai: Shanghai Guji Press, 2007).

[61] Thong and Fu, *Finding God*, 111–55.

were excluded from the worship of Shangdi, similarly to the way in which Akhenaten intended to keep all commoners from worshipping Aten?

It does not. Though not a part of the official ceremonies, and not connected to other Daoist, Buddhist, or Confucian practices, Werner reported that he ran across people who were offering joss sticks or the like to God, perhaps around New Year's, and if asked to whom they were making this gesture, they would reply "Shangdi."[62] Werner interpreted these facts as a display of ignorance on the part of these people because he drew a hard-and-fast line of distinction between Shangdi, who may only be worshipped by the emperor, and Tian, who may be worshipped by anyone. So the people who thought they were worshipping Shangdi were actually worshipping Tian. Here is an example of how not to do ethnology or comparative religion. It is appropriate for scholars to question the *interpretation* made by other scholars, but it is never acceptable to be a *Besserwisser* when it comes to what adherents of a religion are actually practicing—no matter whether it fits our expected pattern or not. All reports by adherents are data and need to be respected, even if, to our eyes, they clash with what we think we know of a religion. To go one step further, even if, by our understanding of the religion, what someone is doing is a violation of their religious beliefs (e.g., terrorism as contrary to the principles of Islam), we still cannot say that what the person is doing is something different from what he or she is self-reporting (e.g., that the terrorist claims he is fulfilling the commandments of the Qur'an).

Thus, the memory of original monotheism is alive and well in China. Efforts by Thong and others to revive this part of their ancient heritage are spreading. Personally, my concern is that the strong case for the reality of Shangdi as the original god in China could be weakened by tying it to other issues which carry far less certainty.[63]

---

[62] Werner, *Myths and Legends*, 93.

[63] I'm thinking here, for example, of the attempt to see the first eleven books of Genesis reflected in the characters of Chinese writing (Thong and Fu, *Finding God*, 45–72), an undertaking that I find unpersuasive because, among other things,

Conclusion

The history of religions subsequent to the *Primitive* era bears out two important consequences. We see the expected degeneration but also the fact that numerous cultures did not do away with the entire idea of a single God above all other spiritual beings, even when the culture as a whole has been tainted by incompatible beliefs and practices. And second, we see how even for the much more developed and enscripturated religions of the Indo-Europeans, various Semites, and the Chinese, there is solid evidence for a monotheistic background.

---

it appears to be tied to an arbitrary selection of words to represent a picture. Even if it should turn out that the advocates of this phenomenon are right, the case for Shangdi is clear enough that tying this material to the matter of Shangdi is only adding a hurdle that needs more support in its own right. At a minimum, the two issues should be treated separately. And, as I have stressed before in some other writings—and I shall not refer to any specific sources here since there is no need to create any further heat—the attempt to find parallels between Chinese pagan mythology and biblical history is to give away the case since (a) it doesn't work and (b) it places the imaginary characters of paganism on the same level as Shangdi or vice versa.

CHAPTER 11

Original Monotheism and Christian Apologetics

As we come to the end of this story of an intellectual quest, we need to ask ourselves: So, what have we proven?

My first inclination is to say, "Not much that wasn't there already." To put matters into a minimalistic form, I think we can express it this way: We have shown that Wilhelm Schmidt's conclusions still stand, and that, consequently, it is more reasonable to believe that the original religion of humanity was monotheism rather than some other alternatives, such as animism. We have done so primarily by following the course of the often-heated discussion on the subject, learning about the evidence brought up by Lang and Schmidt, demystifying Schmidt's method, and by showing that the criticisms brought up against these two writers did not stand up. If I may be forgiven for a possible understatement, we could say that the hypothesis of an original monotheism stands so far unfalsified.

Still continuing to speak in understated terms, this is a helpful hypothesis; I would suggest that if we had done nothing more than sustain its plausibility, we could be satisfied. Some hypotheses are more important than others because they constitute the fountainhead of further truths. Furthermore, there are degrees of plausibility, and when I say that hypothesis A is more plausible than hypothesis B, the difference in meaning may range all the way from (1) "All things considered, I'm more inclined toward A than B"; to (2) "A is clearly supported by the best evidence, and B stretches one's credulity to the breaking point." In the latter case we're clearly not merely expressing a subjective preference between two hypotheses of almost equal standing but a rather well-grounded theory and a highly dubious attempt at an alternative to it. That does not mean, of course, that, therefore, the entire academic world would subscribe to theory A. As a matter of fact, in order to preserve theory B, a large part of this world unto itself may just decree that one should no longer ask the question to which A is clearly the better answer.

So, if I may be forgiven for possible overstatement, I suggest that the standing of original monotheism is more in line with the second meaning of "plausible" than the first. It is supported by data based on a strong, though admittedly not infallible, method, and its most formidable competing hypotheses are—well, absent. For the past fifty years the issue of the origin of religion in a genuine historical sense has been brought up, if at all, almost entirely by the occasional Christian apologist; and it has been shouted down by scholarly publications and textbooks alike, for the most part by the technique of one writer citing the authority of another writer, who is relying on the judgment of a third writer. Such maneuvers in the halls of academe say nothing about the truth status of the theory of original monotheism.

The Issue Is Still Alive

As a matter of fact, evolutionism and misdirection continue to have a palpable impact. The feeble theories, born and buried in the nineteenth century, continue to influence our culture on a daily basis. Earlier in this book we quoted Tomoko Masuzawa and Mircea Eliade, as they asserted that the quest for a historical origin of religion was dead and predicted that its resurrection was highly unlikely. I also promised that in this chapter I would come back to the question of whether it really is dead. Please understand that I am not thinking of a conspiracy or formal agreements. Still, it appears to me that scholarship at large has settled for a halfhearted moratorium on the question of origins and has informally agreed to let the matter lie there unless required to borrow from it under pressure. Such a consensus would have originated in convenience, not in conviction, though at times it may look as though it has become a universally acclaimed creed. Still, due to its origin in convenience, it is not surprising to find any number of scholars violating the dogma if they perceive a necessity for doing so. To continue with the clerical analogy, we may just find some deacons smoking in the church parking lot.

Evolutionism Applied to Specific Religions

Despite the formal renunciation of an evolution of religion, writers frequently make use of it when analyzing specific religions. In the previous chapter we saw David Noss try to force the origins of Hebrew religion into an unconvincing evolutionary scheme. The same tactic comes out as well, for example, when scholars describe the nature of *kami*, the spiritual power(s) in Shinto, the Japanese national religion. One finds this word used rather indiscriminately to refer to objects, spirits, and deities in temples, as well as to gods in mythology. To explain this diversity, one looks at the underlying nature of *kami* and finds that writers frequently liken it to *mana*, the spiritual force described and named after a belief in Melanesia,[1] which is not problematic per se. But then many authors casually make reference to it as the foundational preanimistic idea that gave rise to religion, an idea that simply does not square with the facts as we have come to know them.

---

[1] C. H. Codrington, *The Melanesians* (Clarendon: Oxford, 1891), 118–20. It is interesting to note that even though subsequent scholars made use of the idea of mana as nothing more than a force pervading the world, Codrington insisted that mana is never found apart from personal beings.

So Daniel Clarence Holtom wrote: "*Kami* in its original meaning is practically identical with *mana* the name adopted by science from the language of the Melanesians to indicate the occult force which preliterate man found emanating from objects and experiences that aroused in him emotions of wonder and awe."[2]

We are by now sufficiently acquainted with the language used here to recognize that it relies directly on the scheme advocated by J. G. Frazer. The point is that the concept of *mana* was not in itself religious and gave rise to magic (the attempt to manipulate *mana*), which, in turn, due to its lack of success, gave rise to animism. Although the above quotation comes from fifty years ago, it continues to be cited in contemporary books.[3] In the world religions textbook authored by Niels C. Nielsen Jr. et al., Alan L. Miller wrote:

> The Japanese scholar Motoori Norinaga (1730–1801) derived the term *kami* . . . from a word written with a different character but pronounced the same, which means "above," "high," "lifted up"; by extension it also means something unusual, special, and powerful; and finally it can also connote something august, awe-inspiring, mysterious, and divine. This understanding accords well with the modern Western notion of **the most elemental form of religious experience**: the discovery of *mana*, that is an undifferentiated power inherent in all things that gives each its peculiar nature, efficacy, and attributes. When this power becomes concentrated for some reason, it is believed to manifest itself as a sacred object or event, which in turn gives rise to special activities called religion.[4]

The evolutionist legacy lives on.

---

[2] Daniel Clarence Holtom, "Shinto," in *Living Schools of Religion*, ed. Vergilius Ferm (Paterson, NJ: Littlefield Adams, 1965), 19–43.

[3] See Lewis M. Hopfe and Mark R. Woodward, *Religions of the World*, 9th ed. (Boston: Pearson, 2009), 223.

[4] Niels C. Nielsen Jr. et al., *Religions of the World* (New York: St. Martin's Press, 1983), 322 (emphasis added). In fairness I must state that the phrase in question is not found in the 3rd edition of the book, though the reason probably lies in the fact that it is an abridgement of the former editions.

Wellhausen: Evolutionism Is Thriving in Old Testament Studies

Furthermore, if the idea of an evolution of religion has been repudiated, the obituary has not reached the field of Old Testament studies. One of the most successful corollaries of Tylor's theory was Julius Wellhausen's history of the evolution of Israelite religion. Julius Wellhausen (1844–1908) did far more than sort out the supposedly intertwined strands of documents underlying the Pentateuch, usually labeled as J, E, D, and P, a technique known as the "Documentary Hypothesis" or "Source Criticism." Those alleged discoveries had been made by others before him. Wellhausen's contribution was to lay them out in a coherent narrative thanks to Tylor's Procrustean bed, which enabled him to force the biblical material into his expectations of how Israelite religion must have developed. A centerpiece of his major study was that the so-called Mosaic law was not fully invented until after the Babylonian exile, and, thus, strict adherence to the Torah did not become a central part of Judaism until long after the prophets had proclaimed their messages and their teachings had been written down.[5] Obviously, with this rewriting of the biblical account, he turned the entire history of Israel topsy-turvy.

Wellhausen, when he was a professor of theology at the University of Greifswald, realized that his theory was incompatible with his job of preparing students for Christian ministry. Robert J. Oden places Wellhausen's voluntary resignation as a theologian into a favorable light.

> Wellhausen resigned from Greifswald in 1882. His letter of resignation is a classic testimony both to Wellhausen's integrity and to the internal tensions experienced by a historian who was also a theologian: "I became a theologian because the scientific treatment of the Bible interested me; only gradually did I come to understand that a professor of theology also has the practical task of preparing the students for service in the

---

[5] Julius Wellhausen, *Prolegomena to the History of Israel* (1883; repr., New York: Meridian, 1958).

Protestant Church, and that I am not adequate to this practical
task, but that instead despite all caution on my own part I make
my hearers unfit for their office. Since then my theological
professorship has been weighing heavily on my conscience."
The career of Wellhausen then ended where it had begun, at
Göttingen, where from 1892 until his death he was a professor
of Semitic languages.[6]

Robert Oden is making it appear as though there had been a ten-
year hiatus before Wellhausen stood behind the lectern again, but he is
leaving out the fact that Wellhausen immediately went from Greifswald
to the University of Halle as professor of philology, followed by a few
years at Marburg, before his final appointment at Göttingen. During
this time he taught the same subject matter but now without feeling
the restrictions that had bogged him down at Greifswald. I cannot say
whether Wellhausen had any further regrets on what his ideas were
doing to the faith of his students; if so, he did not let them influence
his teachings or writings. Significantly for us today, the reality is that
many institutions across the world are attempting to prepare their
students for future ministry by indoctrinating them with ideas that its
author thought were counterproductive for such a purpose.

Even though Tylor has been repudiated and Wellhausen's theory
is firmly based on Tylor's ideas, classrooms devoted to the study of the
Old Testament still reverberate to the recital of Wellhausen's theories
and its offspring. The idea that the Documentary Hypothesis has been
superseded by other approaches, such as form criticism and redaction
criticism in Old Testament, may be true. But by and large the newer
theories presuppose the Documentary Hypothesis and build on it;
they certainly disqualify Mosaic authorship of the Pentateuch on an
a priori basis. Even in some supposedly evangelical schools, some faculty trained at liberal seminaries or universities have no other story
to tell their students.

---

[6] Robert J. Oden Jr., *The Bible Without Theology* (New York: Harper and Row,
1987), 20.

Origin Without Beginning

In addition to the remarkable fact that Tylor's theory is alive and well in Old Testament studies, it also continues to remain true that in religious studies, insofar as the word *origin* is used at all, its meaning continues to be something that the word actually does not mean, nor has ever meant outside of this contrived context. Durkheim, Otto, Eliade, or Kitagawa notwithstanding, if "origin," *Ursprung,* or *l'origine* do not entail the concept of a "beginning," they have been given the meaning outside of the standard use in their home languages. (We will have to leave it up to the descendants of Raffaele Pettazzoni to clue us in on whether *origine* in Italian contains a special meaning known only to the initiates—see chap. 8.) As we saw, Otto responded to a historical question, or, rather deflected it, with a psychological answer. Émile Durkheim addressed the issue of an origin head-on by developing a long and highly complex historical narrative on the origin of religion in totemism but informed us along the way that the word *origin* did not really mean "origin." Masuzawa observes the irony intrinsic to those contemporary theories that present us with a diagnosis of religious people as supposedly yearning to return to an origin outside of time.

> What does this reflect vis-à-vis the modern scholarship on myth and ritual, the scholarship, that is, that rather emphatically denied itself the quest for the origin of religion some time ago? This scholarship is peculiarly marked by its obsession with cosmogony, paradigms, and archetypal narratives—in short, a preoccupation with the question of origin.[7]

The question of origins will not disappear, and metaphysical answers to historical questions will never be satisfactory, but the perpetuation of this category mistake continues. And as long as metaphysical counterfeits are permitted to be substituted for historical

---

[7] Tomoko Masuzawa, *In Search of Dreamtime: The Quest for the Origin of Religion* (Chicago: University of Chicago Press, 1993), 29.

conclusions, the vacuum created by the absence of a historically validated theory will be filled by evolutionism when a scholar has nowhere else to turn. Thus, he or she will dismiss history on a routine basis but also invent it if needed to sustain a metaphysical allegory.

Even if such bizarre moves were not intended to sidestep the truth of Christianity—though in many cases they were—they would be still draining the lifeblood out of biblical Christianity. Christianity is not compatible with the trivialization of history. It is founded on the historical events of God's people in the Old Testament and the person and work of Jesus Christ as described in the New Testament. By sending historical events to the margins of relevance, Christianity becomes pointless. As Peter says, "For we did not follow cleverly contrived myths when we made known to you the power and coming of our Lord Jesus Christ; instead, we were eyewitnesses of His majesty" (2 Pet 1:16).

Take away the historical events of Christ's life, in particular his physical death and physical resurrection, and we have nothing left of Christianity but Christ's teaching. And what Christ taught set an impossible requirement of righteousness (Matt 5:20),[8] so that it required the historical events connected with his atonement and resurrection, which are the foundation of divine justification, to make sense out of them. By those who are not willing to take the words of Jesus literally, let alone accept his death on the cross and supernatural resurrection as historical realities, the alternative has been to trivialize his teachings to the level of greeting-card wisdom. Biblical Christianity without biblical history is meaningless, and, in fact, biblical content without biblical history makes no sense. And that includes an origin. Apart from a direct initial encounter between God and human beings, the Old Testament loses its point.

All three of these concerns—the unjustified ad hoc resorts to religious evolutionism, the continuing propagation of Wellhausen's

---

[8] "For I tell you, unless your righteousness surpasses that of the scribes and Pharisees, you will never enter the kingdom of heaven" (Matt 5:20).

evolution-based theory, and the sleight of hand that substitutes the stone of metaphysical speculation for the bread of historical inquiry—are clearly rendered unnecessary and unsustainable by the reality of primitive monotheism. We can then see that emergency resorts to evolutionist explanations are appeals to an "evolution of the gaps" mentality. The Wellhausian myth can be understood as the subjective contrivance that it is. And subjective and phenomenological approaches, though potentially helpful in understanding *how* religion works in the lives of individuals and groups, can no longer be palmed off as the "real" answer to the "real" question of the origin of religion, which is not at all the real question. But how sure can we be of this conclusion?

Careful Assessment

Let me reemphasize a point I made earlier. The more we claim, the harder it is to prove our claim. In light of the benefits of establishing the reality of original monotheism as stated above, whatever parsimony it may take to uphold a fundamental belief in primitive monotheism is well worth the price because the implications will produce a great amount of profit. Once we have shown that humanity's first religion was monotheism, the structures established by evolutionism or misdirection must crumble, but we could not do it all at once, and we need to trust God to take the basic information further in the hearts and minds of people. In this connection, let me raise some questions of varying degrees of importance.

1. *Have we (that is to say Wilhelm Schmidt and those of us who support his cause) really shown that original monotheism is true beyond all conceivable objections?* Of course, we have not. It would be impossible for any human to do so. There is no limit as to what human beings can "conceive" of, but that's not relevant. There is no scientific enterprise where eliminating all "conceivable" objections is the point. For example, someone could object to the idea of a monotheism of the past by saying there actually has been no past earlier than, say,

fifteen seconds ago. At that time the entire universe came into being complete with history books and artifacts, giving us the misleading impression of a genuine past. Then a theory for a monotheism in the remote past has no meaning since there was no past. Now, if you've followed the silly idea I just advanced, you are able to conceive of it, and it is, thus, a conceivable objection. Furthermore, I cannot think of any way to refute that objection, as absurd as it may seem. Anything I could bring up as evidence of there having been a significant past could simply be labeled as included in the makeup of the world when it popped into existence a short while ago. So here is an extreme case of a conceivable objection against which I have no defense.

But we must ask: Are we going to approach this scientific issue as rational people and scholars, or are we going to let it degenerate into an empty debate between ourselves and the ad hoc objections dreamed up by the village atheist? The topic here is what is actually plausible within the boundaries of empirically recorded data; it is not a thought experiment. As we said in the preface, first place of importance goes to the researchers who collected the information. A long history of ignoring the evidence or treating it selectively makes no difference. The reports are still there for anyone to read. Scholars must be able to defend their theories against reasonable objections, not against the absurd fantasies concocted by someone intent on demonstrating their cleverness. There is no need to defend a theory against an objection that no sane and rational human being actually believes.

The same thing applies to mantra-like repetitions of formulas of dismissal. As we have mentioned so many times, the literature is filled with pronouncements such as, "It is impossible ever to uncover what the earliest human religion may have been like." Again, there is no rational defense against an empty assertion of this kind presented as unassailable dogma. It is true that logically contradictory statements can never be true. But these assertions concern methodology and empirical facts. In that case stating it does not make it true, and the person making such an assertion is entering the realm of the agnostic's dilemma: To be able to say categorically that some knowledge is in principle unattainable requires knowledge of all the methods of the past, the present, and the future, as well as the further knowledge that none of those methods have ever worked, are not now working, nor will ever work in the distant future. In other words, it requires virtual omniscience, and I cannot see the point in my trying to defend the theory against someone who, whether he realizes it or not, is assuming such an exalted position.

To repeat once more, the culture-historical method does not grant the ethnologist omniscience, and if someone presumes to know in advance what can or cannot be proven by means of this or any other method, those of us who are not as fortunate to know the truth about things that we have not studied can only respond in humble silence unless we find it impossible not to give vent to our horrified amazement.

2. *Is the god of original monotheism real?* This is the first of three questions which do not have straightforward answers, but this is not a straightforward question. Undoubtedly, the answer to this is uppermost in the minds of numerous readers, and many readers may want me to give an unequivocal answer of yes. But I cannot do so yet. We need to be careful because there are corollary issues. The subject of our investigation has been the religion of earliest humanity, and we have found the solution to that matter to be monotheism. This phenomenon is not what one would expect on a purely naturalistic basis, and we should take seriously that people testified to have experienced something real. However, so far it cannot be more than a strong pointer that enhances greatly the probability of the reality of this single God, Creator, Sustainer, and Moral Lawgiver. But it would take more to turn this point into a genuine argument, such as the cosmological one that holds that any finite thing (e.g., our **idea** of God) is an effect that needs to be rooted in an infinite God, and, though not impossible, we can spare ourselves that exercise for now.

3. *Is the god of original monotheism the same god in all of the cultures in which he appears?* This can be a slippery question, and I don't

want to be accused of special pleading. One could simply define the relevant cultures by the degree to which their monotheism fits into a standard we have created and then marvel at how amazing it is that all of these cultures have such similar forms of monotheism. In order to avoid such circular reasoning, we first of all took recourse to the culture-historical method in order to isolate the cultures that apparently demonstrate the oldest ages and only then came up with a description of the God of original monotheism based on what we found there. If we are faithful to that approach, our generalizations are not arbitrary axiomatic definitions, but they are and will remain to be strong and plausible generalizations.

So how can we tell when two objects or concepts are identical? In strict logical terms two things are identical if whatever can be said of one can also be said of the other. In that case, none of the gods of original monotheism found in any of the tribes are identical with one another because all of the mythologies concerning the gods, including their descriptions—not to mention anthropomorphisms— are frequently incompatible. But we need to realize that this way of establishing identity is limited by our epistemological capacity. The classical example in philosophy, due to Frege, is the statement that "The Morning Star is the Evening Star." Today we know this statement to be true because astronomers have assured us that both descriptions apply to the same planet, namely Venus. However, to the ancients, this identity would not have been clear at all due to the obvious difference that one appears in the morning and the other in the evening. Clearly some aspects of a description are essential to the object while others are contingent or accidental.

What's worse, one may even get some facts wrong in talking about someone or something even though our agreement concerning their identity is correct. You and I may disagree on whether a specific person has blue eyes or green eyes, which means that at least one of us is wrong; but the entire discussion would presuppose that we are referring to the same person, known to us by other essential properties. Now, as soon as we decide which attributes are essential and which are accidental, there is a risk of a certain amount of sub-jectivity or arbitrariness, which can, however, be severely overstated as long as we remain in the real world and not in some realm of the conceivable but implausible.

Let us not lose sight of the point of this whole enterprise. What we see in these cultures, which have qualified on the basis of the culture-historical method, is that each of the supreme beings, regard-less of surrounding mythology, bears the essential attributes of deity. They have personhood. They created the world and are now oversee-ing a moral code. They are all-powerful, all-knowing, eternal, and all good, to mention just some of the most outstanding attributes, which certainly puts them all into the same rubric labeled "supreme being." So, does that mean that we can say that Baiame of Australia is identi-cal with Gitche Manitou of the Algonquins? It appears that we can say so but only within certain severe restrictions, as revealed in the next question.

In short, they are alike insofar as they all share in the attributes of a monotheistic deity, but whether they are truly identical requires some further critical thinking.

4. *Is the god of original monotheism the God of the Bible?* In light of the answer to the question above, we need to be even more careful in responding to this question. Furthermore, it can become danger-ous to answer affirmatively without getting caught up in syncretism or an unbiblical inclusivism in which we just brush aside differences. Andrew Lang devoted an entire chapter to contrasting Jehovah of the Bible with the god of original monotheism, and concluded that, on the whole, he preferred the supreme being of the Australians to Jehovah.[9] I am mentioning this fact because it illustrates that there certainly are significant differences between the gods, and, even if they all qualify for being classified as the god of a monotheistic belief system, that does not necessarily entail their being identical to the

---

[9] Andrew Lang, *The Making of Religion*, 2nd ed. (Charleston, SC: Bibliobazaar, orig. 1900), 253–69.

one God of biblical monotheism. I am afraid some Christian authors
who have mentioned original monotheism have drawn the equivalence with more enthusiasm than reflection. Thong, the subtitle of
whose book reads *How the Ancient Chinese Worshiped the God of the
Bible*, says:

> The picture that emerges dovetails so neatly and corresponds
> so closely with the One described in the Hebrew and Christian
> Scriptures that we can recognize Him as one and the same. . . .
> Only by taking all of [His] attributes together can we gain a
> proper understanding of the nature and person of the One True
> God. It is important to understand that His attributes are not the
> same as His works or manifestations.[10]

Similarly, Don Richardson's book is subtitled *Startling Evidence
of Belief in the One True God in Hundreds of Cultures Throughout the
World.*[11] We need to trim down such triumphant expressions a little
bit before we can assent to them. For one thing, it is important to realize that though the attributes (or essence) of God are not the same as
his works (or energies), there is strong continuity between his being
and his works and manifestations. The latter are as much a part of the
criteria for his identity as an abstract catalog of his attributes; in fact,
one might argue that God's actions and manifestations demonstrate
to us how we are to understand his attributes. When we have finished
such an analysis, we are certainly still left with a God who shares his
attributes on the whole with the God of the Bible, but differences
remain differences and stand in the way of easy identification.

There is a plausible way of establishing identity, even on the grand
scale Richardson promises, but we need to be careful to observe the

---

[10] Chan Kei Thong and Charlene L. Fu, *Finding God in Ancient China: How the
Ancient Chinese Worshiped the God of the Bible* (Grand Rapids, MI: Zondervan, 2009),
86.

[11] Don Richardson, *Eternity in Their Hearts: Startling Evidence of Belief in the One
True God in Hundreds of Cultures Throughout the World*, 3rd ed. (Ventura, CA: Gospel
Light Publications, 2005).

important distinction between the historical origin of an idea and the manner in which this concept is now understood by various people.

As an example, the issue of the identity of the gods in the monotheistic cultures comes up frequently in comparisons of Allah in Islam with Yahweh of the Bible. Now, I mentioned earlier that there is good reason to believe that a monotheistic tradition, propagated by the Hanif, survived on the Arabian Peninsula independently, and then was combined by Muhammad with insights from Christianity, Judaism, and Zoroastrianism, as he constructed his conception of Allah. So there can be little doubt that the origin of God in Islam stems from the one true God, whom we Christians recognize as the God of Scripture. However, when we look at the utterances Allah purportedly speaks in the Qur'an, we find that he directly contradicts the biblical view of God. Specifically, he denies being a triune God; he denies that Jesus Christ is the second person of the Trinity; and he denies Jesus, God's incarnation, died on the cross. Now, regardless of what other attributes we may apply to him, it is clear at this point that Allah of the Qur'an and the God of the Bible cannot be identical. Thus, we must come to a two-sided conclusion: God and Allah share the same origin, which by our best lights is the one true God who has revealed himself in the Bible. However, as presently conceived, they are not the same being.

This is the answer we also must apply to the attempts at comparison between the God of original monotheism and the God of Scripture. As to origin, we are happy to accede to the proposition that he is identical in origin with Yahweh, the Creator, Redeemer, and sovereign Lord that we read about in the Bible. But when we analyze the concepts ascribed to these beings on the indigenous level, chances are that there are sufficient differences in the nature of the beings that prevent us from asserting identity. I could be tempted to set up a hierarchy of different conceptions of God in various cultures, based on how likely it is that they might be identical with the God of Scriptures, but that would not be helpful since there is no reason my judgment on such a call should be authoritative. People who make such claims for "their" God need to be careful to avoid misleading people into syncretism. It would appear to me that a common origin is highly plausible; present identity with Yahweh is subject to debate.

Reversing Direction

Still, again, we must remind ourselves what the whole point has been and what we have achieved. The overall picture is this: The conventional wisdom, so to speak, has been that religion is a part of human culture, developing along with the inventions of writing, pottery, and long division. In short, it is of human origin and, whether we explain it psychologically, socially, or symbolically makes no difference for that larger assumption. Let us put this statement negatively for a moment: Religion is not something that stems from outside of human beings, as would be the case if it were based on a revelation. However, it appears to be evident to most critics, who reason less carefully in that regard than I did above, that a universal monotheism would ultimately be inexplicable without a historical self-disclosure of the God of original monotheism. Antagonists to Lang understood this better than Lang did because Lang insisted on denying a revelation, while others laid one at his doorstep. (Some people, e.g., Eliade, missed Schmidt's affirmation of a primordial revelation for the simple reason that they had not read that far, I guess.) A global prohibition of revelation and a global prohibition of an original monotheism without a prior set of stages of development have gone hand in hand. This sanction applies to the declaration that the issue is out of bounds as well. To say that we may not ask the question concerning the original religion of humanity is tantamount to forbidding us to say that the original religion of humanity was monotheism. But that's precisely what we're saying.

The Original Religion of Humanity Was Monotheism!

If that's what we have shown to be true (and I believe that Lang and Schmidt did, and it would be a great honor if I have managed to clarify some of their ideas), then we may have demonstrated that the ideological foundation of virtually all of today's anthropology and ethnology is insufficiently substantiated.

That's the real outcome of this study. Let me repeat what we have not done: (a) We have *not* proven the theory of original monotheism beyond all conceivable doubt. We have, however, shown that it is true beyond any reasonable scientific doubt, which acknowledges the truth of the source material. (b) We have *not* demonstrated that all supreme beings contained in cultures with an original monotheism are real. We have, however, indicated that the fact that the oldest cultures consistently manifest a monotheism lets us establish a high probability that they experienced something real. (c) We have *not* shown that all the supreme beings are identical with one another. Still, by looking at their attributes, they all fit into the category of deity and, therefore, share a likeness on a foundational level. (d) Finally, we did *not* argue that the supreme being of original monotheism was necessarily the God of the Bible. However, insofar as he is real, and since there can only be one being with all of the attributes of the one and only God, he must be identical with the biblical God in origin. The attributes of the god of many monotheisms today are such that we can say pretty confidently that they all may have a common origin with the one true God, but they are not necessarily identical with the one true God when we consider all of their attributes.

This much, I would humbly contend, is sufficient to accomplish the apologetics purposes we had in mind for this study. We have shown that there is good reason to believe that human religion began with monotheism, and we have demonstrated that there simply are no viable, rational alternatives. In other words, we have shown that the commonly accepted notion that religion is merely a product of human culture cannot be maintained as a globally true statement. To be sure, this is a negative result, not to be considered a "proof" for the existence of God. However, we can say that we could not have hoped for a better outcome for the study as a whole. After all, we have just potentially put some gaping breaches into the ideological structure on which contemporary anthropology has been erected. The next step can be filling in the holes with the patterns based on the self-reports of the people concerning their own belief as well as reconfirm the chronological sequences. From there we can ask the same question that presumably many humans in prehistory did: "Who made all of this?" With a traditional argument, akin to the cosmological argument, we can then demonstrate that the beliefs of the people on Schmidt's *Primitive* level are actually more reasonable than those of many people advocating contemporary secularism. I will settle for that.

Relationships among some Indo-European Languages[1]

PROTO-INDO EUROPEAN (PROTO-IE)

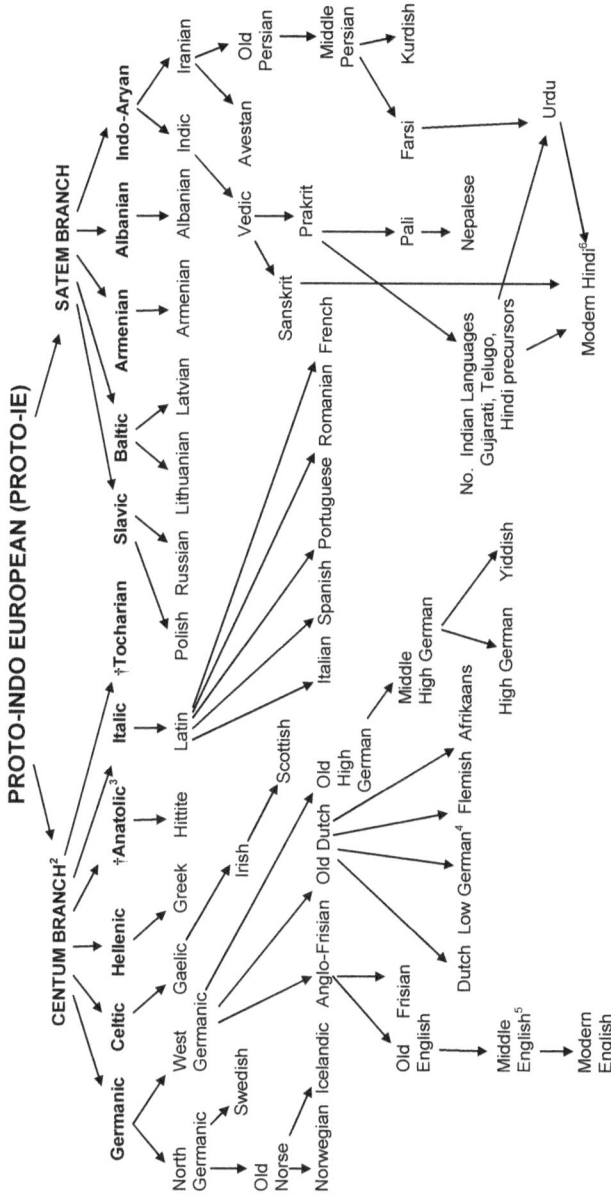

---

[1] Please note that in this diagram the lengths of the arrows indicate neither extent of time nor degree of affinity, only an attempt to maintain some clarity.

[2] The words for "hundred" in Latin (*centum*) and Avestan (*satem*). This division indicates a very early split among IE-speaking tribes.

[3] There are two branches that are now extinct, Anatolic and Tocharian. Tocharian was spoken by a people in the Tarim Basin of Central Asia (the vicinity of Afghanistan).

[4] Note that "Low German" is an altogether different language from "High German," not just a different dialect. The number of its speakers is actually increasing.

[5] Middle English developed side-by side with the version of French spoken by the Normans. Their language, in turn, was a combination of Old Norse and medieval French.

[6] Modern Hindi is the result of an intentional nineteenth-century attempt to build a more Indic language by retrofitting Urdu with native Indic languages and even Sanskrit.

Appendix B
Some Cautions on
Brandewie's Translations

D r. Brandewie has done us all a great service in keeping a fact-based interaction with Schmidt alive, so I'm bringing up this example merely to emphasize the need to approach his translations critically, not to embarrass him. A glaring example of translation by surmise occurs in a passage I cited in the last chapter, which comes from *Der Ursprung*, vol. 6, 480. I will set my translation and that of Brandewie (*Wilhelm Schmidt*, 279) side by side flanked by Schmidt's original German and my explanation why the differences are important. See chart on the next page.

Am I just nitpicking here? I'm afraid that "nitpicking" is no longer an appropriate word if substance is lost in a translation, and there certainly is a significant difference in this case whether the testimony comes from some unnamed experts or from the adherents of a religion. Furthermore, I would not have gone through this example if similar incidents were not found throughout Brandewie's book. I conclude by saying: Please use Brandewie's work and his translation, but please use it carefully and, if possible, double-check the translations on the Internet or with software, which I'm sure Dr. Brandewie wishes he had at his disposal when he wrote the book!

Schmidt's German	My Translation	Brandewie's Translation	Comment
Alles in allem genommen, die Nachrichten die wir von den Bekennern der ältesten Religionen selbst haben, sind der Annahme, daß diese von den Menschen suchend und forschend geschafften worden seien, nicht bloß nicht günstig, sondern, was schlimmer ist, sie erwähnen sie nicht einmal mit einem Worte.	The bottom line is that the reports we have from the adherents of the oldest religions themselves are not only merely disinclined towards the supposition that the religions were created by seeking and searching human beings; rather, worse yet, they do not even mention it with a single word.	All in all, the reports I myself have received from those who know these oldest religions well do not accept the assumption that early man, through his own effort, created his religion. They do not mention this at all.	*Alles in allem genommen* conveys a finality stronger than the English "all in all," which has the connotation of a loose generalization similar to "on the whole," leaving room for exceptions, which is not Schmidt's meaning.

I have no idea why Brandewie turned *wir* ("we") into "I," except that he may have been misled by the word *selbst* ("self"), which refers back to the *Bekennern.*

As to the *Bekennern,* a quick consultation of a dictionary would have revealed that *bekennen* means "to confess," and the *Bekennern* of a religion are those who confess it, viz. its adherents. Brandewie apparently recognized the word *Kenner,* which means literally "a knower" and usually refers to an expert, and presumably surmised that the *Be-* could be ignored so that the *Bekennern der Religionen* are still experts on the religions rather than its "confessors," which, I believe, translates into more readable English as "adherents."

Finally, Brandewie's translation loses some of the force of Schmidt's statement by not bringing out the incremental increase in the negative sentiment expressed. Schmidt asserts that the indigenous believers don't just think of the human origin of their religion as something they reject, they don't even think of it at all.

The overall intention of the passage is conveyed, but Brandewie's translation is not what Schmidt wrote. |

Name Index

Subject Index

www.ingramcontent.com/pod-product-compliance
Lightning Source LLC
Chambersburg PA
CBHW031041110426
42740CB00047B/767